THE MYTH OF JAPANESE UNI

'This book is an original contribution not only to the study, but also to the sociology and psychology of ideology.'

Arthur R. Gould, *British Book News*

'anyone long bored and saddened by the bland, arid, and graceless prose predominant in contemporary American fiction and scholarly treatises will be delighted to rediscover the nearly sensuous spell of the English Language, with all its evocative nuances, incisive edges, and rich resonance.'

Chieko Irie Mulhern, *Japan Quarterly*

The 'nihonjinron', a vast body of academic writing, analyses Japanese character, 'race' and culture as fundamentally different from all other known societies. Insisting on Japanese 'uniqueness', it has influenced profoundly linguistic, sociological, psychological and philosophical discourse on Japan.

This critique of the total field of this modern 'mythologic' system attempts to elucidate the structure of assumptions concerning Japanese identity, revealing its origins in Western nationalism. It endeavours to provide not only a critical introduction, but also a socio-historical deconstruction of discourse on identity in Japan and, implicitly, elsewhere.

THE NISSAN INSTITUTE/ROUTLEDGE JAPANESE STUDIES SERIES

Editorial Board

J.A.A. Stockwin, Nissan Professor of Modern Japanese Studies, University of Oxford and Director, Nissan Institute of Japanese Studies
Teigo Yoshida, formerly Professor of the University of Tokyo, and now Professor, Obirin University, Tokyo
Frank Langdon, Professor, Institute of International Relations, University of British Columbia, Canada
Alan Rix, Professor of Japanese, The University of Tokyo
Junji Banno, Institute of Social Science, The University of Tokyo
Leonard Schoppa, University of Virginia

Other titles in the series:

The Emperor's Adviser: Saionji Kinmochi and Pre-war Japanese Politics, Lesley Connors
A History of Japanese Economic Thought, Tessa Morris-Suzuki
The Establishment of the Japanese Constitutional System, Junji Banno, translated by J.A.A. Stockwin
Industrial Relations in Japan: the Peripheral Workforce, Norma Chalmers
Banking Policy in Japan: American Efforts at Reform During the Occupation, William M. Tsutsui
Education Reform in Japan, Leonard Schoppa
How the Japanese Learn to Work, Ronald P. Dore and Mari Sako
Japanese Economic Development: Theory and Practice, Penelope Francks
Japan and Protection: The Growth of Protectionist Sentiment and the Japanese Response, Syed Javed Maswood
The Soil, by Nagatsuka Takashi: a Portrait of Rural Life in Meiji Japan, translated and with an introduction by Ann Waswo
Biotechnology in Japan, Malcolm Brock
Britain's Educational Reform: a Comparison with Japan, Mike Howarth
Language and the Modern State: the Reform of Written Japanese, Nanette Twine
Industrial Harmony in Modern Japan: the Invention of a Tradition, W. Dean Kinzley
Japanese Science Fiction: a View of a Changing Society, Robert Matthew
The Japanese Numbers Game: the Use and Understanding of Numbers in Modern Japan, Thomas Crump
Ideology and Practice in Modern Japan, Roger Goodman and Kirsten Refsing
Technology and Industrial Development in Pre-War Japan, Yukiko Fukasaku
Japan's First Parliaments 1890–1905, Andrew Fraser, R.H.P. Mason and Philip Mitchell
Emperor Hirohito and Showa Japan, Stephen S. Large
Japan: Beyond the End of History, David Williams
Understanding Japanese Society, Joy Hendry
Ceremony and Ritual in Japan: Religious Practices in an industrialized Society, Jan van Bremen and D. P. Martinez

The Myth of Japanese Uniqueness

Peter N. Dale

London and New York

First published 1986 by Croom Helm Ltd.
Reprinted 1988 by Routledge
11 New Fetter Lane, London EC4P 4EE

New in paperback 1990, reprinted 1995

Simultaneously published in the USA and Canada
by Routledge
29 West 35th Street, New York, NY 10001

© 1986 Peter N. Dale

Printed and bound in Great Britain by
Mackays of Chatham PLC, Chatham, Kent

All rights reserved. No part of this book may be reprinted or reproduced or utilized in any form or by any electronic, mechanical, or other means, now known or hereafter invented, including photocopying and recording, or in any information storage or retrieval system, without permission in writing from the publishers.

British Library Cataloguing in Publication Data
A catalogue record for this book is available from the British Library

Library of Congress Cataloguing in Publication Data
A catalogue record for this book has been requested

ISBN 0–415–03002–1 (hbk)
ISBN 0–415–05534–2 (pbk)

"'The Japanese spirit!' the Japanese shouted, while coughing like someone infected with tuberculosis... 'The Japanese spirit!' say the journalists. 'The Japanese spirit!' say the pickpockets. The Japanese spirit has crossed the ocean in a single bound. In England, lectures are given on the Japanese spirit. In Germany, they stage dramatic spectacles on the Japanese spirit ... Admiral Tōgō possesses the Japanese spirit and the local fishmonger has it as well. Swindlers, mountebanks and murderers also have the Japanese spirit... Now if you ask, 'Well, what exactly is this Japanese spirit?' they say in reply 'Why it's the Japanese spirit of course!' and walk on. Then, after they've gone five or six paces, one can hear them clearing their throats with an hrrumph ... Is the Japanese spirit triangular, or is it quadrangular? As the name indicates, the Japanese spirit is a spirit. And since it is a spirit it is always blurry and fuzzy. There's no one in Japan who hasn't had it on the tip of his tongue, but there's no one who has actually seen it. Everyone has heard about it but no one has yet encountered it. Is it, perhaps, a kind of that long-nosed braggadocio, the goblin?."

Natsume Sōseki, *Wagahai wa neko de aru* (1905-6)
(Shinchō Bunko ed. 1961 pp.221-2)

To the memory of my parents
Florence Maria Dale (1907-70)
Frank Melbourne Dale (1903-78)
   in gratitude.

εὐτυχῶς μέν, ἀλλ' ὅμως
τὰ τῶν τεκόντων ὄμμαθ' ἥδιστον βλέπειν.

CONTENTS

List of Tables

Introduction

1.	On 'The Otherness of the Other'	1
2.	The Quest for Identity	12
3.	A Uniqueness Rare in the World	25
4.	The Dialectics of Difference	38
5.	The Warp of Language	56
6.	The Linguistics of Silence	77
7.	Silence and Elusion	100
8.	Omnia Vincit Amae	116
9.	The Complex of Japanese Psychoanalysis	147
10.	The Shame of a Shame Culture	176
11.	Monkey Business	188
12.	On Identity as Difference	201
Index		228

TABLES

1.	Geoclimatic Base	42
2.	Racial Base	42
3.	Productive Base	42
4.	Social Base	44
5.	Socio-Cultural Mode	45
6.	Intellectual Style	46
7.	Principles of Indigenous Efflorescence	51
8.	Language	78
9.	Loan Words and Indigenous Words	87
10.	Characteristics of Japanese and Other Languages	100
11.	'Public' or 'Private'?	105
12.	Abstract *v.* Colloquial	123
13.	*Ki* Equivalences	130
14.	Interpretations of 'Compulsive'	132
15.	Bee Behaviour	189
16.	Progress Towards Cultural Autonomy	213

INTRODUCTION

The subject of this book is that vast array of literature comprehensively referred to under the rubric *nihonjinron*. Literally, this term refers to 'discussions of the Japanese'. As such, it might at first glance appear to entail virtually everything written about the Japanese, enclosing within its ample embrace the whole field of discourse on Japan and its people. The *nihonjinron*, in their attempt to define the specificity of Japanese identity, range over the whole complex of Japanese historical culture, choosing their illustrative material from classical records, folklore materials, historical chronicles, contemporary news, dictionaries of Japanese usage etc. They include highly abstruse discussions of oriental thought and ephemeral journalism on characteristic knacks of behaviour in everyday life. Yet we would do well to draw a distinction between the *nihonjinron* and serious empirical research on Japanese society, even if, for a variety of reasons, the disciplined academic study of the Japanese often betrays either a tacit or explicit endorsement of judgements which we may identify with the ideological analyses common to the *nihonjinron*.

In contrast to modern empirical research on Japan, the *nihonjinron* are characterised by three major assumptions or analytical motivations. Firstly, they implicitly assume that the Japanese constitute a culturally and socially homogeneous racial entity, whose essence is virtually unchanged from prehistorical times down to the present day. Secondly, they presuppose that the Japanese differ radically from all other known peoples. Thirdly, they are consciously nationalistic, displaying a conceptual and procedural hostility to any mode of analysis which might be seen to derive from external, non-Japanese sources. In a general sense then, the *nihonjinron* may be defined as works of cultural nationalism concerned with the ostensible 'uniqueness' of Japan in any aspect, and which are hostile to both individual experience and the notion of internal socio-historical diversity.

Given the pervasive impact and presence of ideology and nationalism in the intellectual and cultural life of the Japanese, the distinction I have drawn is a rough one, and hardly watertight. We are dealing with a climate of received ideas, commonplace

Introduction

assumptions and accepted principles which, for complex historical reasons, have conditioned the very atmosphere in which all those who concern themselves with Japan think and work. In a sense the *nihonjinron* do not constitute a specific genre of scholarship. Rather, they are concentrated expressions of an intense tradition of intellectual nationalism whose broader impact on both our general way of interpreting Japan and specialist studies remains to be analysed.

Outsiders may have difficulty coming to grips with the precise dimensions of the *nihonjinron*. Just imagine the situation which might ensue had English letters over the past 100 years been singularly preoccupied with the clarification of 'Englishness', not only as an essayistic form but as a major subject of austere academic research. Imagine then dozens if not hundreds of works pouring from the presses of Oxford and Cambridge, in which the Hare Professor of Moral Philosophy discussed the uniqueness of the English ethical tradition, or Wittgensteinians examined at book length hundreds of terms in the Oxford English Dictionary to derive concepts of Englishness in such terms as 'fair play' 'good form' 'gentleman' 'guvner' etc., or wrote books on the influence of bad weather on parliamentary institutions and democracy, of cricket on the outlook of the English people, on matriarchy as a constant element underlying British institutions from the times of Boadicea through to Mrs Thatcher; treating everything under the English sun as consequences of some peculiar mentality unchanged since one's ancestors first donned woad and did battle with Caesar; imagine this as something which filtered down through newspapers and regional media to everyday life, and you have something of the picture of what has taken place in Japan, where almost any discussion from the formally academic to the colloquial market-place exchange can reflect this ideology of nationhood. What we are dealing with is not a national 'mentality', a way of thinking intimately related to that complex and intricately interwoven meld of institutions of social and economic organization but rather a fictional mentality constructed by innumerable thinkers and writers over a considerable length of time, through whose lens, due to the impact of constant discussion and exposure, the people often tend to interpret their world.

This book is an attempt to write out formally the groundrules which govern the production of this kind of nationalistic idea through successive layers of thought, from linguistics, through to family structure theory, sociological concepts, and psychoanalytical notions to philosophical constructs, in order to show that this established way of interpreting Japan is formally invalid, and that much work has to be done afresh because this kind of approach has influenced even western scholarship.

The present work, a much reduced version of a manuscript completed in 1981, while aspiring to provide an overall introduction to the central notions of the *nihonjinron*, scratches the surface of a far more extensive network of ideas.

A book produced through a chain of apparently random circumstances, and one which, by its own inner momentum, has relentlessly swept its reluctant author from his chosen field into areas beyond his formal competence, perhaps requires a note of clarification. Though trained primarily in Greek, I was particularly interested in the influence of shamanism on epic poetry. When an opportunity arose to pursue these studies in Japan, I seized it in the desire to complement my Western research by examining this theme in the context of Sino-Japanese mythology.

In reading Japanese materials, my increasing fluency in the language appeared to be rewarded by mounting difficulties in following many arguments. Were my original work to progress, I gradually realised that I should have to clarify the array of specific assumptions which often influenced the orientation of many popular and academic interpretations of the past in terms of a search for uniqueness. It soon became evident, however, that racial, linguistic, sociological, philosophical and psychological premises about the Japanese, past and present, were tightly intertwined. To illuminate any one supposition, one was forced to elucidate its connection with an extensive and intricate network of associated ideas.

The ideological code I began to unravel was queer enough in its own terms. But the discrepancies between national image and existential reality were even more glaring when one contrasted the projected ideal of an harmonious public identity with the vivid, complex and often tormented witness of the novel. Neither my preparatory reading of authors like Benedict, Gorer, Hearn and Maruyama before coming to Japan, nor my personal experience once there, had given me the slightest impression that the Japanese were radically different from the rest of humanity. Yet little, if anything, in the vast postwar Western literature on Japan had forewarned me of the existence in Japan of a pervasive academic

Introduction

approach which sustained precisely this thesis of uniqueness. From my first acquaintance I presumed that however much the particular forms of Japanese history and socialisation might have structured the impact of power over the individual's frail autonomy, one could readily recognise the usual symptoms and pathologies of an all too familiar malaise.

Initially, I undertook to accompany with a formal analysis every example of intellectual aberration I came across, an approach which quickly swelled my material beyond manageable proportions. In reviewing these results, however, I found that the material fell naturally into twelve chapters which appeared thematically unrelated to one another. Later it struck me that the techniques used in the structural analysis of primitive myth would enable me to elicit and give form to the logic of cultural oppositions in these texts, and thus I began to rework these ideas as if they constituted an essentially mythological universe. But while this anthropological approach brought to light the binary code (of East-West antitheses) underlying these arguments, it failed to explain the presence and function of such an archaic procedure in modern Japan.

Another, deeper order of intelligibility was discerned when I tried to treat this mythological ensemble as a social ideology. Guided by certain trends in neo-Marxism, I undertook to relate these fictions of cultural identity to social contexts. This approach yielded up a rich array of contradictions between the formal code of interpretation and the Japanese situations it claimed to analyse. Yet the reductive unmasking of this ideological facade in terms of economic interests and social control appeared insufficient. One sensed the presence of an unconscious element of individual motivation in the production and consumption of these books. Therefore I began to rework my material in the light of the psychoanalytic problem already exposed to view in chapters eight and nine.

It was through a re-immersion in Freudian literature, and a concomitant analysis of my own critical, negative fascination with this imaginary world of unique identity that I managed to dredge up the theme which gathered into a single pattern the disparate threads of this ideological tapestry. But, to complete the picture, it then became necessary to trace back the historical origins of these concepts and, strikingly, it emerged that virtually every key axiom in the contemporary literature on Japanese identity could be

Introduction

tracked down to work done in the critical years of 1909-11. A sociological explanation of the ideology, as a reaction to the crisis of late Meiji, thus presented itself. Further, the analysis of the intellectual systems propounded by Japanese thinkers around these seminal years revealed an uncanny coincidence in theoretical affirmations in otherwise distinct and independent disciplines, and this in turn yielded me the key to the philosophical error underlying the whole project of nationalism outlined in this book.

Given the character of the book's gestation, the reader may find these successive layers of interpretation and cross-reference rather perplexing. He would do well to bear in mind that the work should perhaps best be read as it was written, as a labour of slow detection in which every casual clue yields up, on examination, its meaning for the eventual solution. Despite what might appear to be disconcerting jumps in analysis over a variety of apparently unrelated details and intellectual disciplines, nothing in these pages is arbitrary. Each chapter highlights a puzzle which, when partially deciphered, throws up yet another problem to be studied in the subsequent chapter, until the elements of the jigsaw puzzle can finally be pieced together in the concluding pages.

Finally, I should like to thank Karl for the two years of almost daily argument; Professor and Mrs Crawcour for reading part of a draft on Kuki and Doi, and for the encouragement to persist; Mr L. Oates for comments on a very early outline; Professor I. Cubeddu, my brother G. Dale, D. Kishere, and Dr P. Toohey, for procuring books and checking various references, and my wife Angela for her stylistic strictures. I owe above all a profound debt of gratitude to Professor J.A.A. Stockwin for his timely intervention, his unlimited patience with untidy drafts, and for the exceptional liberty he has conceded me to present this *mongai shoken* in the form which the nature of my inner engagement with these texts demanded. Given the origins of this book as a private intellectual exercise that did not anticipate publication, the responsibility for both style and content, not to speak of any errors that may emerge, is wholly my own, and the views herein expressed may in no way be attributed to those who have, at various stages, occasionally offered me advice.

1 ON 'THE OTHERNESS OF THE OTHER'

'the odds is gone,
And there is nothing left remarkable
Beneath the visiting moon.'
Anthony and Cleopatra, 4.15: 66-68.

From Greek antiquity down to present times, the Orient has exercised a peculiar hold on the Western imagination. If the scorched deserts of Africa were seen as the breeding quarters of death, pestilence and the monstruous, Asia by comparison was a 'land rich in everything',[1] a wealthy, barbarous rival, a secret adversary pregnant with queer contrasts. Man's inveterate habit of investing the unknown with visions of furtive desire, or of inculpating it with his own latent anxieties, has always found ample scope for untrammelled speculation in the vague and abstract vastness of the Asian world. The more distant the country, the greater is the temptation to extend the submerged landscape of private fantasy into the hearsay reaches of an exotic geography, to populate it with creatures of the imagination whose existence is otherwise rendered improbable by the dulling pressures of a known and banal reality. The mind abhors a vacuum, and where facts are in short supply, myth stands ever ready to cast its narrative nets over the yawning gaps.

The great voyages of exploration which, from the Renaissance onwards, ventured into this once mythical realm did not at first subvert the classical vision by the preciser knowledge of factual reportage and first hand observation. If anything, the detailed information now gleaned tended to be filtered through, and subsumed by, the framework of earlier preconceptions, thus lending a kind of empirical substance to traditional fantasies. The East was not demystified by encounter; rather, the old myth of the Orient was revarnished with an impressive structure of concrete particulars drawn from the real. Asia became recognisably exotic, and centuries were required to appreciate the view that the odd was not just queer but simply an appearance of difference.

With the Enlightenment, this perception of radical difference assumed great tactical value in the philosophical assault on the prerogatives of rule of the *ancien régime*. The profusion of Asian polities bore eloquent testimony to the thesis that custom was relative, that social institutions were circumscribed more by convention than by natural law. Reason was to supplant convention as arbiter of social life, and Asia, with its diverse repertoire of exotic states, suggested a rich range of alternative models to replace or supplement the moribund systems of aristocratic Europe. But the picturesque images of Siam, Persia, Turkey and China were still overwhelmingly conditioned by mythopoetic vision. Asia was useful to the degree that it lent itself to fabrications of utopian possibility.

The notion of Asia as utopian exemplar suffered rapid eclipse after the French revolution. With the emergence of civil, secular society, European debates on social reform were to be dominated by the prospects opened up in the aftermath of the spectacular events of 1789. The succeeding emergence of nationalism and Imperialism dealt a double death blow to this ideological value of Asia. Nationalism was, naturally, inward-looking, while Imperialism could perceive in Asia only the profits of conquest. Evolutionism, with its concomitant faith in progress, contained deep implications for the way the non-European world was to be seen. Differences in culture and society became quaint tokens of benightedness. Diversity was no longer a spur to emulation but rather a ground for unctuous self-esteem or the proud benevolence of a dutiful pity, a warrant for assuming the white man's burden with its paradoxical ethic of charitable predation.

The internal failure of nerve suffered by European civilization consequent on the catastrophic holocausts of two world wars not only undermined imperial pretensions, but led to a radical switch in attitudes towards the non-European world, a readiness not only to accept its 'otherness' but often also to insist on it. Anthropology sought to investigate the primitive through the lens of a sympathetically indigenous focus, while sociology began to explain alien societies in terms of native historical patterns. True, the theory of unilinear development surfaced in various forms of modernisation thought, but in all save one version, its inexorably eurocentric presuppositions were easily exposed. The exception, Marxism, the most radical form of that concept of unilinear progress which flourished under nineteenth century capitalism, survives with relative immunity to this charge precisely because it readily lends itself, in revisionist versions, to any type of hostility to the West.

The new preparedness to study, listen to, and learn from Asia, understood as constituting a tradition radically different from anything in the West, is shared by people with widely differing outlooks and interests, from the Zen-infatuated *aficionados* of pop mysticism and Third Wave industrialists enthusiastic about the futuristic technology of the Tsukuba exposition, to neo-Maoist revolutionaries and exponents of the higher Japanology. Some seek a spiritual anodyne for the crisis-ridden West in oriental religions, others discern in Japanese capitalism or Chinese Communism alternative socio-economic systems to replace those of the stress-prone world of post-industrialism. Oriental culture, as constructed by many of its interpreters, presents a seductive image of harmonious sociality in raw contrast to the 'alienated' structure of Western life.

This quest to discover revitalisingly exotic patterns of life-style, industrial management and existential outlook, as a means towards a radical transcendence of a West exhausted of everything save, apparently, its intellectual aggressiveness, recapitulates the Enlightenment trend touched on above. It is not, therefore, without regressive traces, such as, for example, a programmatic disarming of critical consciousness. Franco Ferrarotti ingenuously illustrates the point with dramatic eloquence:

> It is above all important for Western European and North American analysts to learn how to 'let go', how to let themselves be penetrated by the new and the different, to accept the otherness of the other (*l'alterità dell'altro*) ...
>
> For starters the researcher does well to renounce those concepts and means of a technical and notional kind to which he has become accustomed. It is not as easy as at first appears. One cannot change one's mental habits as simply as one changes one's shirts, for example. No doubt, I journey with my thoughts, with those logical and political categories which have served me well over the years in my analyses. What I must not forget, and what I otherwise murmur in my inner ear incessantly, is that I may not allow myself the luxury of being eurocentric, of yielding to the temptation of nostalgia, to the flavour (certainly sweet but mortally deceptive) of returning home, of not breaking out of that cosy familiarity with one's habitual mental landscape. The categories of political-ideological reasoning of the kind we find in Western Europe

cannot be applied, mechanically, to the reality of Japan. I know that I cannot permit these categories to drop away without risking the chance of emptying myself intellectually. All I forbid myself is the act of projecting them upon Japanese reality. I decide that I prefer not to understand, rather than to colour and imprison the object of analysis with conceptions that are, in the final analysis, preconceptions.[2]

In encountering the 'supplementary reality' of a country like Japan, we must, in this view, bereave ourselves of 'rigid logical defences', sloughing off that hard skin of intellectual habit which, analytical in the West, becomes prejudicial when applied to Eastern realities. Remaining ignorant of others is to be preferred to inadvertently misunderstanding them; better to lapse into a passive silence than to imprison and contort the sacred 'alterity' of the Orient within the conventional framework of Western knowledge.

In its most extreme form, this desire not to compromise the 'otherness' of the East by the symbolic nomenclature and projective categories of Western cognition leads to the disarming avowel by writers like Barthes that, in order not to traduce the Orient by imposing on it the interpretative bias of occidental discourse, they will make no claim to speak about Japan when writing about a country they elect to call 'Japan'. The exotic label is a mere device around which the writer assumes a complete liberty to weave 'orientalist' fictions.[3]

The ultimate form of this intellectual modesty assumes the lineaments of an ill-disguised, racist intimidation of theory itself when it is exploited by oriental nationalists to invalidate as tendentially imperialist any Western interpretation of Asian realities, however benign or sympathetic. In this view, the projection of analyses derived from a Western interpretative mode is all the more insidious in its imperialism because it annuls and disguises its colonialist roots while preserving its covert values in the specifically occidental framework of modern thought. Edward Said implies as much when, in speaking of Western images of Islam, he remarks: 'it is a contradiction to speak of "Islam" as neither what its clerical adherents in fact say it is nor what, if they could, its lay followers would say about it.'[4]

In the Japanese or Chinese context, this sophisticatedly xenophobic thesis would suggest that a Western orientalist dooms his work to contradictions whenever he steps beyond mere citation of indigenous authorities to advance his own, dissenting, interpretation. In addition to the old criteria for informed competence in a foreign culture (language competence and empathy) we are presented here with an additional rider, critical self-lobotimisation. Western studies are valid only in so far as they approximate to the original force of hermeneutics, i.e. translating pure and simply.

The formal doctrine underwriting this studious evasion of comparativist temptations is known as cultural relativism. According to Redfield, this view holds 'that the values expressed in any culture are to be both understood and themselves valued only according to the way the people who carry that culture see things.'[5]

The anthropologist subscribing to this notion must prorogue or suspend those terms of critical evaluation inherent in his original social and intellectual milieu, and supplant them with the value judgements provided by the informants of the society he happens to be studying. Given the universality of prejudice, the inherently subjective character of all interpretation, this naive 'elevation of the native informant to the status of ultimate judge of the adequacy of the observer's descriptions and analyses'[6] merely shifts the locus of bias from the foreigner to the insider. While ethnocentrism may be the occupational hazard of both anthropologist and traveller alike, the burden of subjectivism is by no means relieved by training the 'other' to be his own ethnographer. Eliciting information does more than draw out neutral data; the foreign presence of the anthropologist as interrogator prods, spurs and conditions his informants to objectify and reflect upon their world in a way perhaps formerly alien to them.

Even the cultural relativist, then, may risk merely rendering in a more subtle form that intellectual 'imperialism' his professed technique formally disavows. He solicits, as much as he elicits, his facts. Equally troubling is the fact that cultural relativists frequently assume the existence of a coherent world view shared by all members of a tribe or a non-Western society, and thus run the risk of disindividualising the 'other'. The informant is useful is so far as he succeeds in mirroring by his views a wider social order and outlook. To each group, tribe or nation a cohesive *Weltanschauung* is attributed, which tends to exclude *a priori* the possibility of pluralism, of the coexistence of conflicting notions of the world and diverse value-systems. This is particularly evident in works which treat non-Western nations from the perspective of cultural anthropology.

In essence then, this investigative tendency views occidental cognitive patterns as a kind of Procrustean rack upon which the profuse diversity of existential types is stretched into a uniform shape congruent with the particular structure of Western experience. That there is considerable force in this view I do not wish to deny. Curiously Marxism, the analytic mode which most readily exposes itself to precisely this charge, seems far less subject to the insinuation than other eurocentric approaches. We are, in any case, on difficult terrain here and no sure path has been mapped around or between the Scylla of eurocentrism and the Charybdis of an informant's subjectivism or tendentiousness.

What I wish to do in the present work is to explore critically some of the problems which arise from working on the assumption, when studying modern oriental societies, that they define a 'radical alterity', and that canons of Western reasoning and analysis are best replaced by ostensibly indigenous, 'informant' models of method and approach. The assiduous attempts made in Japan to construct a consciously unwestern epistemological mode to calibrate the distinctive features of that socio-cultural reality prove to be either incoherent, or mere pale imitations of theories indirectly derived from the abandoned cognitive luggage of earlier Western intellectual and nationalist fashion.

The introduction of the modish anthropological distinction between *emic* (native informant's judgement) and *etic* (foreign observer's analysis) into the study of modern(ising) societies in Asia has wrought considerable mischief, and mystification, in the field of interpretation. The relativity of values and concepts implied by these terms may prove innocuous when deployed in the study of small, cohesive and primitive social groups, of tribal and ethnic culture. But as Redfield argues persuasively, it is altogether another matter when we use them with regard to major societies. For, logically, we can 'anthropologise the Nazis' or the white supremacists of Mississippi.[7] Modernisation introduces a culture of change which obliterates or destabilises that unity of vision or social style in smaller communities upon which the anthropologist dwells. An ideology of national homogeneity, manipulated for specific social ends, takes its place whose function is to mobilise supra-communal sentiment. Control over interpretation becomes a key element of successful statecraft, which tends to fear that, 'when in a nation the mass refuses to be a mass — that is, to follow the directive minority, the nation breaks down, the society is dismembered, and social chaos, historical invertebration, supervenes.'[8]

In complex societies like Japan, the 'indigenous' version of how that world is perceived is often deeply coloured by ideological interests. In such cultures, there are no longer 'native informants', but only other interpreters who are subject to the same tendentiousness that afflicts all thought. The outsider who confuses such interpretations with authentic, 'raw' information may, far from transcending the parochial limits of his eurocentric code of understanding, merely subject it to the programme of an exotic nationalism. Applied in this way, cultural relativism connives at the importation of value judgements all the more subversive of reality because camouflaged as empirical views. The visible, familiar assumptions of the Western intellectual tradition are replaced by the submerged, ill-recognised and fugitive presuppositions (often substantively analogous in kind) of an ostensibly alien *Weltanschauung*.

The premise that a different logic underlies societies of the non-Western world inhibits comparisons and highlights real or putative contrasts. It also tends to dismiss resemblances as superficial and tries to dissolve apparent similarities by applying indigenous interpretations biased towards the perception of local peculiarities. Those who advocate the approach of cultural relativism often find themselves operating in a double mental universe characterised by a schizoid tendency towards making contradictory judgements. Once the possibility of a tellingly congruent analogy between a Western and Oriental phenomenon is ruled from consciousness, once homologies are denied between otherwise similar situations, prejudice is exoticised. If the provincial is prone to extol even the vices of his own country, the rootless academic, as intellectual entrepreneur for the alien, begins to admire in exotic shape anything which, in the more familiar idiom and dress of his own social world, excites in him only vehement disapproval. Radical psychiatrists who enthuse over otherwise extremely authoritarian forms of Japanese 'therapy' are a case in point.

Erich Fromm's study of aggression provides a striking illustration. In his polemic against behaviourism, he trenchantly shows that the theory of operant conditioning mystifies the nature of the aggression, in that it views the relationship between aggressor and victim simply in terms of a mechanical cause-and-effect operating between reciprocal stimuli. The essential element of psychological intention is suppressed, and thus it follows that 'the tortured, by his manifestation of pain, conditions the torturer to use the most effective instruments of torture.'[9] By excluding the motivation which leads the torturer to torture, the theory makes his victim an accomplice to his own suffering. Behaviour cannot, Fromm insists, be understood if divorced from the psychology of the behaving person, for: 'A man fires a gun and kills another person; the behavioural act in itself — firing the shot that kills the person — if isolated from the 'aggressor', means little, psychologically. In fact a behaviouristic statement would be adequate only about the gun; with regard to it the motivation of the man who pulls the trigger is irrelevant.'[10]

Two hundred pages on, however, Fromm discusses what he calls 'benign aggression' by an illustration from Zen Buddhism, namely of an exponent exercising his martial prowess with the sword.

> A Zen master of sword-fighting *does not harbour the wish to kill or destroy*, nor has he any hate. *He makes the proper movement*, and if the opponent is killed, it is *because the latter 'stood in the wrong place'* (personal communication from the late D.T. Suzuki). *A classic psychoanalyst may argue that unconsciously the sword fighter is motivated by hate and the wish to destroy his opponent; this is his privilege, but he would show little grasp of the spirit of Zen.*' (my italics)[11]

It requires little reflection to remark the absurd incongruity of this double standard. It is nonsense, Fromm tells us, to divorce the gun from the gunman, but eminently reasonable to detach the sword from its wielder. 'Culture' as 'radical alterity' has intervened to disrupt and obfuscate the obvious, and instructive, homology. The trigger-happy gunslinger of the familiar West is neurotic, it would appear, but his slashing samurai colleague in the Orient is mystically sane.

Deeper acquaintance with Suzuki's writing, and the neat ideology of mystical justification it provided to the practice of beheading prisoners during the war might just have enlightened him. Suzuki's views here read remarkably like the very behaviourist mode of interpretation which Fromm elsewhere so vigorously condemns. Of the swordsman he wrote that, 'it is really not he but *the sword itself that does the killing.* He has no desire to do harm to anybody, but *the enemy appears and makes himself a victim.*' (my italics)[12]

Such a swordsman is, for Suzuki, an 'artist of the first grade engaged in producing a work of genuine orginality', an 'emic' explanation that is undoubtedly of great, if posthumous, consolation to the beheaded whose severed bodies bear witness to creative genius. The culpable perpetrators of such exquisitely benign aggression during the Pacific War, many of whom had no doubt read Suzuki on the sword, may refresh themselves with such texts to soothe any residual pangs of guilt. But the cause of intercultural understanding is ill-served by these cosy mendacities.

My purpose in this book will be to survey, and occasionally analyse in depth, certain currents in Japanese thought and scholarship which, though marked by a highly tendentious strain of nationalistic feeling, have exercised a considerable impact on the way Japanese culture is perceived and discussed, both within Japan and abroad. When not treated with a quiet and discreet neglect, this genre of work has often succeeded in establishing itself as the authentically indigenous view of Japanese realities, and is often reported as such in foreign publications of both a specialist and general nature. Unfamiliarity with the ideological sources of many Japanese images and interpretative concepts, when mixed with a mode of analysis which has consistently failed to distinguish the methods of an empirical sociology from the assumptions of an ingrained nationalism have often compromised the objectivity of Western reportage.

The postwar period has witnessed the emergence of a vigorous, indeed booming, industry of national self-appraisal in Japan. The temptation to sidestep the ethnocentrism of eurocentric approaches by treating this burgeoning field of interpretation as an authentic, autochthonous expression of Japanese realities is strong, and often results in the marriage of Western scholarship with native forms of ethnocentrism masqueraded under the formal garb of 'oriental thought'. In consequence, what we often read in translations, and Western books which draw upon this tradition, is not Japan as experienced by Japanese individuals. Rather, we encounter a 'Japan' as that society and its people tend to be interpreted by conscious nationalists working in an intellectual framework out of touch with both reality and the most elementary principles of logic and method.

My intention here is not therefore to add another volume to the endless pile of interpretations of Japan. If I have occasionally sketched out certain socio-psychological dimensions that would appear to underlie the mythology, it is because the analysis of contradictions in this mode of ideological representation consistently suggests them. It is common enough in Western thought to read discourse as concealing an unpalatable inner or external reality. In applying these techniques here, the structures I refer to are only those which might account for the form which the specifically Japanese ideology of nationalism has assumed.

The generalisations made here refer thus to very specific social contexts, such as those of corporate life. They are therefore not necessarily representative, and are not obtained from an empirical sociology as much as by deductions from the character of the ideology of these mythological representations. Yet, if it is imprudent to try and generalise about Japanese society on such evidences, it would err on the side of excessive caution to wholly exclude them. If the mere complexity of socio-economic life in Japan should suffice to expose the presumptuousness of a style of pseudo-intellectual chat about 'us Japanese',[13] powerful institutional forces and interests still aspire to sustain the fictions of socio-psychological and racial homogeneity. The problems addressed here relate exclusively to the subtly coercive cooption exercised over unconscious thought in Japan by 'entrepreneurs of identity' in their relentless endeavours to maintain over other Japanese an hegemony of cultural interpretation.

Finally, this book is not an introduction or survey of 'Japanese thought' or a guidebook to the Japanese academy. In a country of such commendable literacy and intensively productive scholarship, the range of methods and ideas is vast, and includes such masters of critical scholarship as Maruyama Masao, Murayama Shichirō, Nakanishi Susumu, to name but a few, whose rigorous work has often cut the ground from under those engaged in propping up the old mythological pyramids. But if the profound desire of such men to know and scrupulously explain constitutes a different mental universe from that which is presented here, it would appear unfortunately true that their representative labours have, for a variety of reasons, exercised far less influence on internal popular and official opinion than the sensationalist interpretations of 'national identity' propounded by those thinkers presented here, whose understanding is continually pre-empted by a stubborn, parochial tendency to regress from the modern.

Notes

1. M. Manilius, *Astronomicon*, IV, 671.
2. F. Ferrarotti, 'Innovazione e Continuità nella Società Giapponese', in *Notiziario* (Instituto Giapponese di Cultura Rome, 1980) pp.3-15, pp.3-4.
3. R. Barthes, *L'Empire des Signes* (Éditions d'Art Albert Skira, Geneva, 1970) p.9.
4. E. Said, *Orientalism* (Random House, New York, 1978) p.283.
5. R. Redfield, *The Primitive World and its Transformations*, (Peregrine ed., Harmondsworth, 1968) p.148.
6. M. Harris, *Cultural Materialism*, (Vintage Books paper, New York, 1980) pp.32f. For a typical confusion of 'emic' models and native ideological constructs see Harumi Befu's paper, 'A Critique of the Group Model of Japanese Society' in Ross Mouer and Yoshio Sugimoto (eds.) *Social Analysis* (Adelaide, 1980) nos. 5/6 pp. 41ff, and the afterthought, pp. 190ff.
7. Redfield, *Primitive World*, ibid. p.149.
8. J. Ortega y Gasset, *España Invertebrada*, 1922 (Revista de Occidente en Alianza Editorial, Madrid, 1981) p.76. On the Meiji élite's awareness that 'manipulation of affects is the key to socialisation through indoctrination in patriotism', see K. Tsurumi, *Social Change and the Individual*, (Princeton University Press, Princeton New Jersey, 1970) p.103. Kawamura Nozomu writes that 'The early Meiji élite was keenly aware of how the vocabulary associated with Japan's "traditional" past would facilitate its ability to maintain autocratic control'. See Kawamura Nozomu, 'The Historical Background of Arguments Emphasising the Uniqueness of Japanese Society', in *Social Analysis*, ibid pp.44-62.
9. E. Fromm, *The Anatomy of Human Destructiveness*, (Penguin, Harmondsworth, 1977) p.70, n.4.
10. Fromm, *Anatomy*, ibid p.75.
11. Fromm, *Anatomy*, ibid pp.255-6.
12. D. Suzuki, *Zen and Japanese Culture*, (Princeton University Press paper, Princeton New Jersey, 1973) p.145. Compare the rationalisation of killing, displacing culpability from the self to the gun, acutely described in Ōoka Shōhei's novel *Nobi*, 1954 (Shinchō Bunko ed., Tokyo, 1978) pp.87-8.
13. *Cf* 'To say "we" and mean "I" is one of the most recondite insults', T. Adorno, *Minima Moralia*, trans. E.F.N. Jephcott (verso ed., London, 1978) p.190.

2 THE QUEST FOR IDENTITY

'(I)n Japan, as elsewhere, insularity, a sense of isolation, and the resultant paranoia, persecution mania, and belief in uniqueness all combine to lead nationalism into dangerous channels.'
Ivan Morris, *Nationalism and the Right Wing in Japan*, (Oxford University Press, 1960) p.424.

The student of Japanese, once he has passed the initial difficulties posed before his entry into that culture by the formidable script, often finds his fluent immersion in this new world hindered by a second order of difficulty. In reading many works that come his way, both popular and technical, he often finds his progress impeded by the discovery of a densely woven network of assumptions which, at first sight and second thought, are both alien and hostile to common principles of logic. If he persists past this initial sense of oddness, he will often find any resolution he makes to map the capricious topography of such thought subject to repeated frustrations. Like Ulysses in his travels, he will frequently find himself adrift in unfamiliar seas, bereft of the usual landmarks. Or like Alice, he may feel condemned to bumbling about in a topsy turvy terrain of defiant queerness that seems to deny him the usual euclidean props at every improbable turn of the page.

The temptation to assign these exploratory difficulties to some inner resistance to exotic conventions of understanding can prove seductive. Perhaps, he may well reflect, the 'common principles of logic' which constitute his 'euclidean props' are eurocentric in design and therefore inapplicable to the study of the novel cosmology of oriental thought. The texts themselves frequently encourage this view in their repeated stress on the inadequacies and subjectivism of Western thought. Increasing familiarity with the codes of association and notional context adopted in the literature may tend to assuage his original sense of strangeness. Habituation, rather than breeding a contempt that risks the accusation of residual ethnocentrism, may breed in his mind a growing sense of at-homeness in this increasingly recognisable world of ideas. Indeed the tradition constituted by these very texts openly highlights the apparently innate character of paradox and puzzle in

The Quest for Identity 13

'Japanese thought', as if enigma itself were congenial to that culture. Over-exposure to such discourse may easily accustom the initially sceptical mind of the outsider to a breezy connivance with the enigmatic as a defiant scandal to 'occidental' reason. Charles Moore for one will tell him that,

'The Japanese thought-and-culture tradition is probably the most enigmatic and paradoxical of all major traditions, but — partly for that very reason — it represents more intellectual and cultural challenges, more unique and interesting suggestions, and more provocative reactions than any of the other great traditions of Asia.'[1]

If by 'enigmatic' we are to understand something which disconcerts, or which has yet to be fully explored and explained, then the Japanese tradition certainly brims with unplumbed riches. And yet, the very terms in which this 'tradition' is expounded by those who consider it unique, far from clarifying, only compound one's perplexity. Can one speak, for example, of a system of thought when its expositors so insistently concur in describing it as lacking in either philosophical or logical form?

For it is indeed an 'enigmatic thought tradition' which, in the words of one writer in Moore's anthology, exhibits a 'mentality ... unfit for abstract thinking'.[2] Perhaps there may in fact be something 'unique' and 'provocatively challenging' in thinking characterised by 'non-logical tendencies' or a 'weakness in ability to think in terms of logical consequences',[3] especially when those who describe it thus are themselves deficient in analytical coherence. They tease us by asserting on the one hand the paradox-ridden uniqueness of the Japanese heritage of thought, and by coyly refusing to furnish us, on the other hand, with any logical key from within that same tradition to enable us to analyse this quizzical universe. Why an intellectual patrimony marked by incoherence should be more challenging than those rich worlds of philosophical and scientific discourse in India and China is left unexplained. Why should lack of logic constitute a major philosophical tradition when we would normally assume that it simply indicates rather an absence of significant thought?

Reflection on his materials will perhaps provide our hypothetical reader with the clue to the underlying problem. For side by side with this massive genre of works which endlessly extol and puzzle over the quixotic strangeness of the Japanese tradition, there exists another variety of works, informed by methods of critical analysis he may readily understand, which sees nothing essentially odd or queer in this same patrimony. Where the one train of thought uses mysterious methods to identify what it conceives to be the ineffable peculiarities of the indigenous culture, the other school works in the mainstream of modern thought to clarify the past. A comparison between these two streams of analysis hints that the crux of the issue lies not in the past itself, but rather the methods used to analyse it. The former style of approach is consciously nationalistic and obsessed with any idea which might confirm the belief that the Japanese are unique. The latter approach is guided by methods which exclude speculative hypotheses until the facts have been ascertained. Unfortunately for the way in which the image of Japan is projected within and without, the former school has exercised a marked ascendency in propagating its ideology of culture.

I refer here on in to works which emerge from the former, nationalistic current, books which may be summed up under the general heading of *nihonjinron* or discussions of Japanese identity. The *nihonjinron* constitute the commercialised expression of modern Japanese nationalism. The rubric resumes under one genre any work of scholarship, occasional essay or newspaper article which attempts to define the unique specificity of things Japanese. It gathers within its ample embrace writings of high seriousness, imbued with a deep, often specious, erudition, and the facile *dicta* of interpretative journalism. Its theme — the quest for autochthonous identity — answers to profound needs, since it is echoed repeatedly at every level of discourse; and yet the massive energy invested in these inquiries has ended invariably with, at best, trivial results. Over time the successive attempts of such works to define the Japaneseness of the Japanese have merely enhanced the mystery, adding glaze on glaze to the over-lacquered idols of traditional forms of national self-deification.

But trivial and illogical as the varied contents of such works may prove to be, their mere existence and popularity, from production to consumption, demand explanation. If all we are given in the end is a series of Japanese versions of Roland Barthes' *peuple fictif*, it is nonetheless true that cultural fictions are not incubated and hatched in a vacuum. Claude Lévi-Strauss somewhere remarks that, *(d)errière tout sens il y a un nonsens*, but the converse may be argued with equal cogency. There must be some meaning or function beneath or behind what appear to be logically incoherent or empirically meaningless ideas.

If read in a critical light, then a whole, massive genre of comment and study upon the Japanese collapses into a patchwork of *non sequiturs* and ideological clichés. But we cannot explain the allure of such works unless the mythical images they purvey touch, however indirectly, on critical problems in Japan. Studying such highbrow and popular trivia may provide us with an anatomy of misinterpretation, whose consistency of deception betrays in turn an inadvertent kind of self disclosure. Occasionally the exposure of the contradictions in this rhetorical discourse on identity may yield a rich, negative witness to the hidden reality it traduces, a reality that proves to be less exotically alien and, indeed, strikingly familiar in its estrangements. It is in this sense that I would like to understand Andreski's reference to a possible 'sociology of nonsense' or Turkle's notion of a 'sociology of superficial knowledge'.[4]

According to the Nomura survey, in the roughly 30 years from 1946 to 1978, approximately 700 titles were published on the theme of Japanese identity, a remarkable 25% of which were issued in the peak three year period from 1976 to 1978.[5] This formal listing may well underestimate the extent of the literature, since the *nihonjinron* as a distinctive genre merely exemplifies and intensifies the focus of a mode of thinking, of an ideology of cultural and ethnic sentiment, which has influenced generations of Japanese in the way they perceive and discuss themselves and their history and culture. The *nihonjinron* have become a force in society conditioning the way Japanese regard themselves.[6] In this sense, we cannot draw a neat distinction between the *nihonjinron* and other media. The problem consists in defining the organising principles and the ideology of the literature on Japanese identity in order to be able to discern where it is operant, and where it is ignored or excluded.

The *nihonjinron* I have selected for study here are, predominantly, the handiwork of upper echelon scholars in the Japanese academy who have chosen to elect themselves as proxy spokesmen for the inarticulate soul of the national essence. These thinkers occupy a singularly privileged position in their society, whose social and educational ethic strongly favours those who by persistence manage to secure their intellectual credentials from such élite centres of learning as Tokyo and Kyoto Universities.

Despite their prestige as reception centres for the best and brightest, such universities have invited conflicting judgements from outsiders. Where one visiting scholar can write that they are characterised by an: 'openness, vigour, and imagination — probably reaching as close to the ideal of free inquiry and the unbiased search for truth as has any other institution in Japan or elsewhere',[7] another can write on equally good grounds of evidence that: 'little of what contemporary Japanese scholars write and publish in Japanese could be published intact in a literal English translation without becoming the butt of amazement and even ridicule abroad. Yet these works, which are widely read in Japan, are by eminent men writing in their own fields.'[8]

Reading the *nihonjinron* is an exact task. The unflagging productivity of the genre, the extremely broad parameters of its cultural references, its mingling of trite opinion with obscure erudition, and particularly the way one text plays off another, accepting a silly idea thrown into the ring of debate only to modify it with a further twist of absurdity, make inordinate demands even on those prepared to wade and sift through what is in good part merely the intellectual fast food of consumer nationalism. It would be a simple matter if the material could be circumscribed by Gellner's dictum that, 'the nationalist process is inversely related to its own verbiage, talking of peasants and making townsmen,'[9] since it would suffice for interpretation to simply turn the myths inside out in order to discover the embarrassing realities they disguise. But the *nihonjinron* subsume under their scrutiny virtually anything in Japan, from *pachinko* (i.e., pinball as Zen *satori* in the machine age) to nosepicking and toilet functions (behavioural and olfactory emblems of East-West differences).[10]

Because the competition for this lucrative market is fierce, new ideas and angles are at a premium in a literature all but exhausted of interpretative novelty by over one hundred years of intensive discussion. One well-worn technique is to comment on contemporary news in terms of the hackneyed concepts of national character. The news justifies the recourse to the banal clichés of nationalism, while the nationalist concepts are renewed and sustained, vindicated by their apparent relationship to ever-changing events. Another technique consists in the eclectic melding of sociological jargon with older ideas, which enables writers to repackage ideas almost moribund in the worn language of an earlier idiom. Behind the dizzying proliferation of terms, therefore, there lies hidden and retained the inveterate shortlist of key concepts of national identity, which survive from earlier decades solely by virtue of this flashy linguistic transvestism.

Related to this trend is the perturbing device of ransacking prewar texts of an ultranationalist cast of thought for cultural insights whose freshness for the younger generation stems from a diffuse ignorance of a specifically fascist interpretation of Japan. This conceptual counterfeiting rephrases extreme right wing notions in terms of a modish jargon borrowed from foreign disciplines of analysis, thus safeguarding and preserving the earlier totalitarian theorems under the impenetrable alias of an ostensibly value-neutral, empirical sociology or psychology. Despite the proliferation of titles and the rapid flux in idiom, the *nihonjinron* often merely recycle, in scientific garb, the ideological forms of the past, and show themselves impervious to the instructive movement of time.

As an easy source of extramural income, writing on cultural identity is often inspired by the allure of money. But it would be wrong to reduce the phenomenon to the corruptions of mercenary interests. The mandarinate is heir to a tradition of Confucian bureaucratic moralism, and their functional effectiveness as promotional agents stems from the fact that often both writer and reader have been reared within a propagandistic milieu of cultural education permeated by controls on critical dissent. The ideology of Japaneseness has exhibited a tenacity of life denied more formally political doctrines precisely because political discourse was inculcated as cultural values with strong moral overtones. Concepts grounded in this earlier, albeit contrived, 'tradition' are thus not understood as intellectual constructs but rather as objective descriptions of social mores.

The literature on identity in this sense is the subtlest of instruments of ideological coercion, and a 'self-fulfilling prophecy' since it reflects and conditions in turn manipulated categories and modes of expression diffused for the discussion of how the Japanese are supposed to perceive themselves. Such an enculturation of political discourse is potentially a more powerful form of social control than prewar 'thought policing' since, though demonstrably heir to the ideological patrimony of Japanese fascism, the ideological roots of these ideas have been forgotten, while the ideas themselves are hailed as new conceptualisations and ethnological descriptions of Japanese realities.[11]

Given that the bulk of the more recent material consists in pep talks dishing out the sweet anodynes of national uniqueness to a mass audience, the popularity of the *nihonjinron* may in part be explained by the way they gloss the ritual banalities and oppressive formality of everyday life with the rich lacquer of cultural traditions vibrantly alive through successive upheavals in society from the hoary past to present times. Couples who silently spend their time in front of the television are not suffering from communication problems, as in the West, but merely engaging in a novel version of the ancient art of oblique discourse. Girls who have been sexually assaulted may console themselves with the learned view that, in Japanese tradition, rape is followed by love.[12]

Thus everything, from the distasteful tedium of the factory line to daily violence can be made to resonate with archaic significances. In this way the *nihonjinron*, through the consistent linking by analogy of the hallowed past with the haggard present, tend to sanctify the hollow banalities and estranging dimensions of the profane, contemporary world. Just as the new religions cater to the alienation of rural immigrants to the great urban centres, to people suffocated by the rootless yet dense anonymity of the great metropolis, so these books on cultural identity service the semi-bourgeois strata of the new state with a sense of national community, as a kind of emotional ersatz for a wanting sense of either real social solidarity or individual selfhood.

In their self-elected function of being the interpreters of the world, the mandarins exercise an enormous power of conditioning influence on the way not only other Japanese but also on the way foreigners perceive Japan. The language barrier insulates the full contextual picture of much pulp scholarship from the critical glance of foreign eyes, and the bewildering jargon built up through decades of intertextual commentary constitutes itself a formidable barrier in its obscurity and apparent incoherencies, a kind of intellectual bamboo curtain even for those with some control over Japanese materials. The practice of editorial censorship, suppression and discrete paraphrase in books translated from this literary deluge naturally tones down accents of waspish nationalism, speculative eccentricity or cultural point-scoring rendering them all but opaque to the foreign readership. Dialogue under these conditions assumes the form of a superficial consensus based on shared mystifications, and Kiernan's fear that the meeting of East and West might prove less an amalgam of enlightenments as much as an encounter of minds in mutual regression[13] threatens to approach its sorry realisation.

The extension of the images packeted by the *nihonjinron* to external markets is increasingly important in an age of Japanese internationalisation. Spreading knowledge of Japan abroad has been seen as an indispensable device for bolstering Japan's national security.[14] Scholars have buttressed their arguments for larger investments in the establishment of language programmes and cultural centres abroad by suggesting that 'the coming economic war' will be 'a war of cultures' in which the way foreigners interpret the Japanese mind will prove decisive for the outcome.[15] The country's international success will hinge, according to one foreign commentator, on its ability to convince a sceptical outside world of the uniqueness of its racio-cultural traditions.[16]

Since the *nihonjinron* assume that culture itself precedes and determines existence, economic frictions with the outside world are reduced to unfortunate clashes in cultural style. Discussions on economic and diplomatic conflicts are entangled in dubious references to the decisive differences in mentality and culture, a tactic which often relies upon the outsider's ignorance, or his inability to verify such claims. Often the argument of culture is used astutely and consciously to deflect attention from the real problems at issue, or to rationalise a refusal to concede ground on issues that primarily involve economic interests.

A case in point was the suit brought by American employees of C. Itoh and Co Inc of New York over discriminations in wages and benefits against the non-Japanese staff. Management rejoined that salary differentials and perks reflected, not parochial favouritism, but rewards for the added linguistic and cultural skills of the Japanese staff. American executives were advised to live in Japan and study *haiku* composition and the rituals of *sake*, in order to make up the leeway.[17] This specious defence runs counter to what some *nihonjinron* maintain, namely that rewards for work in Japanese groups are not measured in economic, but rather in social, terms.[18]

The case illustrates well how the projection of 'culture' abroad, the deft publicitarian manipulation of national images often contrived by government-linked circles in close collaboration with journalists, intellectuals and business groups, is believed to have a key role in furthering Japanese economic interests.[19] The tie-ups between trade interests, politics and the packaging of the ideological software of culture by coopted intellectuals in the nationalist current in order to influence the way Japan is seen by the outside world, is a subject which has received scant attention. We lack *expéditions en haute intelligentsia* like that conducted by Hamon and Rotman within the intellectual freemasonry of the Parisian *cumulards* (intellectual entrepreneurs with a finger in every pie). Their conclusion that there are no more than 200 *intellocrates* with real social power, of which perhaps no more than 30 are able to propose or block a course of ideas,[20] may well prove suggestive for the Japanese situation. The élitist character of the school system encourages such networks, and Mori Arinori specifically designed education so that:

> the higher schools should cultivate, among those who are headed for the upper crust (of society), men worthy of directing the thoughts of the masses: be they bureaucrats, then those of the highest echelon, be they businessmen, then those for the top management, be they scholars, then true experts in the various arts and sciences.[21]

The use of the words 'culture' and tradition in these contexts suggests how the interpretation of social realities in terms of continuities with the pre-industrial past has proved of great advantage and tactical force in the pursuance of social control via the ideology of authenticity, and the ambitious quest for a position of self-determined status and image in the world at large. Consciously or otherwise, the intervention of the mandarinate, by which I understand those intellectuals who sponsor the politicisation of culture for nationalistic ends, has been decisive in the betrayal of the past in the service of contemporary deceptions. Their insistent habit of entrapping social life, history, culture and politics within the confounding, entangling nets of archaic 'traditions' and 'unique characteristics' has deprived their audience of the linguistic and conceptual resources indispensable for understanding the socio-economic roots and historical contexts from which that culture and its interpretations have emerged.

When culture is seen as infrastructural, as determining all of the forms of social and economic life, history is made irrelevant, and social praxis is emptied of any element of liberating force and illuminative power, since everything is seen as a symptom of the higher spirit, that enduring, omnipresent yet ineffable entity which is called 'the Japanese spirit'. Witness the remarks of an Aida Yūji in discussing the nature of economic competition in Japan:

> It is not a matter of saying that excessive competition is due to the extreme overcrowding of our society, but rather that it is first and foremost due to the fact that the mental structure (*seishin-kōzō*) itself of the Japanese produces a peculiar kind (*tokuyū*) of excessive competition. Is it not then possible for this kind of defect to be rectified? No, for as these racial characteristics (*minzokuteki-tokushitsu*) are a product of ethnological, climatic and historical conditions, they do not easily allow of rectification. Furthermore, these matters are not so much questions of 'good' and 'evil' as much as problems of 'character' (*seikaku*).[22]

In displacing empirical investigation with cultural and characterological prognosis, the mandarinate catapults itself from a position of marginal relevance to centre stage. It is to such stewards of tradition that the 'meaning' of pollution, alienation, suicide, monopolies, political manoeuvrings and social crises is referred. These sleuths of autochthony, while anchoring the contemporary world to the bedrock of ancestral race consciousness, profit from key deficiencies in the educational system, such as the lack of training in clear thinking and debate. It is as if an erudite immersion in tradition were an adequate substitute for analysis, whereas in fact such historical cultivation is often little more than a cultural placebo for a modern malaise. When all social phenomena are riveted to the cast iron moulds of ahistorical identity, there can be no redress from crises, personal or national, but only a perpetual recursion to cultural renewal as expressed in mindless solidarity with the pristine virtues of the tribal past.

The *nihonjinron* not only entrap people with a contrived discursive tradition to insulate the social structure from effective critique, but also militate against the emergence of an autonomous and individual search for identity. Adjudicating on 'Japanliness' (*nihonrashisa*) is an academic or media-controlled monopoly whose very terms of debate exclude competitive dissent from the Japanese, as individuals, themselves. The Japanese are as the clerks choose to define them: *cogitor ergo sum* (I am thought therefore I am). Where Erikson has accustomed us to think of identity in terms of that complex process of inner struggle and growth through which the individual realises himself, the *nihonjinron* insist that in Japan identity is invariably 'group-orientated', and the term comes to imply the submergence of the individual within society, his coalescence with others, and the identity of subject and object, the inner and the outer world.

Therefore, that complex fusion of felt estrangement of self and society leading towards a dialectical reequilibrium between the two, in which the individual realises himself within society, is alien to the notion of identity as understood by the *nihonjinron*. Every inch of autonomous self-assertion by the individual is contested as threatening the hegemonic reach and authority of the corporate, national ideal. While intent on projecting an image of Japan's national uniqueness abroad, the *nihonjinron* vigorously deny the very possibility of individual, uniquely personal identity within Japan itself.

Take the following testimony from a book on a form of Japanese psychotherapy claimed to be unique. Patients in Japanese mental homes rebel, as do patients the world over, against the way their doctors label and categorise them:

> His case is not exactly like other people's, he may claim, though similar perhaps. The doctor handles such *a plea for uniqueness*, however, by eliciting reports from other patients which indicate congruency between their symptoms and those of the patient in question. Furthermore, he continues to make accurate predictions about the symptom complex. *How could he understand it so well if it were so unique? Finally, the doctor defines the desire to be 'special' or different from other people as part of the neurosis itself, as something to be eventually overcome by the treatment.* (My italics)[23]

In prewar Japan people suspected of thought crimes were arrested, and pressured to renounce their subversive ideas, and any such 'thought criminal' (*shisō hannin*) 'was not recognised as fully cured until he did so'.[24] In the somatic totalitarian order of Huxley's *Brave New World*, '(a)ll the people who, for one reason or another, have got too self-consciously individual to fit into community life',[25] are exiled to an island. In democratic, postwar Japan people are apparently interning themselves in asylums in order to be healed of their pathological sense of private identity. But in the last instance, despite the similarities in theory and technique to the diagnoses and 'health care' meted out to dissenters and anti-social individuals in the Soviet sphere and countries where authoritarian psychiatry is used, the Japanese approach has frequently been hailed as a unique ethno-psychiatric method which may prove a valuable contribution to an alternative psychotherapy.

We may take the liberty of borrowing this insight from Morita therapy and redeploying it back against the obsessional claims for uniqueness in the *nihonjinron*. In doing so, we are enabled to diagnose such assertions as neurotic symptoms of derangement in the intellectual asylums of nationalistic learning. By analysing these exclamations of peculiar identity and national idiosyncrasy we may pick up a clue here and there as to the underlying disorder. Persistence in our critical attention may enable us to understand the paradoxical insistence on the uniqueness of Japan among the community of nations side by side with a consistent refusal to recognise the individual uniqueness in the Japanese themselves. How, after all, can a society be exalted as *sui generis* if those who constitute it are much of a muchness, mere clones of an invariant national type?

Notes

1. C.A. Moore (ed), *The Japanese Mind: Essentials of Japanese Philosophy and Culture*, (University of Hawaii Press, Honolulu, 1967) p.1.
2. Yukawa Hideki, 'Modern Trend of Western Civilisation and Cultural Peculiarities of Japan', in Moore, *The Japanese Mind*, ibid. pp.52-65, p.56.
3. Nakamura Hajime, 'Basic Features of the Legal, Political and Economic Thought of Japan', in Moore, *The Japanese Mind*, ibid. pp.143-63, p.143.
4. S. Andreski, *The Social Sciences and Sorcery* (Penguin, Harmondsworth, 1974) p.12. S. Turkle, *Psychoanalytic Politics* (MIT Press paper, Cambridge, Massachusetts, 1981) p.19.
5. Y. Sugimoto and R. Mouer, *Nihonjin wa 'nihonteki' ka* (Tōyō Keizai Shinpōsha, Tokyo, 1982) p.13, citing a survey by the Nomura Sōgō Kenkyūjo.
6. Sugimoto and Mouer, *Nihonjin wa 'nihonteki' ka*, ibid. p.15.
7. T.R.H. Havens, 'Changing Styles of University Life In Japan' in *The Japan Interpreter*, 8:3 (autumn 1973) pp.285-91, pp.290-1.
8. R.A. Miller, *The Japanese Language in Contemporary Japan: Some Socio-linguistic Observations*, AEI-Hoover Policy Studies, 22 (Stanford University Press, Stanford, California, 1977) p.2.
9. E. Gellner, *Nations and Nationalism* (Basil Blackwell paper, Oxford 1983) p.107, cf.p. 57.
10. On *pachinko* see F. Maraini, *Ore Giapponesi* (Leonardo da Vinci, Bari, 1962) pp.65-7; on nosepicking, Kenmochi Takehiko, *'Ma 'no nihon bunka*, (Kōdansha Gendai Shinsho, 1978) pp.68-9; on excrement and identity, Aida Yūji, *Honne no jidai* (Kōdansha, Tokyo, 1981) pp.72-3, and Watanabe Shōichi, *Nihon soshite nihonjin* (Shōdensha, Tokyo, 1980) pp.39ff.

24 The Quest for Identity

11. Ideology in Trilling's sense, cf. 'Ideology is not ideas; ideology is not acquired by thought but by breathing the haunted air ... Ideology is not the product of thought; it is the habit or the ritual of showing respect for certain formulas to which, for various reasons having to do with emotional safety, we have very strong ties, of whose meaning and consequences we have no clear understanding.' L. Trilling, *The Liberal Imagination* (Doubleday & Anchor paper, New York) 1953 p.277.

12. D. and E.T. Riesman, *Conversations in Japan*, (Allen Lane, London, 1967) pp.114, 224.

13. V.G. Kiernan, *The Lords of Human Kind*, (Pelican, Harmondsworth, 1972) p.xxxviii.

14. Mr Takahashi Hisatsune as reported in *Mainichi Daily News*, 10 February 1979.

15. Kimura Shōsaburō, *Seiyō no kao. Nihonjin no kokoro*, (PHP, Kyoto, 1977) p.194. Cf. Suzuki Takao, *Kotoba no ningengaku* (Shinchō Bunko, Tokyo, 1981) pp.119ff., recommends teaching Japanese abroad to guarantee world peace, since it will be easier for foreigners to be ordered out of the way as the economic elephant of Japan moves.

16. G. Clark in *Shūkan Asahi*, 27 May 1977 p.137. See also G. Clark with Takemura Ken'ichi, *Yuniikuna nihonjin*, (Kōdansha Gendai Shinsho, Tokyo, 1979) pp.106ff.

17. As reported in *Time*, 13 June 1977, p.15.

18. C. Nakane, *Japanese Society*, (University of California Press, Berkeley and Los Angeles, 1970) pp.82-3.

19. Some aspects of this are touched on in R.A. Miller, *Japan's Modern Myth*, (Weatherhill, New York and Tokyo, 1982) pp.12-13, 17-18, 140-3, 196-9.

20. H. Hamon and P. Rotman, *Les Intellocrates* (Editions Ramsay, Paris, 1981) pp.11, 27.

21. Cited in D. Roden, *Schooldays in Imperial Japan* (University of California Press, Berkeley and Los Angeles, 1980) p.40.

22. Aida Yūji, *Nihonjin no ishiki kōzō* (Kōdansha Gendai Shinsho, Tokyo, 1972) p.30. For a rational explanation see Martin Bronfenbrenner, '"Excessive Competition" in Japanese Business', in *Monumenta Nipponica*, 21:2 (1966) pp.114-124.

23. D. Reynolds, *Morita Psychotherapy* (University of California Press, Berkeley and Los Angeles, 1976 p.204.

24. R.H. Mitchell, *Thought Control in Prewar Japan* (Cornell University Press, Ithaca and London, 1976) p.185.

25. A. Huxley, *Brave New World* (Penguin, Harmondsworth, 1955) p.178.

3 A UNIQUENESS RARE IN THE WORLD

'Si je ne vaux pas mieux, au moins je suis autre'
J.J. Rousseau, *Les Confessions*, book I.

The vapidly reiterated refrain underlying the literature on Japanese identity is that of uniqueness. An insipid enough catchword in English, where it is frequently used by clever admen in publicity campaigns to flog mass-produced goods to a market of anonymous consumers, it constitutes the cardinal verbal and conceptual pivot around which Japanese writers hinge their manifold claims for the peculiar status of their national culture.

The concept in Japanese is handsomely served by an ample vocabulary, headed by the egregious loanword *yuniiku* (imported perhaps to suggest a foreign endorsement of local narcissism). Such words as *tokuchō, tokushoku, tokuyū, tokuisei, dochaku, dokutoku, dokuji* and *koyū*, to name but a few, run the range of implication from 'distinctive characteristic', 'singularity', 'idiosyncrasy', 'peculiarity', 'indigenous to', 'unique' to 'autochthonous', '*sui generis*' and 'originality'.[1] The undertone of uniqueness to which such varied terms allude is frequently strengthened by such qualifying expressions as *rui no nai* (unparalleled), *takoku ni nai* (not in other countries) and *gaijin ni totte wakarinikui* (difficult for foreigners to understand), which tip the balance of connotation from the mere 'distinctively different' to the 'absolutely unique'. Theoretically, any Japanese phenomenon is natural grist for the uniqueness mill, and is presumed not to exist elsewhere by virtue of the fact that it exists in Japan. Further such uniqueness is unable to be perceived by foreigners, or understood by them, since its cognition is grounded in social consciousness, in the epistemology of the blood.[2]

The word 'unique' is used in very peculiar ways, in a manner consistent with the rigorous illogicality of the *nihonjinron*. In normal parlance, unique properly means 'the only one of its kind'. Yet in Japanese it assumes the connotation of referring to the unusual, the different. Thus we read of references to 'something (Japanese) which is unique, with *very few* parallels in foreign countries',[3] where the final phrase compromises the very assertion it qualifies. Within the genre it is a tacit convention that the word and concept of uniqueness are co-terminous and indeed synonymous with Japan. Pearl Buck reflects this view when she remarks that, 'If there is one single truth about Asia, it is that while each country there is totally different from every other, Japan is the most different of all. Here people are unique, even among Asian peoples.'[4]

The real distinction in such gobbledegook is obscure, though as we see by comparing this with the remark of Charles A. Moore cited earlier, it reflects a curious preference and esteem for the Japanese against other Asian peoples. Pearl Buck concedes that all Asian countries are 'totally different' from each other which, logically, should imply that each equally warrants the epithet 'unique'. But this, by some unexplained convention, is reserved for Japan. Whereas other countries are totally different from each other in their unlikeness, Japan is, we are given to believe, unique in its dissimilarity. The point of such semantic finesse is justly lost upon the reader.

Another writer has it that, 'Japan ... is unique in being almost as unique as its people like to think.'[5] Again, it is recognised that, the world over, people tend to consider themselves unique, but the author will accept this claim only in the Japanese instance. What is meant by 'almost as unique' is not clear, since something is either unique or not so. Clearly, the word is used as a talismanic password: like the mason's handshake, it signals to others that one is privy to the secret knowledge accorded to the initiated insider. Protest at the solecistic way this word is used, and at the relentless repetition of the term, and one usually receives an amicable rejoinder along the following lines: 'If the Japanese are to do better in the vital task of effective communication with other peoples, they need to understand themselves better, starting with the fact that *they may be unique but not that unique.*' (my italics)[6]

The ritual incantation of the word 'unique' in this vague, solecistic fashion suggests the essential mystifying nature of such discourse, the appetite for the odd and enigmatic. It is no coincidence that these books are peppered with allusions to riddles and puzzles (*nazo*), since the purpose is to acclaim the ineffable rather than to explain. A priestly caste of interpreters like the mandarinate must make reality mysterious before it can assume an oracular posture, and the mere evocation of the word 'unique' is a guaranteed device for popularising one's works on Japan.

Gregory Clark's recent volume, *The Japanese — Sources of their*

Uniqueness, is an easy digest of trendy themes in the *nihonjinron* which owed its success to the way in which a foreigner managed to 'transcend' his Western prejudices by echoing the general line of the *nihonjinron* world view. After an extended elaboration, in episodic and anecdotal fashion, of the various clichés of Japanese uniqueness, Clark rather curiously suggests that the only other civilisation to share the traits that render Japan *sui generis* was that of Minoan Crete.[7]

Two points might be made here. If Minoa may be properly adduced as a parallel to Japan, then neither can be considered unique. The second point is that Clark recapitulates the highly tendentious image of the Minoan thalassocracy constructed by Sir Arthur Evans, which emphasised the *sui generis* character of this island kingdom. Yet even if scholars do not share the thesis of Hans Wunderlich concerning the Egyptian character of the Minoan palace,[8] they are generally in agreement that Crete was nothing of a *lusus naturae* in the Aegean world, but drew off inspiration from many civilisations in the Mediterranean basin.

Could we say then, in retrospect, that Japan is thus truly unique in that Clark's parallel with Minoa is wrongheaded? Another possibility suggests itself. Namely that the constituent elements of the image of Japanese uniqueness are founded on the same prejudicial reading of the evidence, on the same hollow ignorance of comparative cultures, which marred Evans' interpretation of Crete.

But then Clark remains ineluctably a foreigner, and by definition lacks that power of authoritative introspection into the unique which, according to the *nihonjinron*, is the birthright of those born of Japanese blood. For all of his sympathetic attempts to don the mask and mimic the voice of 'Japaneseness', his cast of mind must betray the perceptual bias of Western consciousness. As we are repeatedly told, 'Japaneseness', and the 'power to perceive the unique' are immanent in the blood, and thus a primary qualification for theorising on Japan is that one be of Japanese racial origin. Japanese folklore is defined as 'research undertaken *by* Japanese' on Japanese customs.[9] To research Japanese grammar it is necessary that one be nursed and reared on the Japanese language (*nihongo de sodatta ningen*),[10] a condition which implicitly snubs and invalidates the work of generations of Western philologists. Japanese archaeology is defined as the study of the material artefacts of people who in childhood mastered Japanese, within Japanese society, and thus, it seems, excludes the archaeological study of any other ethnic group (Korean, Chinese, Ainu, etc,) in primitive Japan.[11]

A second prerequisite is that, in order to calibrate the unique, the Japanese scholar must consciously divest himself of, and repudiate, any kind of thinking and concept derived from Western tradition. This is no small matter, since the formal study of Western scholarly techniques is an integral element of any academic course in Japan, and the intellectual culture has been overwhelmed by the introduction and discussion of Western ideas for over one hundred years. Yet nationalist philosophers like Ueyama Shunpei protest at the taking over of the prejudices of Western research, and historians like Egami Namio insist that it is unscientific to attempt to read Japan through the epistemological lens of alien traditions.[12] What is required is the cooperative building of a conceptual framework from within the immanent resources of Japanese experience itself. The *nihonjinron*, when not merely anecdotal pastiches or episodic reflections, form a kind of testing ground for 'autochthonous' theories, putatively free of any traces of Westernism.

First arguing that Western-style approaches smash themselves against the obdurate rocks of Japanese uniqueness, the mandarins then essay to discover a key term or concept through which the quirkishly elusive shapes of this peculiar reality of Japaneseness may be captured and analysed. Hamaguchi Eshun remarks programmatically that:

> Many of the authoritative theories and concepts employed in the analysis of the national characteristics of the Japanese in research to date have their provenance in the West. And yet, notwithstanding this, students of these problems have adopted and used these theories uncritically, even without scrutinising them from a cultural perspective. For instance, the concept of 'personality', as I shall presently touch upon, and the psychoanalytic theories which are related to its core, are not necessarily suited to the clarification of the humanity and cultural patterns of either orientals or the Japanese. Nevertheless, hardly any investigation has been undertaken of the appropriateness or inappropriateness of these (Western theories) up to the time of writing.

Hamaguchi is no extremist. He assures us that some value is to be found in Western work, and that foreign images of Japan do have some, if limited, value for the Japanese themselves. Yet he continues:

> 'Japanliness' (*nihonrashisa*) as seen from the outside world does not always neatly coincide with that Japanliness which we ourselves feel as Japanese. It is therefore also necessary to portray the Japanese by employing a conceptual scheme thought out from an immanent standpoint, that of the Japanese themselves. As Japanese researchers, we must not be confined to using the framework of Western analysis in order to supplement and reinforce their research on Japan from the inside. Rather, I should like to attempt as far as possible to rediscover an original 'Japanliness' as observed from our own perspective. In short, this work will be an immanent exhumation of the 'emics' (as Kenneth Pike puts it) of our culture.[13]

It is enough to identify a theory as alien to contest its validity and pertinence; there is no attempt at logical rebuttal or at demonstrating empirical shortcomings. Furthermore, we are never told in what precisely this Western perspective or analytical framework consists, the assumption of his work in general being that all outsiders are constrained to see and study Japan through a unitary set of assumptions. He shows no awareness of the fact that anthropologists can come to diametrically opposed conclusions when studying the same socio-cultural reality. Where Redfield's work on Tepoztlán depicts an atmosphere of amicable community, Lewis's research highlighted their factional strife and endemic suspicions.[14] Yet both were Westerners using similar ethnological tools.

Indeed, the premise that Western research is somehow ideologically or culturally cohesive in its assumptions and conclusions reflects more the nationalists' conviction that his own culture is homogeneous. Hamaguchi projects onto Western scholarship his own presupposition that Japanese thinkers share a latent perspective which, in turn, reflects immanent socio-cultural values. Were theory merely the objectification of cohesive national sentiment, then why the historical inability in Japan to achieve any firm consensus as to precisely what constitutes the nature of this 'unique' Japanliness? The Mexican case is instructive since the difference between the two interpretations lies in the divergence between a study which describes how the people *like to see themselves*, the official version, (cf. Redfield), and the analysis of how they actually think and behave, the inner reality (Lewis).[15] What Hamaguchi and others are upholding in their exclusion of Western analytic concepts is their right to see themselves as they would like to be seen.

The entity called a 'Western perspective' is, then, never delineated and exposed. It hovers about like a shadowy bogey in the mandarins' nightmares of being culturally infiltrated, a noxious poison ever suspected of contaminating the pristine wishing wells of native authenticity, despite the fact that it has never been distilled for analysis by the counter-insurgent alchemists of autochthony. And this elusiveness is understandable since what is being referred to by a Western framework is simply a set of analytical procedures which threaten to shake and undermine the illusions of wishful sentiments like the presumptions of uniqueness.

The bogus character of the contrasted procedure of immanentism is evident from the fact that, as we shall see, Hamaguchi's work and its ostensibly 'emic' perspective betray telling traces of a fascist theory imported under an astute linguistic alias into prewar Japan from a Western country. In any case, to speak of introspecting a purely immanent framework when to graduate, teach and think about such problems in Japan one must read a mass of Western works, is very much like insisting on one's virginity several decades after a polyphiloprogenitive marriage. For better or worse, Japanese intellectual culture is profoundly conditioned by ideas (if often ill-digested) derived from the massive impact of Western (and, in an earlier period, Chinese) civilisation.

If the *nihonjinron* are concerned with studying Japan from what is passed off as a Japanese perspective (= any ideological fiction of a nationalist scholar's choice), it is also true that a part of the genre is concerned to interpret the West consciously from the same ethnocentric standpoint. As we shall see, the definition of how the Japanese are 'unique' implicitly requires a model of adversary contrast — namely, the West, against which the *sui generis* nature of things Japanese is set in relief. In this sense, these books are as much *seiyōron* (discussions of the West) as *nihonjinron*. But these interpretations of the West are vitiated by the same defects which characterise the 'emic' analysis of Japan, namely, provincialism, irrationality and mere silliness.

For example, Sabata Toyoyuki attempts to explain Western

institutions, values and intellectual history in terms of the effects of meat-eating and pastoralism. To mix classical proverbs, for Sabata, the belly is the mother of invention. He prefaces his quaint volume *Concepts of the Carnivores*, with a plea for studying the Occident in terms of Japanese notions of culture, to redress the balance for the fact that Westerners like Ruth Benedict have taken the liberty to look on Japan from a Western angle.[16]

The point is that whereas Benedict shows herself acutely aware of the dangers of ethnocentric bias, and consciously attempted to avoid making value-judgments, Sabata makes a conscious effort to ground his theories in nationalistic perspectives. Whereas relativism for Benedict implied the need for continual critical scrutiny of the eurocentric assumptions in her work, for Sabata the doctrine is useful only in dismissing the relevance of ideas of foreign provenance and replacing them with the intrinsically valid presuppositions of his native perspective. The one attempts to de-ethnicise, the other to renationalise, the study of comparative cultures.

Nakane Chie highlights the problem from another angle. She discerns two independent streams in Japanese sociology, both of which suffer from a profound discrepancy between the models they construct and the reality they aim to depict. On the one hand, there are Japanese who work within the mainstream of Western thought, and on the other there are those who, like Hamaguchi and Sabata, strive to elaborate an intrinsically Japanese theory in order to isolate the unique specificity of their own world. For her, each approach embodies insuperable difficulties.

On the one hand, scholars who try to engage the elements of putative distinctiveness by means of 'emic' concepts (the *tokushokuha* or uniqueness clique) are hampered by their dogmatic rejection of Western theory and tend towards 'off-the-cuff theorising'.[17] Then again, thinkers who deploy foreign sociological models often discern a divergence between the model and the quirky character of the Japanese data. She illustrates this with an analogy drawn from traditional dressmaking.

In cutting Japanese cloth, it was customary to employ a standard called the 'whale measure' (*kujira-jaku*, 14.91 inches). Since this measure evolved indigenously and involved no fractions, it is quite 'rational'.[18] Yet under contemporary law, this ancient system has been replaced by the foreign metric system, which exposes the presence of fractions, which she considers 'irrational', since now the dressmaker must add a 'plus alpha' to his calculations. In similar wise, she argues, the imposition of Western models onto Japanese reality reveals a 'plus alpha' fractional residue which the imported theory cannot account for, and it is this element which constitutes the unique aspect of Japan. But since these unique fractional elements do not fit into the model, Western-trained sociologists in Japan are apt to dismiss them as 'feudal residues,' as indices of backwardness. This is a grave error, since it is precisely the plus alpha which constitutes the core of Japaneseness. What is required is an immanent approach but one which has theoretical power and credibility.

Nakane's way out through the Scylla of Western sociology and the Charybdis of 'emic' improvisation is the methodology of British social anthropology, which does not make the West the basis for comparative analysis. In this way, she considers that she has found an 'outsider method' for analysing the 'insider's uniqueness'. The trouble is that Nakane's work displays a diffuse ignorance of the very sociological method she exalts, being unempirical and consistently tautological, or question-begging. She can write without any sense of circularity that, 'It is well known that Japanese women are nearly always ranked as inferiors; this is not because their sex is considered inferior, but because women seldom hold higher social status.'[19] This cannot be another famous example of uniquely Japanese logic since Nakane herself disclaims such methods. In any case, when not marred by *non sequiturs*, her studies merely naturalise in an apparently scientific jargon certain key concepts of the ideology of Japaneseness, and have very little to tell us about social realities.

Since the aspect of uniqueness is apparently precipitated and crystallised into view by the imposition of Western models, albeit as 'alpha plus fractions', this would mean that ironically it is precisely these alien theories which enable us to observe the uniqueness of Japan. Nakane fails to appreciate that sociological models are valuable as much as for what they, in retrospect, fail adequately to explain as for what they do explain. Her analogy itself is false. The British Imperial Measure, when supplanted by the metric system devised in France, forced the English to work, as it were, with alpha plus fractions. But does this imply, by Nakane's logic, that existentialism, structuralism or deconstruction have no relevance to the study of English literature and thought?[20]

What Nakane's remarks do reveal is a latent sense of irritation at the cost to tradition of applying Western sociological notions. She testifies that they show up 'feudal residues' which, from an immanent perspective, are to be valued as repositories of uniqueness. Even if she is protesting at the way Marxist models are imposed, with unbending, unempirical rigour and fidelity, onto the Japanese scene, she aims her shaft at all Western thought, even of the most flexible and undogmatic kind and, in doing so, inadvertently betrays a resistance to Western thought as undercutting and subverting a nostalgia for the pre-modern past. Indeed the persistent failure of thinkers in the uniqueness school adequately to conceptualise indigenous realities in native terms derives precisely from their principled refusal to think in the way demanded by contemporary realities, to acknowledge the modern within themselves.

To cite one final example of this method, interesting in that like Nakane the writer appreciates the fatal weakness of the *nihonjinron* in theory while desiring to salvage somehow the research object of isolating aspects of uniqueness, we may remark Take Sugiyama Lebra's attempt to conflate Western method and Japanese intuition. For her, the orientation of 'universality', which she calls the *nomothetic* approach, is good in so far as it goes, but is vitiated by its irreducible eurocentrism. Agnostic with regard to such 'universals' of human behaviour, she advocates an 'idiographic' approach which might enable one to describe the peculiar features of a culture area.[21]

She is justly cautious, however, to qualify this veiled commitment to the cause of uniqueness. She concedes that unique systems are intelligible only in reference to wider, general propositions, and in the context of Japanese research daringly suggests that, 'it would be legitimate to observe Japanese behaviour as a sample of the behaviour of homo sapiens.'[22] This guarded concession is quite a breakthrough in a literature which, like ufology, expresses an overwhelming passion for discussing sightings of unidentifiably familiar objects. Yet it is only a minor retreat, a *reculer pour mieux sauter*, for she declares somewhat programmatically that, 'Universally applicable concepts and theories derived from social science will be freely imposed in order to locate Japan *uniquely* in a *universal* map.' (my italics)[23]

We are back where we began, with Pearl Buck's contradiction. For logically all societies might be placed uniquely on a universal map. Why this insistence, when dealing with Japan, on the exclusive mania of presuming it is uniquely unique? The result in Lebra's case is the same as we have discussed in Nakane's; her exposition consists in the main of citing ideological testaments from the *nihonjinron* as if they were digests of empirical description and scrupulously statistical fieldwork.

In conclusion, let us return to the problem posed by the shibboleth (a word, we recall, used to detect foreigners) of uniqueness. As Andreski remarks, 'The only kind of admissable explanation of a unique event consists of showing either that it comes under a known general rule, or that it can be resolved into elements which all come under some known general rule.'[24] That is, the unique can only be conceptualised if it has an element of recurrency. The study of Japanese uniqueness should, therefore, subsume the phenomena in question under general laws. But the *nihonjinron* exclude even this possibility because, as I hope to show, it is one of their fundamental axioms that concepts and laws with a general or universal validity (*fuhenteki datōsei*) are characteristic of occidental tradition and thus, by definition, inapplicable to Japan. Andreski concludes that, 'Elements of irreducible uniqueness ... can be apprehended but neither explained nor described — for even description involves analysis of a phenomenon into elements which are sufficiently recurrent to fit meanings of words.'[25]

As the 'ineluctable residue of a phenomenon that has eluded all classification',[26] the unique cannot therefore be conceptualised even by endogenous models conceived from within Japanese traditions of nationalist thought. The fact is that it can only be apprehended and remembered in silence, something which the garrulous profusion of *nihonjinron* overlooks. Whereas Toynbee defined the unique as 'a negative term signifying the inapprehensible', and held that the 'absolutely unique is, by definition, indescribable',[27] the *nihonjinron* insist that the uniquely Japanese is only 'inapprehensible to, and undescribable by, foreigners.'

By this peculiar discrimination therefore, those who tend the cult and culture of uniqueness may dispense with the burden of proof. The truth of their injunctions is entrusted to the felt belief of partaking in an irreducibly ineffable experience by virtue of being born Japanese. The very failure of its numerous hierophants to concur on a rational formulation of such experience is felt to lend a negative witness to its elusive presence. As Sir Banister Fletcher, following Japanese sources, once put it in discussing the uniqueness of Japanese roof design, this differs from Chinese roof architecture in having 'some intangible quality which stamps them as indubitably Japanese'.[28] That is, the very fugitive indefiniteness of what is acclaimed as unique stamps it as being quintessentially Japanese. The chic of indigenous peculiarity thus thrives on the delicious impalpability of its felt truisms.

In the course of these pages we shall encounter many attempts to break out of the constricting bonds of 'Western thought' and develop a specifically Japanese mode of analysis. Extravagant claims will be made for the existence of intellectual revolutions which, curiously enough, have remained shyly hidden from the outside world. Miura will tell us that Tokieda Motoki's theory of language 'has as great a significance (in linguistics) as that of Copernicus in astronomy'.[29] We shall hear Imanishi Kinji acclaimed for revolutionising ethology by thinking through an oriental alternative to Western Darwinism. We shall study claims that Doi Takeo's Japanese version of psychoanalysis has refurbished its Freudian parent with a wide-angled lens of a more general, because orientally-based, concept. We shall hear that Nishida Kitarō, proudly proclaimed as 'the most difficult (thinker) in the whole history of philsophy',[30] has devised a new epistemology whose grandeur lies in its unprecedented synthesis of oriental and occidental thought. Underlying these claims is the assumption that, 'To the extent that we continue our cognition of nature through this windowframe borrowed (from the West), (we) Japanese shall never give birth to a Japanese kind of originality thought out by Japanese brains'.[31]

No one would consider it improbable that people of Japanese birth may produce work of great originality in any field of endeavour. Noble prizes in physics, the brilliance of its literature, and the research of scholars indifferent to national self-intoxication bear witness to the obvious. But to the degree that intellectuals devote themselves to isolating these ghostly entities of cultural uniqueness, they consign their lifework, unawares, to the rubbish-dumps of provincial intellectual history.[32]

Notes

1. *Dochaku*, 'autochthonous', for example, derives currency from the Confucian Kumazawa Banzan (1619-91)'s works which emphasised the need to 'return to the land' (*dochaku*). It thus bears physiocratic undertones. See Henry D.

Smith II, 'Tokyo as an Idea: An Exploration of Japanese Urban Thought Until 1945', in *Journal of Japanese Studies* 4:1 (winter 1978) pp.45-80, pp.50-1.

2. Suzuki Takao writes that, 'To be Japanese is a question of the blood' in his *Tozasareta gengo — Nihongo no sekai*, (Shinchō Sensho, Tokyo, 1975) p.177. Kimura Bin speaks of the Japanese 'historical kinship of blood identity' in his *Hito to hito to no aida*, (Kōbundo Sensho, Tokyo, 1972) pp.12, 75, p.118. This discourse is a postwar oriental revival of what German ultranationalists were wont to call the *Urahnungen von Blut und Boden*.

3. Watanabe Shōichi, *Nihongo no kokoro*, (Kōdansha Gendai Shinsho, Tokyo, 1974) pp.59-60.

4. P. Buck, *The People of Japan* (Robert Hale, London, 1966) p.11.

5. G. Murray, 'Uniqueness is Japan's Strength and its Weakness' in *The Japan Times*, 28 June 1979, p.14.

6. Matsumoto Michirō, 'Haragei as Communication: No. 23', *Asahi Evening News*, 24 October 1978, p.10.

7. G. Clark, *Nihonjin — Yuniikusa no gensen*, trans. Muramatsu Masumi, (Simul Shuppankai, Tokyo, 1977) pp.219-20. Cf Clark, *Yuniikuna nihonjin*, ibid. pp.69ff.

8. H.G. Wunderlich, *The Secret of Crete*, trans. Richard Winston (Fontana Collins, London, 1976), esp pp.46, 66-7, 74, 127, 143, 157ff.

9. Ikeda Yasaburō, *Nihon no yūrei* (Chūkō Bunko, Tokyo, 1974) p.235. Ueyama defines '*nihongaku*' as research done by Japanese on Japanese questions, and insinuates that outsiders' research is imperialist. See Ueyama Shunpei and Umehara Takeshi, *Nihongaku kotohajime*, (Shōgakukan, Tokyo, 1972) p.30.

10. Ōno Susumu, *Nihongo no bunpō o kangaeru* (Iwanami Shinsho, Tokyo, 1978) p.3.

11. See Miller, *Japan's Modern Myth*, ibid. pp.151-2 on an article by Higuchi Yoshio.

12. Tada Michitarō, Umesao Tadao hen, *Nihon bunka no kōzō* (Kōdansha Gendai Shinsho, Tokyo, 1972) p.67.

13. Hamaguchi Eshun, *'Nihonrashisa' no saihakken*, (Nihon Keizai Shinbunsha, Tokyo, 1977) pp.2-3.

14. R.H. Murphy, *The Dialectics of Social Life*, (George Allen and Unwin, London, 1972) p.103.

15. Murphy, *Dialetics*, ibid. p.104. It might be remarked that the same applies to the recent Mead-Freeman dispute on Samoa.

16. Sabata Toyoyuki, *Nikushoku no shisō*, (Chūkō Bunko, Tokyo, 1966) pp.3-4.

17. Nakane Chie, *Tate-shakai no ningen kankei*, (Kōdansha Gendai Shinsho, Tokyo, 1967) pp.14f., 20.

18. The Japanese word used to translate 'rational' (*gōriteki*) bears a strong connotation of pragmatism, with overtones of ruthlessness. This is due to the influence on common usage of such works as Aida Yūji's extraordinary attempt to link Western rationalism to an outlook rooted in pastoralism and meat-eating! See his *Gōrishugi*, (Kōdansha Gendai Shinsho, Tokyo, 1966). On the word see Ferdinand Basabe, 'Attitudes of Japanese Students Towards Foreign Countries' in *Monumenta Nipponica*, 21:1 (1966) pp.61-96, pp.87-8.

19. Nakane, *Japanese Society*, ibid. p.32. See also the critique by Ross Mouer and Yoshio Sugimoto, 'Some Methodological Reservations concerning Nakane Chie's work on Japanese Society' in *Latrobe Working Papers on Sociology* (Melbourne, 1980) no.53.

20. A perfect parallel to Nakane's assumption may be found in Anthony Burgess's novel *1985* (Arrow ed., London, 1980) pp.33-4., where it is held that the Cartesian abstractions of France tend to dehumanise British empiricism and

common sense, a view supported by linguistic arguments from the metrification of British currency.

21. The 'nomothetic' — 'idiographic' distinction derives from Windelband's typographical contrast between a 'science generating laws and a science of individual events' as Frisby puts it in his introduction to T. Adorno et al., *The Positivist Dispute in German Sociology*, trans. Glyn Adey and David Frisby (Harper Torchbook paper., New York, 1976) pp.xx. It enters the *nihonjinron* from Nakamura Hajime's recycling of this Windelbandian contrast between natural and historical sciences (which he attributes to Rickert) in order to contrast the putatively 'idiographic' character of Chinese thought to the 'nomothetic' thought of India. See Nakamura Hajime, *Ways of Thinking of Eastern Peoples*, rev. and ed. Philip P. Wiener (East-West Center Press, University of Hawaii, Honolulu, 1964) p.594 n.54.

22. T.S. Lebra, *Japanese Patterns of Behavior*, (University of Hawaii Press, Honolulu, 1976) p.xiii.

23. Lebra, *Japanese Patterns*, ibid. p.xiv.

24. S. Andreski, *The Uses of Comparative Sociology*, (University of California Press, Berkeley and Los Angeles, 1969) p.49. Cf. Wunderlich, *Secret of Crete*, ibid p.143, writes, 'Isolation, non-correlation, uniqueness — a scientist who deals with the investigation of nature's laws finds it hard to accept this "individualistic" approach.'

25. S. Andreski, *Comparative Sociology*, ibid. p.49.

26. A. Toynbee, *A Study of History*, vol. 12 (Oxford University Press paper., 1964) p.11.

27. Toynbee, *History*, ibid p.11. See also his remarks on 'Pretensions to Uniqueness' in the same volume, pp.620ff.

28. Sir B. Fletcher, *A History of Architecture on the Comparative Method*, 17th edition, ed. R.A. Cordingley (Athlone Press, London, 1963) p.1219.

29. Miura Tsutomu, *Nihongo wa dō iu gengo ka* (Kōdansha Gakujutsu Bunko, Tokyo, 1976) p.109. His use of the Copernican analogy parallels in its silliness the view of a Nazi writer that Fichte's theory of language was a Copernican turning point. For the example see Watanabe Shōichi, *Gengo to minzoku no kigen ni tsuite*, (Taishūkan Shoten, Tokyo, 1973) p.142.

30. Shimomura Toratarō, *Nishida Kitarō, Hito to shisō*, (Tōkai Daigaku Shuppankai, 1977) p.244.

31. Tsunoda Tadanobu, *Nihonjin no nō* (Taishūkan Shoten, Tokyo, 1978) p.361.

32. Cf Miller, *The Japanese Language in Contemporary Japan*, ibid. p.65 on Sakuma Zōzan's attempt to harmonise Eastern and Western techniques.

4 THE DIALECTICS OF DIFFERENCE

'Most human things come in pairs.'
(Attributed to Alkmaion)

Although the bearish market for speculative works on Japanese culture has capitalised on the affluent alienation of the inchoate middle class in postwar Japan, its ideas trade on resources with profound roots in earlier cultural and intellectual traditions. A literature formed over several decades of intensive inframural debate which feeds off such an intricate, long-lived tradition of nationalism, poses daunting obstacles in the way of anyone rash enough to embark on a systematic description. Any passage in the *nihonjinron* demands several pages of linguistic analysis, socio-historical, cultural and intertextual annotation and crossreference before the full resonance of its implicit meanings may assume an intelligible voice. Analysis is further complicated by the fact that the constellation of intellectual premises, interpretative techniques, talismanic keywords and references built up over time operate, to all appearances, on an un- or semi-conscious level.

Secondly, the curious thing about the *nihonjinron* is that while they express, beneath a bewilderingly diverse range of ideas, a coherent ideology of nationalism, they at the same time deny that they have anything to do with ideology or politics. A key theme of the literature distinguishes the ostensibly ideological, power-fixated character of Western discourse from the putatively aesthetic and sentimental expressionism of the Japanese.[1] This is managed by using muckraking techniques to study Western civilisation, and a 'soft' cultural reductionism when contrastively analysing Japanese realities. Nationalism is an ideological construct in the occident, and a natural outgrowth of the race in Japan. Thus we are informed that:

> Murata *pointed out* that before the Meiji Restoration, a single nation was already present in the sense of a single market, a single tongue, and a single culture; hence there was no need to invent the fiction of a nation, as in Europe, but rather to discover what was already there and bring it to consciousness.

Suzuki added that European nationalism was the creation of the middle class, but there there was no such middle class in Japan seeking a locus for ideology (my italics).

These astute mendacities will not convince anyone who has the slightest grasp of Japanese political and intellectual history. One can hardly speak of a single nation, let alone culture, when an aristocratic, warrior oligarchy ruled over a vast peasantry that was cynically likened to a sesame seed in that the more you squeezed it, the more came out. The mass mobilisation of the people was conducted via educational indoctrination and socialisation for nationalistic ends tightly organised by an autocratic élite which rapidly discovered the utility of conducting the politics of social control by means of concepts of race and culture centering on the Emperor.[3] Postwar *nihonjinron* merely attempt to salvage this discourse by detaching it from the more overtly imperial-political idiom.

Thirdly, the interpretation of 'Japaneseness', as I have noted, necessarily implicates, or perhaps more precisely, inculpates, the outside world. The adumbration of putatively unique traits distinctive to the Japanese negatively engages by contrast foreign societies as the dumb accomplices of endogenous uniqueness. As the anti-image of foreignness, Japanese identity can only be affirmed by stipulating a systematic, if Borgesian, taxonomy of the Other (China, the West). All nationalisms stake out the exclusive boundaries of their claim to uniqueness on the common ground of our collective humanity by categorical expropriations of favoured traits and values. What they attribute to themselves they must deny to 'outsiders', and conversely what is ascribed to others is disclaimed within the indigenous patrimony.

The inveterate habit of sifting foreign chaff from indigenous wheat is conducted *in vacuo*, devoid of dialogue and feedback from the contrasted other. In Tokugawan times, Japanese neo-Confucians who contested the Chinese distinction between their central, civilised selves and peripheral, barbarian others (Japanese included) as intolerably demeaning, tended in Nakai's words 'to become involved in a game of one-upmanship played with an invisible opponent', that is, a kind of oedipal 'shadow-boxing'.[16] This acute observation may be transferred, *mutatis mutandis*, to the *nihonjinron*'s endless discussion of differences between Japan and the West. Behind the contrived image of the 'West', as will become apparent, one cannot but sense a narcissistic antagonism to the father.[5]

In establishing such an adversative typology, nationalistic intelligentsias covertly attribute to the other (nowadays the 'West') social tendencies and behaviour which they view as corruptive of an idealised, archaic and purely endogenous tradition, and take great pains to disrecognise or exclude them from their provincial culture. Such national mythologies, while at a political level functioning as devices of 'negative social integration',[6] serve as techniques of cultural exorcism in the attempt to salvage an infantile ideal of pure unity by casting out the devils of invested heterogeneity. Psychoanalytically, the *nihonjinron* represent a childish revolt from the hostile claims of reality (the 'West'), with all that this implies (i.e., aggression exteriorised and self-inflation).

The image of the West then in these pages has nothing to do with reality. It is a projection onto a part of the outside world of the mandarinate's alter ego, or of those latent facets and emerging trends within modern Japanese society which the nationalists of the uniqueness school, with their archaising nostalgia and romantic reverie for an idyllic (and private) past, seem determined to repudiate or dissemble. Their cleaving of sensibility and values into this dichotomy of us and the other has impoverished themselves in the very act of establishing and affirming the authentic traits of Japaneseness, in that their being unique entails not being like the chosen other. When such discourse proceeds to the extremes that we find in the *nihonjinron*, then subsequent recourse to comparison with other societies serves not so much to enlighten by analogy, as to exacerbate the finicky sense of difference. Such a culture deprives itself of any power to understand its human predicament.

We must always bear in mind, therefore, in reading these texts, that the features of contrast function as polemical units in a schizoid dialogue which mediates private or social tensions, wherein the idealised past and the scathed present are posed in adversary contrast under the aliases of 'Japan' and the 'West'. Just as the 'West' here is a contrived fiction indispensable for the reflected appreciation of Japanese diversity, so 'Japan' too partakes of the same imaginary quality. The very disproportion in contrastive scale between a multinational West and Japan not only betrays a strain of megalomania, but hints at the intrinsic futility of such comparisons. The tacit assumption of equivalence in scale and homogeneity produces errors like the following:

> We say simply 'Japanese', but in fact Japanese is a compound body of a great number of small languages. What one calls the Germanic languages are a bundle of such languages as English, German, Dutch and Danish. Japanese in its totality is equivalent to the Germanic languages.[7]

A moment's reflection might have told the author that Japanese and its dialects may bear comparison to English *or* German and their respective dialects. But the tacit premiss of an equivalence in scale between Europe and Japan leads the writer to equate, in effect, Japanese dialects with national languages which have, in their own right, numerous dialects and subdialects. The result is nonsense.

In attempting to introduce a little provisory order into what appears, on the surface, to be a highly disordered and anecdotal script of culture, one is forced to select only the leading themes which form the basic skeleton key to the *nihonjinron* world view. The technique for reading such works consists in remarking the occurrence of every implicit or explicit contrast or polarity enunciated between Japan and the West, and then ordering the elicited terms in a grid to discover the subliminal episteme of basic cultural antitheses. Like primitive thought, which 'deepens its knowledge with the help of *imagines mundi*', we are dealing here with a 'system of concepts embedded in images',[8] whose ideological character only emerges on a close contextual reading of widely differing texts. In eliciting the terms which underpin this field of mythic discourse, I make no pretensions to either elegance or comprehensiveness, but merely attempt to present the minimum number of contrasts around which the basic logic of the *nihonjinron* hinges.

First and foremost, geo-ecological differences are considered to play a decisive, central role in the determination of different cultural styles.

The fashion for discussing East-West differences and Japanese cultural identity in terms of geoclimatic influences was initiated by Shiga Shigetaka's seminal work *Nihon Fūkeiron* (1894) and found sophisticated philosophical expression in Watsuji Tetsurō's *Fūdo* (1935). Such works drew inspiration from that vein of Western

Table 1: Geoclimatic Base

The 'West'	'Japan'
1 Continent (*tairiku*)	1' Island (*shimaguni*)
2 Desert (*sabaku*); pasture (*bokujō*)	2' Forest (*shinrin*); paddy (*inada*)
3 Nature poor, man dominates	3' Nature rich, nature prevails over man
4 Temperate, regular climate	4' Variable, monsoonal climate

writing, from Montesquieu to Herder, which related the diversity of societies and cultures to geographical factors, and redeployed on the West-Japan axis the common distinction between the desert monotheism of the Semites and the agricultural polytheism of Mediterranean, and especially, Graeco-Roman civilisation. These terms are not value-neutral, but rather understood as crucial determinants for explaining the 'violent' forms of Western life in contrast to the 'peaceful harmonies' of oriental, and especially, Japanese culture.

The ideological character emerges when we consider the next two constellations of contrastive features, which are believed to flow inexorably on from the preceding distinctions. In terms of population this geophysical opposition generates the antinomy illustrated in table 2.

Table 2: Racial Base

'West'	'Japan'
5 Miscegenation of races (*jinshu no konketsu*)	5' Blood purity, one race (*chi no junsui na minzoku, tan''itsu minzoku kokka*)

The five elements in tables 1 and 2 engender the distinctions in economic mode illustrated in table 3.

Table 3: Productive Base

'West'	'Japan'
6 Nomadic-pastoral (*yūboku-minteki*)	6' Settled agricultural (*nōkō-minteki*)
7 Animal flesh food base (*dōbutsuteki, nikushoku*)	7' Vegetable/rice diet (*shokubutsuteki*)
8 Labour based on slaves (*dorei*)	8' Communal cooperation

Dwelling on a continental landmass, inhabited by pastoralists, hunters and nomads, so the argument runs, leads to incessant conflict between races. Aggression is nurtured as a key element of survival in the competition for lands, and insufficient food due to poor soil. The killing and enslaving of hostile neighbours, and intermarriage between tribes, is a natural result of sharing a landmass with other races. Since agriculture is unproductive, the nurture and slaughter of domesticated livestock is a key to winter survival. In Japan, by contrast, we are told (as early as 1916) that isolated as they were, the prehistoric Japanese never came into contact with powerful, alien races, and lived by agriculture in a fertile land where moderate labour guaranteed a moderate harvest. Thus it was possible to secure an easy livelihood in a sparsely populated land occupied by one race, which lacked in consequence experience of violent racial conflict of the kind that gives rise to a life and atmosphere of bellicose culture.[9]

In its popular postwar form this thesis was fleshed out by the work of Egami Namio and Aida Yūji in particular. The former, though he suggested ideas scandalous to the ideologues of purism such as that the tumulus culture of prehistoric Japan was created by an influx of alien 'horseriding nomads' (thus implying a blood mix), popularised the notion of contrasting the West and Japan in terms of the differences in culture style that distinguish nomadic pastoralists from agriculturalists.[10] The latter, in a series of comically eccentric studies, attempted to decipher Western high culture in terms of the psychic effects that ensue from an economic lifestyle based on the slaughter of nurtured animals. The effect was to give specious theoretical backing for earlier impressionistic contrasts dwelling on dietary factors like meat versus rice.[11]

There is no point here in confuting this picture since we are dealing with dream-mongering and not facts. That early Japan was multiracial, that Korean élites operated at the highest levels and that even the Imperial house had foreign blood connections is too well known to warrant annotation.[12] That meat-eating was widespread, and that peasants often had to subsist, not on rice, but on millet and vegetables, is less well known.[13] What must be understood is that these ideas are symbolic, not empirical.

The literature next elaborates a series of contrasts in social structure and belief, the majority of which date back to early Meiji times.

This series of terms gives away much of the *nihonjinron* game.

Table 4: Social Base

'West'	'Japan'
9 Society (*Gesellschaft*)	9' Community (*Gemeinschaft*)
10 Individualism (*kojinshugi*)	10' Groupism (*shūdanshugi*), contextualism (*kanjinshugi*)
11 Horizontality (*yoko*)	11' Verticality (*tate*)
12 Egalitarianism (*byōdōshugi*)	12' Hierarchy (*kaikyūsei*)
13 Contract (*keiyaku*)	13' 'Kintract' (*en'yaku*)
*14 'Private' (*shiteki*)	14' 'Public' (*kōteki*)
15 'Guilt' (*tsumi*)	15' 'Shame' (*haji*)
16 Urban-cosmopolitan	16' Rural-exclusive
17 Rights (*kenri*)	17' Duties (*giri, on,* etc.)
18 Independence (inner-directed) (*jiritsu, dokuritsu*)	18' Dependence (other-directed) (*amae, taritsu*)

*There is a deep conceptual confusion involved in the use of these terms, as there is also with the discussion of shame and guilt, so that there is no consensus as to the location of such terms. See chapters 5 and 10.

For what are here depicted as contrasts in cultural style or social structure are more or less identical with differences between industrial and preindustrial (feudal) civilisation in the West. All it tells us is that 'modern' Japan is conceptualised in terms of feudal categories which social development in the West outgrew and transcended. Feature contrasts 9,9', for example, derive from Ferdinand Tönnies' analysis (1887) of the transition from rural community to social, urban industrial life. The *tate-yoko* opposition, associated wrongly with the name of Nakane Chie, along with the egalitarian-hierarchy contrast, stem from Alexis de Tocqueville's critique in *Democracy in America*.[14] So too, the contract-kintract dichotomy reflects Henry Maine's distinction (*Ancient Law*, 1861) between status-relationships in kinship-based societies and contractual relationships in modern societies, though modulated by Francis Hsu's coinage of the term kintract which, through its use in his student Hamaguchi Eshun's work, is now thought of as specific to Japanese culture.

As conceptualised in the *nihonjinron* therefore, Japan's sociocultural and institutional 'uniqueness' consists in nothing more than the retention through modernisation of feudal structures, and as the example cited from Nakane earlier shows, the repudiation of Western conceptual models stems from the fact that these latter tend to expose, by the force of analogy with earlier Western life, aspects of tenacious medievalism operant in the Japanese version of capitalism. In this sense, then, the *nihonjinron*'s picture of Japan's alternative modernism disguises both a sympathy for feudal values and critical hostility or revolt against the logic and institutions of bourgeois culture. It is no coincidence then that the American fascination with these images arises from the crisis and breakdown within the United States of precisely these middle-class values.[15]

Next we discern a series of contrasts in socio-cultural values (table 5). The argument runs that the existence of different races in the European landmass leads to a struggle for survival, intolerance between tribal groups and a bellicosity which encourages patriarchal (masculine) rule. Such conflictuality lends instability to societies. In order to win over the minds of racial adversaries, a unitary ideology of monotheism is created, aiming to subordinate diverse groups, each with a different *Weltanschauung*, to the one ruling principle. All this follows on from the conditions of pastoral existence in ecologically poor regions. Japan, by contrast, follows a different logic. Since war (*sensō*) is often defined as interracial conflict Japan, given the fiction of one race, is reprieved from such violence, since the chronic internecine slaughter marking Japan's internal history is not so much 'warfare' but a family fight.[16]

Psychoanalytically, the characterisation of Japan here as feminine, animistic and, as it were, ontologically inert (see below on the *kokutai*), conjoined to a polemical resistance to the masculine (the father as bellicose or, in monotheistic terms, Jehovah as a violent God) lends itself to a reading of these myths in terms of a return of the repressed phases between primary narcissism and the oedipal stage.[17] This may well appear a strained interpretation on the thin, schematic evidence presented here. But it not only follows

Table 5: Socio-Cultural Mode

'West'	'Japan'
19 Masculine (i.e. paternal) (*masuraoburi*)	19' Feminine (i.e. maternal) (*taoyameburi*)
20 Bellicose (*kōsenteki*)	20' Peaceful (*heiwateki*)
21 Monotheistic (*isshinkyōteki*)	21' Polytheistic animism (*tashinkyō-teki animizumu/shāmanizumu*
22 Unstable (*fu-antei*)	22' Stable (*antei*)
23 Intolerant (*fu-kan'yō*)	23' Tolerant (*kan'yō*)
24 Materialistic (*busshitsuteki*)	24' Spiritual (*seishinteki*)

from the insistent identification of selfhood with aboriginal archetypes, but from the ideology of identity itself espoused by the *nihonjinron* (see chapter 12).

Finally, we are given a set of contrasts in intellectual style which explain, ironically, why the *nihonjinron* are so illogical, since they are doomed to conceptualise Japanese uniqueness within an intellectual culture they themselves define as emotive, subjective and irrational (table 6). Each term implicitly evokes the whole range of other terms in the series. A discussion on Japanese silence, for example, will suggest that communication is emotive rather than rational-verbal, and may conjure up associative ideas of unitary race (on the same wavelength), rice-cultivation by communal effort (no talk needed to do the same work among people of the same village) etc. Secondly, the opposed terms can be reversed in their location, or, introjected into Japan to set up an East-West (cf. *Kantō-Kansai*) internal opposition.[18] Much depends on historical context and polemical vantage point in a given situation, and on whether one is dealing with an Herodian or a zealotist tract.

These two terms were developed by Toynbee to contrast basic patterns of response in peripheral cultures to the encroachment, militarily or culturally, of external civilisation. The zealot responds to the alien by a reflexive fear of enswampment and loss of authentic identity, and advocates a reactionary intensification of fidelity to what he conceives to be indigenous values. The response is one of 'archaism evoked by foreign pressure'. Herodianism is a form of pragmatism, in that its exponents recognise the material superiority of foreign culture, and strive to absorb, imitate and redeploy that mechanical infrastructure which threatens to overwhelm the smaller nation. The Herodian paradoxically attempts to preserve his culture by imitating his adversary.

Table 6: Intellectual Style

'West'	'Japan'
25 Logic (*ronri*), either/or (*nisha takuitsu*)	25' Ambivalence (*ryōkasei, aimai*) both/and (*are mo kore mo*)
26 Rational (*gōriteki*)	26' Emotional (*kanjōteki*)
27 Objective (*kyakkanteki*)	27' Subjective (*shukanteki*)
28 Rigid principle (*kōchoku-teki genri*)	28' Situational logic, ethic (*jōkyō-ronri, jōkyō-rinri*, TMP)
29 Talkativeness (*oshaberi*)	29' Silence (*chinmoku*)

Both implicitly distinguish spiritual from material culture, and do not necessarily differ in their attachment to native traditions. The difference is tactical, the zealot refusing to compromise his purity by modernising, the Herodian attempting to salvage native autonomy by mastery of that technology whose power constitutes the outsider's superiority. Where the zealot finds his 'spirit' futile before the engines of war, the Herodian discovers that his adoption of foreign material culture to defend indigenous autonomy subtly alters and subverts the very values he strives to protect. He quickly learns that the imported infrastructure has a logic all its own, and that the 'mechanically propelled Trojan horse' of alien civilisation drastically disrupts and reorganises the social fabric upon which the ideology of his traditional outlook rests.[19]

If a culture is to survive, the Herodian must initially prevail, for the zealot has no means other than his fanaticism to repel the challenge of a stronger civilisation. But it is a no-win situation, for the Herodian irredeemably compromises the ideal of autochthony in exchange for political autonomy. In a country like Japan, whose history lends itself to a superficial schema of phasal alternation between openness and closedness to the outside world, Herodian reform is often succeeded by zealotist withdrawal. The former is inspired by the illusory slogan of 'Japanese spirit, Chinese/Western techniques' (*wakon kansai, wakon yōsai*) to justify a modernisation which erodes tradition, the latter attempts intellectually to recuperate lost ground by insisting that tradition remains intact somehow, or that the native spirit has 'naturalised' the alien in such a way that it harmonises and strengthens values pre-existing in the endogenous *Weltanschauung*.

To illustrate this point in the briefest way, in the Nara-Heian period Japan was flooded by a massive infusion of Chinese, Korean and Indian culture. The records of the past were written in Chinese or a Chinese-derived script, which inflected local traditions with the concepts, prosody and values of sinocentric civilisation, so that 'nothing in the Chronicles can be safely assumed to be purely Japanese'.[20] But though the blight of foreignness had irreparably contaminated the granary of endogenous tradition, a vast amount of academic labour, past and present, has persisted in trying to sift exotic chaff from indigenous wheat. We see this in the ensuing age, the inward-looking Kamakura Shogunate, marked by rear-guard attempts to salvage the lost, idyllic world of a pure Japan. Zealots like Nichiren and Kitabatake Chikafusa go so far as to flesh out the bare skeletons of nationalism with the muscular forms of foreign thought, ironically appropriating by tacit or overt larcenies the rich storehouse of classical Indian and Chinese thought.

This period is particularly important for understanding some of the key strategies operant in the contemporary *nihonjinron*. Where Nichiren sequesters a certain chiliastic vein in Buddhist eschatology to 'Japanise' the roots of an alien creed, and Kitabatake Chikafusa and other 'Shintoists' shrewdly plundered ideas from heterodox Confucianism to buttress their fictitious claims for Shintoist succession, present-day mandarins borrow ideas from Hegel to Heidegger, and in modified form, pass them off as indigenous interpretations or uniquely Japanese theories.

This inchoate nationalism legitimated the technique of conceptual table-turning, that is, converting ideas of alien provenance into 'originative' Japanese principles, and the technique flourished in late Tokugawan times, where Motoori's textual criticism, though devoted to the retrieval of the pristine forms of Japanese sentiment, is deeply indebted to trends in Chinese philology, and where 'Shintoist' theologians like Hirata Atsutane were not above rifling even the book of Genesis for material to supplement their reconstructions of ancient 'Japanese' cosmology.

The modern *nihonjinron* draw on the herodian thought of the Meiji period, and the zealotist fictions which flourished under Shōwa fascism. The herodian critiques tend to depict the 'Japanese characteristics' in the paradigm as drawbacks to modernisation, while the zealotist school devoted much labour to excogitating malicious theories which cast the left-hand side, or Western half, of the paradigm into disrepute. Given that key social sanctions like shame, and an acute sensitivity to inferiority-superiority implications in relationships with the outside world, motivate and provide the dynamic emotive power behind these debates, the dominant tone depends very much on how the mandarins perceive themselves in terms of being 'behind' or 'abreast' of the West. Herodianism and zealotism have twice marked the beginning and end, respectively, of 'catching up and overtaking' (*cf. oitsuke-oikose*) modernisation.[21] The crosscurrents and intertextual resonances between these two streams of thought which are only tactically diverse are dense, since they share a hidden sympathy for the ideal of a 'purely autochthonous culture'. If the zealot repudiates 'liberty' and 'individualism' in favour of traditional groupism, the herodian tends to try and discern a 'Japanese form of liberty' in a local tradition of inner exile or reclusion in the mountains, and a 'uniquely Japanese form of individualism' in the figure of the hermit.

As with most systems of cultural nationalism, the *nihonjinron* hypostatise traits, qualities, characteristics and values. Everything within the sphere of indigenous culture, and its foreign contrast, is seen to exemplify or betray traces of an underlying entity or substance, in this case of 'Japaneseness' or 'Westernness'. History and cultural change are therefore merely emblematic symptoms of an unfolding or efflorescence of what was already there, in the national ethos, since prehistoric times. This entity in prewar Japan was called the *kokutai* (national polity) or *kokusui* (national essence). Change in itself then, even if impelled by outside pressure, is not significant, since it is interpreted as merely illustrating, epiphenomenally, the aspects and development of the endogenous ethos. In this insistence on the ontological stasis of Japanese culture, we are reminded of what Freud wrote of instinct, namely that it is 'an urge inherent in organic life to restore an earlier state of things which the living entity has been obliged to abandon under the pressure of external disturbing forces'.[22] The zealot's ideal of autochthony thus harbours elements of instinctual regression.

Thus, for example, Darwin's stress on individual differences, and the competitive struggle for survival is not interpreted in terms of an extension into evolutionary biology of the market theory of bourgeois economics, as a scientific reflex of mercantile values or as the natural outgrowth of empirical research. Rather it is 'explained' as merely the modern, but typical, symptom of the endemic Western tendency towards individualism and bellicosity (*cf* 10, 20 in tables 4 and 5, chapter 4). Conversely, since the paradigm of antitheses poises the 'groupism' and 'pacific harmony' of the Orient against such traits, it follows that a truly 'Japanese' theory of evolution must come up with an alternative concept in which the species (= the group) is seen as the unit of change, and in which the struggle for survival is replaced by harmony between species.[23]

Those who sustain in various forms the thesis of an immutable *kokutai*, in the face of the fact that the growth of Japanese culture owes a massive debt to successive infusions of foreign civilisation, understand that this view entails particular difficulties. How is one to comb or tease out the pure threads of 'authentic Japanese culture' from that huge, tangled bricolage of traditions woven and rewoven over with the warp and weft of Ainu, Polynesian, Korean, paleo-Siberian, Chinese, Indian and Western influences? In defining the 'authentically Japanese' as the pure residuum of an archaic mono-racial culture undefiled by, and predating, foreign contamination, the word 'Japanese' can only refer to speculative entities lying beyond the historical reach of empirical studies. At best one is left with *a posteriori* deductions from historical records coloured by Chinese conventions, records that themselves point to a polyracial, and polytribal (*cf* the Kumaso and the Hayato) complex. As one distinguished merchant in this troubled field of speculation puts it, 'When one investigates what is meant by 'indigenous' (*koyū*), one cannot but trace the phenomenon in question back to its origins in the antiquity of *Jōmon* culture. For extraneous elements have penetrated even into "the world of court Shinto", which otherwise appears to be pure and peculiar to Japan.'[24]

No one can of course know what ethnic-linguistic affiliations the *Jōmon* people (5,000-300 BC) had, and in any case there is no justification for calling them Japanese. The *nihonjinron* (and here we may include a specific genre, that vast number of academic works on Japanese origins) simply assume the existence of a 'Japanese tribe' for the prehistoric period, and read back into its culture those features of outlook which later generations have come to consider as unique to their country.

Once this prehistorical *Weltanschauung* is assumed, then the problem of detecting traits and traces of Japaneseness in the later, pluricultural milieu of the historical period becomes easy. The technique consists in interpreting both the capacity and manner of Japanese assimilations of foreign civilisation as itself 'unique', in that some latent principle in the *Weltanschauung* exists which selectively absorbs, controls, and adapts foreign culture in such a way that, rather than disturbing, it actually merely catalyses the natural growth of the endogenous tradition. The principles which determine the indigenous efflorescence of such 'Japaneseness' under the spur of foreign stimulus, with the contrasting attributes of Western civilisation, are illustrated in table 7. (Principles of Indigenous Efflorescence).

As is readily apparent, these principles are merely reflexes of the various features of contrast listed earlier (A, A' result from I, I', B, B' from 5, 5' (table 2) etc,). These principles define not only

Table 7: Principles of Indigenous Efflorescence

'West' (earlier 'China')	'Japan'
A Universality (*fuhensei*)	A' Particularity-uniqueness (*tokushusei*)
B Heterogeneity (*ishitsu*)	B' Homogeneity (*dōshitsu*)
C Absolutism (*zettaishugi*)	C' Relativism (*sōtaishugi*)
D Rupture (*danzetsu*)	D' Harmony (*wa*), continuity (*renzoku*)
E Artifice (*jinkō*)	E' Nature (*shizen*)
F Abstraction (*chūshō*)	F' Phenomenalism (*genjitsushugi*) Concreteness (*gutai*)
G Donative/active (*nōdōteki*)	G' Receptive/reactive (*juyōteki*)
H Open (*hiraketa*)	H' Closed (*heisateki, tozasareta*)

the structural differences believed to exist between the Western and the Japanese outlooks, but also explain why Japanese culture never fundamentally changed despite massive foreign influences. The right hand side represents the principles of conversion which transmute culture having the left hand side principles into forms congruent with the *kokutai*. The universal is particularised, the abstract rendered concrete, the absolute made relative, and the heterogeneous homogenised.[25]

Thus it is that the *kokutai* is attributed with a 'high capacity for absorbing' foreign culture (G'), it is endowed with a unique faculty, a sort of demiurgic ghost in the machine which creatively tailors extraneous civilisation to the native cut of Japanese tradition. What appears to be *gaihatsuteki* (developed through external stimulus) can be interpreted, in this way, as *naihatsuteki* (originating in internal conditions). The logic is of course circular, as we may quickly observe from such representative statements as the following: 'Japan's constant assimilation was made possible partially by the non-exclusive nature of Japanese animism.'[26] That is, the apparent *assimilative power* (G') exhibited by Japanese culture is interpreted as deriving from some hypothetical *predisposition not to exclude* unique to Japanese animism (*cf* table 5).

Thus the banal fact that the formation and growth of Japanese culture was not autogenic,[27] but rather developed through constant creative stimulation from abroad (like every other culture),[28] is controverted by the astute tactic of arguing that alien culture is somehow invariably naturalised or Japanified at the frontier. Thus, whatever enters, has only a catalytic presence to deepen and hasten processes already inherent in endogenous development. Katō Shūichi, whose writings have otherwise displayed in earlier times a genial grasp of Western culture and a combative attitude to Japanese nationalism, reflects such a deep-rooted preconception when he upholds the view that:

> The historical vicissitudes of the Japanese *Weltanschauung* are characterised by a tenacious maintenance of the autochthonous (*dochaku*) *Weltanschauung*, and therefore by the repeated 'Japanification' (*nihonka*) of alien systems, rather than by the penetration of much alien thought.[29]

Hence the presence of the alien, rather than undermining the thesis of indigenous purity, merely sustains it. If Buddhism appears to have set down deep roots into the soil of Japanese culture, in fact what occurred is that only these elements of Buddhism which conformed to, or were compatible with (*tekigō*) the pre-existing outlook were selected.[30] If the native language was flooded with foreign loan words, this only shows that there must be a predisposition (*soshitsu*) in the national character (*kokuminsei*), or some specific character (*seikaku*) in the language which facilitates the adoption of foreign words.[31] Indeed, we are told that the very expression 'intake of foreign culture' is itself peculiarly Japanese.[32]

In reading not only the *nihonjinron* but also, more broadly, books on Japanese cultural history, therefore, the reader must be on the alert for any reference to some innate 'curiosity', 'selectivity' or 'adaptation' which moulds outside culture into forms congruent with an indigenous outlook. The jargon changes, but the prewar myth of the *kokutai* underlies such an approach. This requires some attention since the fascist notion has been consistently disguised by euphemistic rephrasing, so that even Donald Keene can slip into an inadvertent affirmation of this ideology in writing that, 'What the Japanese have done most adroitly throughout their long history consists in *selecting from* other cultures those things most suitable (*fusawashii*) to Japan.'[33]

I have attempted here to sketch out the basic terms and ideas which, under a vast array of linguistic and conceptual aliases, underpin the discussions of Japanese identity. Within these parameters, the *nihonjinron* may be said to operate within a system of totalitarian thought, in the sense of that phrase defined by Robert Conquest in his study of the poetry of Charles Williams. Conquest detects there what he considers to be the four criteria for totalitarian thought, namely (a) 'the complete acceptance of a closed system of ideas'; (b) 'the manipulation of this system as the only intellectual exercise'; (c) 'the treatment of the outsider with a special sort of irritated contempt, which conceals, or sometimes betrays, other emotions'; and (d) 'the subordination of all ordinary autonomous spheres of thought and feeling to the *a priori*: a lack of humility in the presence of the empirical.'[34]

This fits with uncanny exactitude the intellectual frame underlying the *nihonjinron*. Any study of Japan which omits to address itself to the way in which this vast interpretative tradition has conditioned the way we conceptualise Japan risks compromising and entangling itself with what is, to all extents, a totalitarian world view. In the chapters which follow, I hope to delineate some of the ways in which these *imagines mundi* and their parochial logic operate within special fields of learned discourse. If much of what follows is 'muckraking',[35] the purpose is not for ridicule. Real liberty of thought depends not only on the formal institutions of democracy but also on a constant awareness and scrutiny on the tacit conventions of thought and assumption underlying our everyday conversation. What is true elsewhere has a particular importance for the *nihonjinron*-inundated world of the Japanese media, which must be cleared and scoured in order to allow for an empirical science to grow upon the ruins of this totalitarian universe.

Notes

1. Clark, *Yuniikuna nihonjin*, ibid. pp.11, 77ff.
2. D. & E. Riesman, *Conversations in Japan*, ibid. pp.275-6.
3. For a partial explanation of why a middle class ideology did not develop see Barrington Moore Jr, *Social Origins of Dictatorship and Democracy* (Peregrine ed., 1977) pp.240f. On the educational system's 'socialisation for death' see K. Tsurumi, *Social Change*, pp.99-137. Suzuki would no doubt see this as part of tradition, as witness his remark that '(t)he Japanese may not have any specific philosophy of life, but they have decidedly one of death', *Zen and Japanese Culture*, p.85. Fest remarks on the 'deep-rooted tendency of German educational tradition to prepare the young for death rather than life'. J. Fest, *The Faces of the Third Reich*, (Penguin 1972) p.340-1.
4. K.W. Nakai, 'The Naturalization of Confucianism in Tokugawa Japan: The Problem of Sinocentrism', in *Harvard Journal of Asian Studies*, 40: 1 (1980) pp.157-99, p.173.
5. Psychoanalytically, the obsessive assertion of uniqueness reflects a desire to become father to oneself, and a narcissistic complex. Brown remarks that 'The essence of the Oedipal complex is the project of becoming God — in Spinoza's formula, *causa sui*; in Sartre's, *être-en-soi-pour-soi*'. 'N. Brown, *Life Against*

54　The Dialectics of Difference

Death, (Sphere Books, London, 1968) p.109. It is this which underlies remarks like Suzuki's that in order to create a *powerful* civilisation with a third value system unparalleled in the world, Japan must wake up to its own nature by a parricidal (*chichigoroshi*) rupture of relations with Europe, and a matricidal (*hahagoroshi*) breaking with Asia. See Suzuki Takao, *Kotoba no ningengaku*, p.108. Confirmation of such an underlying complex may be found in my remarks on Kosawa, chapter 8.

6. For this in the Germanic context see G. Field, *Evangelist of Race: The Germanic Vision of Houston Stewart Chamberlain*, (Columbia University Press, New York, 1981) p.8, *Cf* p.329.

7. Kindaichi Haruhiko, *Nihongo*, (Iwanami Shinsho, 1957) p.31.

8. C. Lévi-Strauss, *La Pensée Sauvage*, (Plon, Paris, 1962) pp.348-9

9. Tsuda Sōkichi, *Bungaku ni arawaretaru waga kokumin shisō no kenkyū*, 1 (Iwanami Shoten reprint, Tokyo, 1977), pp.28-9. For the desert-forest contrast see Suzuki Hideo, *Shinrin no shikō. Sabaku no shikō* (Nippon Hōsō Shuppan Kyōkai, Tokyo, 1978). For an historical survey of the climate approach see Minami Hiroshi, *Nihonjinron no Keifu*, (Kōdansha Gendai Shinsho, 1980) pp.40-76. The postwar revival of the fascist myth of a mono-racial society owes much to Masuda Yoshio's *Junsui bunka no jōken*, (Kōdansha Gendai Shinsho, 1967), as we see in Suzuki, *Tozasareta gengo*, ibid. p.131ff.

10. *Cf* Egami Namio, *Kiba minzoku kokka* (Chūkō Shinsho, 1967). It is not coincidental that this theory was enunciated just after the arrival of American occupation troops, in 1947. An English reworking of the theory is available in G. Ledyard, 'Galloping Along with the Horseriders: Looking for the Founders of Japan', in *Journal of Japanese Studies*, 1:2 (1975), pp.217-254; see also W. Edwards, 'Event and Process in the Founding of Japan: The Horserider Theory in Archeological Perspective', in *Journal of Japanese Studies*, 9:2 (1983) pp.265-95.

11. Aida's theory is rooted in his wartime experiences as a POW of the British, which left him with a profound hatred for Westerners. See his *Āron shūyōjo* (Chūkō Bunko, Tokyo, 1963), translated as *Prisoner of the British, A Japanese Soldier's Experiences in Burma*, by Hide Ishiguro and Louis Allen (Cresset Press, London, 1966). This is a key document for understanding the sort of psychological complexes underlying the creation of *nihonjinron* fictions of the West. On the animal thought-vegetable thought contrast see Yamashita Masao's two works, *Dōbutsu to seiyō shiso*, (Chūkō Shinsho, Tokyo, 1974) and *Shokubutsu to tetsugaku*, (Chūko Shinsho, Tokyo, 1977).

12. For an exasperated attempt to reconcile evidence of Koreans among the ancient Japanese poets with the premise of race purity, see Watanabe Shōichi, *Seigi no jidai* (Bungei Shunjū, Tokyo, 1977) pp.85-114.

13. See Katō Hidetoshi and Komatsu Sakyō hen, *Gakumon no sekai*, I (Kōdansha Gendai Shinsho, Tokyo, 1978) pp.217-24 for Shinoda Osamu's heretical views.

14. The *yoko-tate* idiom popularised by Nakane derives from Aruga Kizaemon's war-time work on rural sociology, for which see Kawamura, 'The Historical Background' p.55. It was used generally in discussing the broader society by Kawashima Takeyoshi and Katō Shūichi in the fifties. See the latter's article 'Tennōsei ni tsuite' reprinted in Katō Shūichi, *Nihonjin to wa nani ka*. (Kōdansha Gakujutsu Bunko, Tokyo, 1976) pp.104-136, p.119.

15. For example see R. Sennett, *The Fall of Public Man*, (Cambridge University Press, Cambridge, 1977) and C. Lasch, *The Culture of Narcissism*, (Abacus, London, 1980) esp. pp.27-30.

16. *Cf* Sakamoto Jirō's article, abridged and translated in *Japan Echo*, 2:1 (1975) pp.54-6.

17. See in general, C.R. Badcock, *The Psychoanalysis of Culture*, (Basil

Blackwell, Oxford, 1980), with the schema on p.246.

18. *Cf* Hayashiya Tatsusaburō, *Nihon bunka no higashi to nishi* (Kōdansha Gendai Shinsho, 1972) pp.35ff, 57ff: Hayashiya Tatsusaburō, Umesao Tadao, Yamazaki Masakazu, *Nihonshi no shikumi,* (Chūkō Bunko, Tokyo, 1976) pp.211ff.

19. A. Toynbee, *Civilisation on Trial and The World and the West* (Meridian paperback, New York, 1971) pp.167ff, 270-1.

20. Sir G. Sansom, *A History of Japan to 1334,* (Tuttle reprint, Tokyo, 1974) p.55.

21. See chapter 12, for the periodisation of this cycle.

22. Freud in *Beyond the Pleasure Principle,* cited Badcock, *Psychoanalysis,* p.48.

23. Imanishi Kinji and Yoshimoto Takaaki, *Dāuin o koete,* (Asahi Shinbunsha, Tokyo, 1978) p.21.

24. Umesao Tadao, Tada Michitarō hen, *Nihon bunka no hyōjō,* (Kōdansha Gendai Shinsho, 1974), p.9, where Tada is paraphrasing the views of Ueda Masaaki, contained on pp.94-102 of the same volume.

25. See for example Nakamura, *Ways of Thinking,* chapters 35, 36.

26. So Victor Koschmann in J.V. Koschmann (ed.) *Authority and the Individual in Japan* (University of Tokyo Press, 1978) p.6.

27. The most ambitious attempt yet to naturalise within modern terminology the *kokutai* vision of autogenic development may be found in Murakami Yasusuke, Kumon Shumpei, Satō Seizaburō, *Bunmei toshite no Ie-shakai,* (Chūō Kōronsha, Tokyo, 1979). An English résumé may be found in Murakami Yasusuke, 'Ie Society as a Pattern of Civilization', in *Journal of Japanese Studies,* 7:2 (summer 1981) pp.281-363.

28. The way a culture develops is contingent on its geographical location. As Andreski writes, 'Only a small part of a culture of any given society has originated within it; but what can be imitated depends naturally on contacts with other cultures which, as far as the inner structure of the society is concerned, must be treated as accidental. The fact that China is near to India, whence it could borrow Buddhism, and not to Europe, from which Christianity might have been introduced, cannot be conceived as being dependent on the character of Chinese society and culture. Andreski, *The Uses of Comparative Sociology,* ibid. p.180.

29. Katō Shūichi, *Nihon bungakushi josetsu,* I, p.24 (Chikuma Shobō, Tokyo, 1980). For a critique see R.A. Miller's review, 'Plus ça change ...' in *Journal of Asian Studies,* 39:4 (August 1980) pp.771-82.

30. Tsuda, *Wa ga kokumin shisō no kenkyū,* I, ibid. pp.71-2.

31. Kindaichi, *Nihongo,* ibid. pp.20-1; Tsurumi Kazuko, *Nihonjin to kōkishin,* (Kōdansha Gendai Shinsho, Tokyo, 1972) p.107 writes that, 'Japanese has a structure which facilitates the absorption of foreign words'. Updated jargon like 'structure' is increasingly favoured to replace the language of 'character' and 'predisposition' in earlier *kokutai* literature.

32. Suzuki Takao, *Tozasareta gengo,* ibid. p.132.

33. Shiba Ryōtarō, Donald Keene, *Nihonjin no nihon bunka,* (Chūkō Shinsho, Tokyo, 1972) p.159.

34. R. Conquest, *The Abomination of Moab,* (Temple Smith, London, 1978) pp.32-3.

35. *Cf* the remarks of Kawamura 'The Historical Background,' p.60, who emphasises the need for less theorising on Japan and more criticism of existing theories.

5 THE WARP OF LANGUAGE

'Intelligence, give me the precise name of things! ... That my word may be the thing itself, created by my soul once more.'
Juan Ramón Jiménez, *Eternidades*, 3

In the search for the *sui generis* characteristics of Japan, the Japanese language plays a central role, not only as the medium of discussion but also as the primary object of analysis. As the articulate mother of nursling thought, the enabling idiom of mute, material culture, speech constitutes the very crucible of identity. Early difficulties in determining the genetic affiliation of the Japanese tongue have long conditioned philologists in the mainstream of national learning to doubt that Japanese might ever be shown to be related to a wider linguistic family, and this apparent lack of affiliation (itself the consequence more often than not of an inadequate grasp of comparative linguistics) has tended to buttress the view that the language, and thus the culture which it expresses, is 'unique'.[1] If the vehicle of national thought and sentiment was *sui generis*, then the intellectual culture articulated through its verbal framework could not help but take on the distinctive tonality of such an idiosyncratic language.

For those who operate within the *nihonjinron* tradition, therefore, any semantic element in the native lexicon can be brought to bear on arguments for the uniqueness of the reality denoted. The particularistic structure of indigenous reality may be traced out by simply exploring the nuances of select words in the Japanese vocabulary. The discovery of cultural uniqueness is thus facilitated by an assiduous, if highly tendentious, semantic archaeology, whose site of evidential rubbish lies in the accumulated textual strata of historical usage preserved in the archives of the national literature.

By the Japanese vocabulary, however, we must appreciate that a distinction is made between loan words from Chinese and Western languages, and words that are *supposed to be* purely Japanese. Strictly speaking, the linguistic repository of Japaneseness is seen to reside in that pristine part of the vernacular that, putatively, predates foreign influence and thus constitutes the autochthonous linguistic garment of the archaic *kokutai*.[2] However, given the premise that principles in the *kokutai* work to naturalise the alien, one can on occasion argue about Japanese characteristics on the evidence of even the mass of imported vocabulary.

Some discern the 'essence' of Japaneseness in *iki* (chic), some in *akirame* (resignation), and others in *ukiyo* (the ephemeral world). For others it is crystallised in *mono no aware* (understood as 'the pathos of things'), or in *amae* (coaxing), in *aidagara* (relationship), in *tate* (verticality), in *ma* (interval, space), in *kiyosa* (limpidity), in *ie* (family house), or in *ki* (mind, mood, feeling),[3] and so on. In all of these treatises, the premises are identical and the techniques invariant. Each writer will analyse the whole spectrum of ethnic experience in the light of his single, chosen term. Though they may frequently differ among themselves as to where the quintessence of 'Japanliness' may be found, they all share the same simple faith in the idea that Japan's vast and variegated tradition may be summed up in one 'key word'.

An important point is that informed foreign or Japanese criticism, armed with philology, logic and common sense, can make no critical dent in the myth-making power of this pseudo-linguistic discourse. Japanese censure is disarmed by the insinuation that one's antagonist has sold out to invalid foreign methods. Foreign criticism may be dismissed as due to a lack of understanding of the language, for as a reflex of the principle that what is uniquely Japanese is inapprehensible to foreigners (chapter 3, page 34), the unique 'feeling' of the language is likewise impossible for foreigners to master.[4] If a bilingual outsider refutes the view that a Japanese word entails something unique to the Japanese, it is merely 'proof' that he fails to perceive what makes instinctive sense to people of Japanese blood. When Nelly Nauman contested the idea that the ancient Japanese were particularly sensitive to impurity, she met with the reply that:

> Certainly the Japanese are not a race which particularly seeks after 'immaculateness' (*shōjō*) as Nelly Nauman understands it, namely, to the extent that 'immaculateness' (*shōjō*) is to be taken in the sense of *Sauberkeit* or *cleanliness*. But if we take it that German *Sauberkeit*, English *cleanliness* and Japanese *kiyorakasa* (crystalline limpidity) denote semantic contents that radically differ, then it is altogether another matter.
>
> A spirit (*kokoro*) of seeking after immaculateness (*shōjō*) is probably common to every country in the world. However the

'limpidity' (*kiyorakasa*) which the Japanese never cease to aspire to is a very distinctive Japanese thing unparalleled among other races. Notwithstanding Nelly Nauman's trenchant remarks, it must be said after all that, in the sense of this distinctiveness, a very strong tendency of immaculacy-directedness (*shōjō-shikō*) exists as a matter of hard fact in Japan.[5]

Araki's rejoinder plays on an assumption which is central to the *nihonjinron*'s linguistic logic, namely that Japanese has an authentic and inauthentic component, the former comprising *yamato kotoba* (purely indigenous words), and the latter being *gairaigo* (foreign loan words) from Chinese (*Cf kango*) or Western languages. *Yamato* words are charged with ineffable race sentiment; foreign words harbour only alien concepts. Foreigners can only discuss Japanese phenomena in terms of the *gairaigo* component (here the Chinese word *shōjō*) which, being itself foreign, has precise equivalents in other foreign languages (*Sauberkeit*, cleanliness). But they cannot understand *yamato kotoba* like *kiyorakasa* because, being uniquely Japanese, they cannot be translated. Well may Suzuki tell us, in another context, that it is a misfortune for a member of the human race to die without knowing the Japanese language.[6]

If the key to the mysterious heart of Japaneseness lies in such occult qualities of the language (as glossed by the tendentious hermeneutics of linguistic nationalism), it follows that the influence of foreign loan words or linguistic calques* menaces the pure autonomy of Japanese experience. To sustain the chic of indigenous myth, therefore, foreign linguistic influence must be vigorously combatted. For, to adopt a remark of Laurens van der Post, Western words are seen to 'prevent all those people with ancient cultures of their own from being their own versions of themselves'.[4] In the Japanese context this implies that:

> When Western words are used to analyse a society like Japan's which is heterogeneous (*ishitsu*) to those of the West, what such words pick up are the very same phenomena denoted by these words in their Western context; however, these words will not pick up the heterogeneous phenomena of a heterogeneous society. For these a different language is required.[8]

---

*Words coined or used in one language to translate a concept in another language.

This is the linguistic version of the theory sustained variously by Hamaguchi and Nakane (chapter 3). What in fact this tactic entails becomes clearer if we examine the way Ōno Setsuko develops the idea in arguing that:

> Each Western word is loaded with cultural and historical meanings and associations. A word such as 'hierarchy' means automatically an order of power relationships. It has a connotation of oppression, denial of individualism, its rights and freedoms which should lead to the equality of men. In Japan, hierarchy simply signifies ritual order. It defines neither the location of power nor responsibility. Thus Western words as such are not appropriate for describing non-Western reality.[9]

As Nakane repudiates Western concepts because they make Japan appear feudal, so Ōno denies Westerners the right to discuss Japan because their languages impose concepts of political power where only rituals of culture exist. To accuse the writer of wilful misrepresentation misses the point. Nationalists are of two types; those who are completely ignorant of the past, and those whose enormous erudition lacks any clear critical focus. But whatever the case with Ōno, it is futile to call to her attention the fact that Ogyū Sorai, with his interpretation of *hadō* (way of the overlord), analysed shogunal rule in terms of force; or that Fukuzawa Yukichi observed that the ritual hierarchy of the *meibun* (name defining social role and status) system invested those of superior station with a preponderance of power (*kenryoku no henchō*).[10] For *meibun* and *hadō*, like nearly all words for socio-political analysis in Japanese, are of foreign, Chinese origin. As such they lend themselves to Ōno's argument. She herself probably has in mind the *yamato kotoba* term *tate* (warp), a metaphor drawn from textile language to denote the notion of hierarchy in 'value-free', 'emic' language.

We see then that the conversion of abstract jargon (of Sino-Japanese coinage) into vernacular idioms functions to deflect critical analysis of underlying power relationships by placing the emphasis on cultural structures as determinants of reality. Failure to appreciate these linguistic conventions imperils attempts at refutation, as witness the following remarks by Befu on class stratification:

> Emically Japanese have a wide variety of native concepts

referring to social classes, such as '*jōryū shakai*', '*chūkan kaikyū*', '*kasō shakai*', or '*shakai no teihen*'. Although these concepts are not identical to the classes conjured up in English (e.g. 'upper class', etc), the issue here is not whether Japanese have terms of stratification which are conceptually identical to those in the West, but instead whether Japanese conceive of their society as being made up of horizontal strata. The existence of these Japanese terms clearly indicates that the Japanese conception of society does include the notion of stratification.[11]

The point is that you cannot, in the *nihonjinron* logic, consider as 'emic' evidence words and concepts expressly derived from foreign culture. Ōno could simply counter than the terms Befu cites are not *yamato kotoba* but rather Sino-Japanese calques which contain concepts alien to the authentic tradition of Japan. You cannot argue against one *nihonjinron* stereotype by using *nihonjinron*-type approaches (*Cf* arguments from language, the 'emic' notion) without risking being captured by their logic.[12]

The techniques of semantic analysis employed by this literature are not grounded in any rigorous mastery of the philological sciences. But their sum effect on both disciplinary and public usage is profound. As each verbal argument enters into the intellectual tradition of identity discussions, each key word contributes the force of its eccentrically loaded nationalism to the ideological mainstream. The resulting patchwork of tightly interknitted, woolly threads of semantic assertion presents an order of deliberately constituted unintelligibility. That is, this mosaic of words charged with intense resonances of 'Japaneseness' (which they never bore in the vernacular) begins to constitute an academic metadiscourse, implicated with intertextual reverberations of uniqueness, that raises a semantic bamboo curtain between Japan and the outside world.

The outsider must therefore make special efforts to avoid the pitfalls of simplistic translation. If in terms of formal grammar Japanese presents us with no higher order of difficulty than any other language, it may nonetheless be said that the cumulative effects of decades of semantic tampering with the national language have produced a bedevilled jargon of authenticity, whose timbre of implicit resonances of racial uniqueness easily escapes the studious peruser of dictionaries. One must construct the genealogies of interpretation which have accumulated upon, and in

The Warp of Language

turn informed, the use of words in the *nihonjinron* by the praetorian guards of indigenous chic. One must try, further, to clarify the socio-psychological functions of such insistently wrongheaded hermeneutics. By such annotative reading, we may uncover a rich field for the analysis, not so much of cultural uniqueness, as much as of the nature of those processes of mystification which subsist in the construction of the image and ideology of Japanese 'culture'.

Here I wish to deal with two examples of pseudo-semantic finessing from each of the two glossaries in order to illustrate the basic techniques and logics underlying this closed discursive structure. The first two specimens show the vicissitudes of foreign concepts when translated and 'Japanified'; the latter two sketch out the kind of confusion which ensues from speculative redefinitions of words deemed to be unique *yamato kotoba*.

A highly suggestive, contemporary example of conceptual endogenisation is provided by Doi Takeo's discussion of 'freedom'[13] in the light of his theory of coaxing dependence (*amae*; see chapters 8 and 9). For Doi, the Japanese word (of Chinese origin) *jiyū* normally employed to translate the Western notion of freedom in fact means something distinctly different from what Westerners understand by the idea. In Japan, he argues, freedom (*jiyū*) is always strictly limited to relationships of dependence: 'Originally by freedom in Japan was meant the freedom to presume (*amaeru jiyū*), that is, getting one's way. It was never a matter of freedom from presuming on others.'[14]

Freedom in Japan thus entails seeking the indulgence of others, 'taking the liberty' to presume, and implies selfish caprice (*wagamama*). Where in the West it implies freedom from social constraints, in Japan it requires the indulgent consent of the group: 'Presuming on others (*amae*) requires the presence of others and makes the individual dependent on the group, so that, in this sense, it cannot liberate him from the group.'[15]

Doi's subtext here draws on contrastive features 10-10', 18-18'. (Chapter 4, table 4). By a selective use of proverbs, he tries to show that in the West, unlike Japan, freedom entails a spurning of sentiments of social solidarity. Western liberty is bought off at the expense of compassionate fellowship. Marx, Freud and Nietzsche have shown that such freedom is illusory by describing how choice is constrained by economic, psychological and cultural determinants. Further, Sartre held that unconditional freedom must only lead to 'solidarity with others through participation', and thus finally the West is awakening to the fact, long known to the Japanese, that freedom as independence is impossible. As he puts it, 'It is of value to recall that long ago in this regard, the experience of the Japanese taught them the psychological impossibility of freedom.'[16]

Defining Western and Japanese concepts of freedom as diametrically opposed (as if Japanese black is the antithesis of Western black, being white), Doi then argues that the former is a fiction, the latter the correct view, namely, that one must have permission from the group to be free. This excursus illustrates the *gekokujō* logic of the *nihonjinron*. *Gekokujō* is a medieval term referring to a subordinate's usurpation of his superior. Acute sensitivity to status and rank within a hierarchical society is reflected in the way Japan's position in the world is perceived. Being a debtor to Western intellectual culture invokes a sense of status inferiority, which the nationalist attempts to reverse to his advantage by conceptual table-turning. The notion of freedom itself, as the social tolerance of social and political diversity, derives from the West, but by a pseudo-linguistic sleight of hand which obfuscates the nature of the concept, Doi discredits the idea of freedom itself except in its putatively Japanese form which, in that it is a tolerated caprice, implies a wider social compliance which is the opposite of freedom.

Doi is of course operating in a mythical universe. He shows no awareness of the philosophical history and legal translation of the concept of freedom in the West. The novelty of the Western concept in juridical terms lay in its political expression as tolerance of social diversity in both private and public spheres. In the Orient, freedom was traditionally limited to its religious application as spiritual liberation from the conditionings of social and temporal circumstance.[17] *Jiyū* etymologically implies not dependence on others but 'reliance or dependence on the self'. We might note here that the Buddhist notion of freedom (*jizai*) has been paralleled to the Spinozan conception of *libertas* as *in se esse*,[18] and thus Doi not only misrepresents through ignorance his own tradition, but shows himself unaware of the significant parallel it has here with an earlier phase of Western thought.

But these Humpty-Dumpty semantics of Doi, with their wonderful power to convert the usual meanings of words into contrary senses, come off rather poorly in comparison with the fate of the words 'public' and 'private' in Japanese. A few randomly chosen examples of their usage alerts one to the fact that, in Japanese, these words have nothing whatsoever to do with the Western concepts they originally served to translate.

In a survey of the phenomenon of citizens' action groups (*jūmin undō*) which militate against the encroachment of monopoly corporations into regional economies on the grounds that these tend to restore the hierarchical system of the feudal lords of yore, in which, 'the company is the castle, the white-collar employees are the vassals, and the local people are the townsfolk and the peasants,'[19] a reviewer discerns a radical break with tradition in the way such groups give priority to their own self-interest over the interests of the 'public'. Traditionally, he argues, '*the "public" sector has always overwhelmed the "private" sector in Japan,*'[20] whilst now regional citizens' groups are emphasising their parochial priorities over national development.

The English reader, at this point, is provoked to wonder if there has not been an error in translation, for the writer identifies what we call private corporations with the public, and public interest with private concerns. But the text is unblemished. Japanese usage defines what we call the public sector as the private sector. But then again English public schools are called private schools in the United States, so we may soothe our initial qualms with the reflection that even in English, usage shows considerable variation.

And yet other works only compound our original perplexity. Watanabe Shōichi, in discussing the Lockheed scandals, defends the reticence of company money-runners before the Diet investigatory committee by arguing that their holding to 'private loyalty' (*shiteki shingi*) in preference to 'public loyalty' (*kōteki shingi*), that is to their company's interest over the national interest, is proof of the strength of liberal democracy in Japan. A society where 'public loyalty' is stronger than 'private loyalty' is, in effect, totalitarian. By implication, the failure of the Japanese parliament to make these agents of corruption speak is proof of the healthy state of Japanese democracy, while the success of the US Senate in making Lockheed officials disclose their malfeasance is proof that America has succumbed to the totalitarian temptation. For Watanabe, the tight-lipped bribers of corporate Japan remained faithful to the traditional ethos of the country, since 'it is a tradition of the autochthonous community of Japan that private loyalty takes absolute precedence over public loyalty.'[21]

The writer on the *jūmin undō* asserts that traditionally in Japan, the public interest always preceded private interests. Watanabe insists with an equally impressive reference to tradition that the contrary is the case, that usage sanctions fidelity to private over public loyalties. Their conclusions may be diametrically opposed, but in effect they are saying the same thing; namely, that companies, whether understood as public or private entities, must always have their interests defended against the Japanese people. We begin to appreciate Chesterton's detective Mr Pond, whose 'public powers were very private'. Humpty-Dumptian linguistics win out again.

The words *kōteki* ('public') and *shiteki* ('private') owe their popularity in the *nihonjinron* to the sociological and legal importance accorded this distinction in Western thought. But, though used to translate alien concepts, they bear connotations wildly out of keeping with this tradition inspired by Ulpian, the Roman jurist, (d.223 AD).[22] In keeping with the *yamato kotoba — gairaigo* distinction, the 'authentic' Japanese concepts for these foreign categories are obtained by reading these two Sino-Japanese words (*kō, shi*) with their native glosses, namely *ōyake* and *watakushi*. Now, *ōyake* originally referred to the principal family of Japan, the 'big house' of the Emperor, in contrast to which all the people were called *koyake* (minor families).[23] By extension then, the native term *kō/ōyake* selected, by an astute piece of linguistic statecraft in Meiji times, to do service for the Western notion of public, actually referred to the Emperor's possessions, his activities and those of his functionaries, and ultimately to the spheres of interest of the imperial government itself. Consequently, in Nakamura's words, 'In Japan there was originally no conception corresponding to "public". Among the Japanese, public affairs consisted in nothing but relations with the Imperial family.'[24]

The second part of this judgment is misleading, since it follows from the first sentence that *instead of* public relationships, in Japan there were only duties to the Emperor. *Kō/ōyake* are used to denote the concept of public, but refer to precisely the opposite conception entailed by the words they presume to translate. Public law concerns the commonwealth, the interests of the people, as the etymology itself suggests (*Cf populus*). Likewise, *shi/watakushi* is hopelessly inadequate for translating the notion of private (*privatus*, withdrawn from public life),[25] since it refers to the personal pronoun 'I', and not to the individual who, as a private citizen, can nonetheless make a public action in defence of the common interests of all other individuals in the community against corporations or the state. It is thus wholly pointless to speak of a 'Japanese' concept of public and private since *kō/shi* denote precisely the opposite of what they are presumed to translate.[26]

What the use of these words does tell us is that in Japanese feudalism there was lacking the institutional base which was central to the development of public and private realms in the West. Both these words assume the existence of institutions intermediate between the individual (*shi/watakushi*) and the state-monarch (*kō/ōyake*). In the West, public institutions developed from domainal ones with the growth of administrative *loci* of power distinct from the jurisdiction of the royal house. An important step was constituted by the distinction between the formal legality of the state and the citizens' private values which followed on the Wars of Religion.[27] In Japanese, the word which does (traitorous) duty for the notion of public confounds the distinction between the imperial, shogunal, and popular spheres. Secondly, we cannot but note the crucial advantages to the Meiji state which ensued from this choice of terms. If Meiji controversies often centred on disputes as to the meanings of words[28] coined to translate ill-understood ideas, it is also true that this kind of deliberate *verbicide*, insinuating that the common interest was to be identified with imperial institutions and not with the people's will, was an astute linguistic measure of invisible social control. Its effect is still felt since one can apparently speak of it being a Japanese characteristic *to find the meaning of life in not being oneself*, by denying the 'private' self (*watakushi*).[29]

With Japanese translations of foreign technical terms one has some control on the distortion of concepts. With *yamato kotoba* on the other hand, where the assumption is that these 'unique' words are untranslatable into foreign tongues, the tendency to trust in the reliability of one's 'emic' informants is stronger. The fate of expressions and words like *mono no aware* and *iki* should teach us otherwise.

Any discussion of Japanese aesthetics invariably touches upon the romantic pathos of *mono no aware*, as expressing a distinctively Japanese sense of the *lacrimae rerum*, the sadly ephemeral beauty of things. The expression is usually analysed as meaning 'the pathos (*aware*) of things (*mono*)', though the interpretation, if standard, would appear to bear little relation to the truth.

Aware was originally an ejaculation of surprise before the sight of something moving, often suggesting a reaction of pathos. Hisamatsu tries to sum up the essence of the idea as follows:

> In considering the relationship between '*aware*' (sensitivity) and '*mono no aware*' (sensitivity to things), Motoori Norinaga dismissed *mono no* as relatively meaningless. ... Generally speaking, we can regard *mono no* as a device for calling *aware* into existence. *Aware*'s meaning has been modified, and its aesthetic content has been altered gradually, through various kinds of combinations with other parts of speech, such as *aware naru mono* (a moving thing) and *aware to omou* (to be moved by), but in the phrase *mono no aware* there is no semantic or structural modification, and the aesthetic content remains constant from one period to another.[30]

Hisamatsu's translator clearly renders *mono* as 'things', though Hisamatsu himself does not appear sure of its precise meaning, taking Motoori's gloss as dismissing *mono no* as 'relatively meaningless'. All he can manage is to call *mono no* a device for 'calling *aware* into existence', and suggest strangely that in this combination the aesthetic content denoted assumes a trans-historical value.

Watsuji Tetsurō devoted several pages to the problem in 1922.[31] Noting that Motoori regarded *mono* as 'a word which is added when speaking broadly', Watsuji responds that usage would indicate rather that it expresses some meaning or other, and that *mono* in fact is a general something which comprises both the emotional state engaged by meaning and the material object, the thing (*mono*), perceived. It is thus the ultimate *Es* and at the same time *Alles*.[32] Arima, in commenting on this construction, compares *mono no aware* in this sense to Goethe's *Anschauung*, in which observation united to intuition enables the mind to grasp a visual whole, and concludes that:

> Without doubt, what Motoori proposes is one form of individualism in that one finds oneself at the centre of the universe, the only cognitive being. Yet cognition depends exclusively on one's feeling towards *mono* (a particular object), which is ultimately related to the whole.[33]

Unlike Motoori then, both Watsuji and Arima take *mono* as referring to some *thing*, and *mono no aware* as an experience in which man penetrates through particulars to universals. The psychologist Doi Takeo links *mono no aware* to that 'unique' emotional complex he denotes by the key word *amae* (coaxing in a dependent relationship), and argues that, '"*Aware*" is to be moved by some human or natural object (*taishō*), and by means of this deep emotion to become one with this object.'[34] That is, *mono no aware* is taken as expressing the direction of dependent feelings (*amae*) onto either human or material objects in the external world. *Aware* is interpreted as an emotion which unites the subjective individual with an object (*taishō* = *mono*) or another person.

Though these representative interpretations all betray a difficulty in reconciling *mono* as a modifier, and *mono* as a substantive,[35] they reveal a tenuous consensus that somehow 'things' are involved. When the *nihonjinron* show such signs of consensus, it is always salutary to go back to the origins of the idea. The *locus classicus* for this *aware* is the Genji Monogatari, where it occurs some 1,018 times in a bewildering variety of senses, from 'miserable', 'lovable', 'mournful', or 'happy' to 'compassionate' and 'tasteful'.[36] It was the great scholar of national learning Motoori Norinaga (1730-1801) who seized on the form *mono no aware* to define the essence of Japanese literature. It is to his treatment that the *nihonjinron* refer.

R.A. Miller, taking exception to the typical translation of this phrase as 'the pathos of *things*', has demonstrated that philologically *mono* here does not refer to objects or phenomena in the external world. He relates it etymologically to a Chuvash interrogative particle, *měn* (what), and notes that in Japanese it is used to modify the word which follows: 'For him (Motoori) ... *mono no aware* has nothing to do with "things"; it was rather a feeling or sensibility (*aware*) modified by "some, certain, ... some ... or other" (*mono*).'[37] This acute analysis not only clarifies a vexed philological crux, but also undermines a key concept in the cultural ideology of Japanese nationalism.

Motoori was much concerned with defining the indigenous terms of ancient Japanese culture, and he shows an explicit preoccupation in distinguishing this from the style of Chinese civilisation. His sense of the nature of this antithesis is clearly evident in the following poem:

kusuwashiki	How vain it is
kotowari shirazute	For the men of China
Karahito no	To discuss the reason of things
mono no kotowari	When they know not the reason
toku ga hakanasa	Of the miraculous.[38]

Here Confucian rationality (*Karahito no mono no kotowari*) is set out in sharp, negative relief to the apprehension of the mysterious whose reasons (*kusuwashiki kotowari*) escape the analytical lenses of foreigners. We have then, in a nutshell, a view which emerges as a fully fledged tendency in modern times, when the West replaces China as adversary in the cultural code. Rationality (China/West) is opposed to the mysterious, and contextually here to emotions like *mono no aware* (i.e. features 26, 26' chapter 4, table 6) unique to the Japanese experience. That this phrase is commonly considered to mean a distinctive unity between subjective experience (*aware*) and objective reality (*cf mono*) will assume greater importance in the succeeding chapters. In closing, we should bear in mind that *mono no aware* dissatisfied Watsuji because it was an aesthetic of feminine sensibility, lacking in masculine elements.[39]

The word *iki* has a less elaborate history than the cliché of *mono no aware* but tracing its interpretation can prove no less instructive. The celebration of the term in the *nihonjinron* owes much to Kuki Shūzō's *Iki no Kōzō*, considered itself by some to be a 'unique study'.[40] Count Kuki Shūzō (1888-1941), on graduating from Tokyo Imperial University, spent many years abroad in France and Germany, including a spell at Marburg where he studied under Martin Heidegger. On returning to Japan he obtained a professorship at Kyoto Imperial University, at the time a centre of pronounced right-wing thought, and held it until his death on the eve of the Pacific war. He mixed with philosophers at the forefront of Western thought and is said to have been held in the highest regard as an intellectual prodigy.[41]

Some inklings of his activity may be gathered from Martin Heidegger's *Unterwegs zur Sprache*.[42] For Heidegger, discussion of Japanese values within the system of European discourse is almost impossible. In attempting to unmoor ideas from the anchorage of their native speech by embarking them on the exotic craft of an alien idiom, we make them assume a direction and intent distinct from that which they bore in their original linguistic habitat. Ideas are born of words, words which in each language have a purely national timbre of contextual associations. Translation involves the emigration of thought across semantic borders, and thus a defection from the original matrix of meaning. In the very process of transfer into a new idiom, the original thought is necessarily betrayed.

In Heidegger's dialogue with a Japanese, which fictively recreates his discussions with Kuki, both speakers share the assumption that communication between users of structurally different languages is virtually impossible without doing irreparable violence to meaning. Yet since both concur that Japanese 'lacks the delimiting power to represent objects in an unequivocal order above and below each other,'[43] they concede that, paradoxically, doing philosophy in Japanese demands that one borrow from those very European languages the taxonomic categories required for conceptualising Japanese culture.

Heidegger illustrates this thesis by recalling Kuki's attempts to define *iki* for him. Despite exhaustive plumbings, he could never quite fathom the depth of this aesthetic term *iki*, and his endeavours to pick up from Kuki a precise sense ended in bemused frustration. This is ironical, in retrospect, since the same might be said of those who try to understand Heidegger's use of Greek. In a sense, Kuki steals his mentor's rhetorical thunder by interpreting *iki* in such an impalpably vague manner that it leaves Heidegger pleasantly bewildered, by confirming his original assumptions about the untranslatability of Japanese. We are informed that Kuki paraphrased *iki* to signify, '... the sensuous radiance through whose lively delight there breaks the radiance of something suprasensuous'.[44]

On reading this we are warranted in assuming that *iki* is akin to what Eliot meant by his line about 'the visible reminder of Invisible Light' in *Choruses from the Rock*, or that there is something of *iki* in Dante's Beatrice when she is described in the fifteenth sonnet of the *Vita Nuova*: *e par che sia una cosa venuta da cielo in terra a miracol mostrare* (And seems like something heaven-sent to show a miracle on earth). ... But it is difficult to reconcile all this with what the standard dictionaries tell us about *iki*, namely that it means, somewhat flatly, 'chic, smartness, posh, dapper, stylish,' and so on. This is what *iki* somewhat banally implied before Kuki, fresh from his studies with the semantic sorceror of Marburg, began in his famous opuscule to spin a web, like a spidery trap for the incurious, of hermeneutic profundity around the simple lexical body of *iki*.

In *Iki no Kōzō*, Kuki briefly compares this word to its rough equivalents in Western languages, *chic, élégant, coquet(terie), dandy, Fängerei* and *raffiné*, and concludes that none of them covers the complete range of connotations of his unique word. Having thus summarily adjudged the elusive *iki* to be peculiar to the Japanese language (nothing remarkable since all words are by definition unique), he feels justified in asserting that, 'Nothing stands in the way of our considering *iki* as one of the conspicuous forms of self expression of the unique existential modes of Eastern culture, nay, rather of the Yamato race itself.'[45]

Iki, being untranslatable, must refer to a 'specific character of the race'.[46] With greater precision he goes on to inform us that *iki* is a term used of coquettish chat with the opposite sex, with those in whom one perceives the possibility, not so much of love, but rather of flirtatious dalliance.[47] It embodies the quick-witted sophistication of the chivalrous but unmoneyed samurai who cavorted in the gay quarters of Edo. He links it also to the Buddhist virtue of resignation (*akirame*). In that Japanese 'chic' harmoniously conjoins coquetry, resignation and pride, *iki* is then to be understood as commingling the ethical idealism of *Bushidō* with the religious irrealism of Buddhism.[48]

This provides us with the essential leads to trace back the mystification. Given that Japanese *iki* is the product of a certain mode of aristocratic cultivation among the haughty patrons of the red light distincts, we may venture to suggest that it bears comparison with the ethos of the roués and dandies whose cult of urbane elegance and seductive ennui flourished in Regency England and Baudelaire's France. In fact, we shall see that Kuki's *iki*, a raffish mode of aesthetic nonchalance as both social pose and seductive technique, not only resembles the code of the Western dandy, but explicitly draws on it for its philosophical expression.

Iki belongs to a complex of words in late Edo literature (*cf sui, tsū*) which collectively denote the cool sophistication of one completely at home in the *demi-monde*.[49] Kuki elaborated his image of *sui generis* racial style from terms which had fashionable currency in the bordello world of a particular class and period in Japanese history. He converts an ethos specifically nurtured in the world of feudal prostitution into an 'existential mode' deemed unique to the Japanese race as a whole. If its 'comprehensive elements' consist in the triad of seductive coquetry (*bitai*), the galant's pride (*ikuji*), and resignation (*akirame*), the 'extensional' structure is analysed in terms of *iki*'s relationship to a series of paired antonyms. Thus we have *iki* (chic — *shibumi* (subdued elegance); *amami* (sweetness) — *yabo* (rough, uncouthness); *jōhin* (refined) — *jimi* (plain); *hade* (dandy) — *gehin* (vulgar). The analysis here only confirms one's impression that Kuki's work is trying to particularise what is a very generalised social phenomenon.

The cult of bordello chic outlined here as unique to Japan emerges with equal declarative force in the world of the *nagarika* (sophisticated town-dweller) and *ganika* (courtesan) of India, in the rapport between the urbane (*asteios*) aristocrats and *hetairai* of Periclean Athens, that is, where the new cosmopolitan dynamic of the cities defines itself against the earlier rustic codes of traditional marriage, in terms of the elective sexuality of the brothel culture. We see this in Rome, where *urbanitas* denoted the refined, external expression of an inner culture, developed in a metropolitan setting, involving impeccable manners, correct and witty speech, and the wearing of fashionable clothes with aplomb. In Cicero's time, such an ideal was considered peculiar to the patrician élite, as a mode of demeanour and outlook which distinguished the older families from both rustic and immigrant. Kuki's stress on the influence of Bushidō (*cf ikuji*) and Buddhist renunciation in the development of *iki* in fact recalls the relationship between military honour and stoic resignation in the formation of the Roman ethos.

Indeed, just as the chic set in Edo were mimicked by the dandies (*hadesha*), so the *urbanus homo* found himself parodied by the *perurbani*. Kuki is aware that *iki* suggests the Baudelairean aesthete, with its classical prototypes in Caesar, Alcibiades and Cataline (not to speak of Clodia's set, or Petronius, the *arbiter elegentiarum* of Nero's court) but he holds that such masculine types lack the femininity conveyed by the Edo *tsūjin* (sophisticate). The combination of elegant sobriety and seduction in *iki* may differ somewhat from the sexual propriety of the Ciceronian *urbanus homo*, yet the early *urbanitas* of puritanical Rome quickly develops a tone of feline cultivation in the male (*cf venustus*), and at the same time is extended to the female, to the poised and cultured woman (*culta puella*) of the Propertian and Ovidian smart sets.[50]

But more directly pertinent is the Baudelairean dandy. If

Heidegger provided Kuki with his linguistic and conceptual tools, it is beyond doubt that his reading of the French decadents was critical for his reappraisal of, and sense of affinity with, the dandy tradition of Edo. Kuki's work is essentially one of disguised transposition, of discovering a Japanese counterpart to the occidental coxcomb, with his '*physionomie distincte*', (distinctive and telling cast of features), and then erasing all comparison with his original. We see this clearly in his failure to cite Barbey d'Aurevilly, though his analysis of *bitai, ikuji* and *akirame* derives directly from the latter.[51]

For Baudelaire, whom Kuki acknowledges, the cult of the dandy was an aesthetic epiphenomenon of the transition from aristocracy to democracy, in which the insouciance to the wealth of the former is mixed with a contempt for the drudgery of the latter. As the 'last burst of heroism in times of decadence',[52] it faced extinction before the rising tides of a levelling plebianism. The appeal of this to Kuki, scion of a declining nobility in a country whose rapid industrialisation was destroying Edo culture, is evident.

Kuki's book exploits the new rhetoric of existentialism and Husserl's phenomenalism for nationalistic ends. Published around the time of the Manchurian 'incident', it subtly clothes a spirit of reaction in the idiom of racial uniqueness. We remind ourselves of the intimate conjunction between Heidegger's boldly obscurantist philosophy and the brash jargon of Nazi rhetoric. The cosy affinity of this perplexing philosophy with *völkisch* thought suggests hints as to the character of Kuki's own brand of aesthetic nationalism. In effect, he conflates Nishimura's studies of Edo chic with the philosophy of both German reaction and decadent antimodernism in order to generalise as a peculiarly Japanese ethos what, on inspection, appears to be his own specific crisis.[53] We shall see (and this is true of most *nihonjinron*) that the writer's theorising simply furnishes a rationale for an otherwise impermissable narcissism. Baudelaire's dandy, with his '*espèce de culte de soi-même*', marked by '*le besoin ardent de se faire une originalité*',[54] (the burning need to make oneself original) is expropriated for nationalist ends to mask Kuki's cult of himself.

Heidegger's final definition of *iki* as 'the swaying of the quiet of luminous rapture'[55] provides us with an exemplary anecdote of the romantic mystification suffered by Japanese culture through literary emigration to the West, an obscurantism connived at by accomplices from both sides of the border. Kuki's attempt to impress his *maître à penser* with his own inimitable 'sophistication' (*iki*), his staunch grasping for that nebulously equivocal phrasing beloved by the master, succeeded in giving exotic confirmation for Heidegger's own linguistic mysticism. The dapper *savoir-faire* of the Edo dandy and brothel habitué assumes the odd form of a kind of suprasensually sensuous metaphysics.

But it does not surprise that Heidegger found common ground with Kuki's semantic musings. The pseudo-linguistic finessing of concepts of identity in the nationalistic self-appraisals of the *nihonjinron* remind one of similar trends in the West. The rhetorical mode of vaporous yet plausible profundity, of 'dressing up empirical words with aura',[56] is the polemical tool favoured by the reactionary in his battle to preserve the mystique of tradition from the logic of a mature modernity.

The pathology of language manipulation obliquely encountered in these texts coincides *mutatis mutandis* with the techniques familiar to anyone versed in writers like Fichte and Heidegger, and it is perhaps for this very reason that Japanese nationalists sense an elective affinity for the negative German tradition. In both we discern an anti-modernist thought system based on displaced categories of affective experience, which obtains its dynamic energy of analytical 'dyscription' from a fundamental and willed misunderstanding of speech as communication.

Notes

1. R.A. Miller, *Origins of the Japanese Language*, (University of Washington Press, Seattle, 1980) ch. 1, esp. pp.27ff; Miller, 'The Relevance of Historical Linguistics for Japanese Studies' in *Journal of Japanese Studies*, 2:2 (summer 1976) pp.335-88, pp.364-7. Miller's pioneering analyses of socio-linguistic aspects of the *nihonjinron* have been a constant aid in organising my own material, and in this and the following chapter I am indebted to him to an extent that I cannot always acknowledge fully for reasons of space.

2. On the meanings of *kokutai* see R.H. Minear, *Japanese Tradition and Western Law* (Harvard University Press, Cambridge, Massachusetts, 1970) pp.64-71.

3. Akatsuka Yukio, '*Ki 'no kōzō*, (Kōdansha Gendai Shinsho, Tokyo, 1974) constitutes perhaps the most outstanding example of linguistic monomania in the genre.

4. Suzuki, *Kotoba no ningengaku*, ibid. pp.109ff; Itasaka Gen, *Nihongo yokochō* (Kōdansha Gakujutsu Bunko, Tokyo, 1978) pp.69ff. See Miller, *The Japanese Language in Contemporary Japan*, ibid. pp.82ff.

5. Araki Hiroyuko, *Nihonjin no shinjō ronri*, (Kōdansha Gendai Shinsho,

74　The Warp of Language

Tokyo, 1975) p.4.

6. Suzuki, *Kotoba no ningengaku*, ibid. pp.100, 123. Miller, *Japan's Modern Myth*, ibid. p.255.

7. L. van der Post, *Jung and the Story of Our Time* (Pantheon, New York, 1975) p.31.

8. Kawashima on Doi's views, in Ōtsuka Hisao, Kawashima Takeyoshi, Doi Takeo, *'Amae' to shakai kagaku*, (Kōbundō, Tokyo, 1976) p.29.

9. Ohno Setsuko, 'Fragile Blossom, Fragile Superpower — A New Interpretation', in *Japan Quarterly*, 23:1 (1976) pp.12-27, p.26.

10. On Sorai's interpretation of 'The Way of the Overlord' see D.M. Earl, *Emperor and Nation in Japan* (University of Washington Press, Seattle, 1964) pp.16-17, 35. On Fukuzawa, see C. Blacker, *The Japanese Enlightenment*, (Cambridge, England, 1964) pp.9, 70-3.

11. Befu, 'A Critique of the Group Model', ibid. p.34.

12. *Cf* Sugimoto Yoshio, '"Nihon tokushū shūdan setsu" no kōzui no naka de', in *Asahi Jānaru*, 14 November 1980, pp.10-14, p.11 concludes that the Japanese have strong individuality on the same data that Suzuki Takao, *Kotoba to bunka* (Iwanami Shinsho, Tokyo, 1973) pp.129ff, uses (Japanese personal pronouns) to argue the opposite case. Compare Okonogi's view in Miller, *Japan's Modern Myth*, p.118.

13. Doi, *'Amae' no kōzō*, (Kōbundō, Tokyo, 1971) pp.94-108.

14. Doi, *'Amae' no kōzō*, ibid. p.94.

15. Doi, *'Amae' no kōzō*, ibid. p.95. *Amae* (coaxing) here is the *yamato kotoba* for the *gairaigo izon*/dependence, and *wagamama* (caprice) the same for *jiyū*.

16. Doi, *'Amae' no kōzō*, ibid. p.108 (freedom only exists in death).

17. *Cf* Yamazaki Masakazu, Ichikawa Hiroshi, *Gendai Tetsugaku Jiten* (Kōdansha Gendai Shinsho, Tokyo, 1970) p.309.

18. Nakamura Hajime, *Parallel Developments*, (Kodansha Ltd, Tokyo, 1975) pp.506-8. Elsewhere Nakamura defines Japanese freedom as 'compliance with the human nexus — through devotion to secular activities' in contrast to China where it means 'liberation from the human nexus'! *cf* His *Japan and Indian Asia*, (Mukhopadhyay, Calcutta, 1961) p.25.

19. Editor's comment, 'Peasant Uprisings and Citizens' Revolts' in *Japan Interpreter* 8:3 (autumn 1973) pp.279-83, p.280.

20. 'Peasant Uprisings' ibid. p.280. The editor notes however that 'The "public" sector ... has always been uncomfortably like the "private domain" of officialdom and its handmaidens'.

21. Watanabe Shōichi, *Seigi no jidai*, (Bungei Shunjū, Tokyo, 1977) pp.147-77. p.156.

22. See in general, S.I. Benn and G.F. Gaus (eds.) *Public and Private in Social Life*, (Croom Helm, London, 1983): Sennett, *The Fall of Public Man*, ibid. ch.1, esp. pp.16ff.

23. Nakamura, *Ways of Thinking*, ibid. p.469.

24. Nakamura, *Ways of Thinking*, ibid. p.469.

25. R. Williams, *Keywords*, (Fontana paper, London, 1976) pp.203-4.

26. The key text for the *nihonjinron* formulation of 'public' and 'private' is Aruga Kizaemon's long essay, '"Kō" to "shi"-giri to ninjō', available in *Aruga Kizaemon chosakushū*, 4 (Miraisha, Tokyo, 1966) pp.177-283. However Aruga may owe something to Watsuji Tetsurō, for which see below, chapter 12, n.54. A useful bibliography may be found in Koschmann, *Authority and the Individual*, ibid. p.284, n.32.

27. For various aspects of the problem see R. Pipes, *Russia Under the Old Regime* (Peregrine, Harmondsworth ed., 1977) p.68; Maruyama Masao, *Thought*

and Behaviour in Modern Japanese Politics, ed. Ivan Morris (Oxford University Press, 1963) pp.2ff.

28. Sir G. Sansom, *The Western World and Japan* (Random House, New York, 1973) p.311.

29. Isobe Tadamasa, *'Mujō' no kōzō*, (Kōdansha Gendai Shinsho, Tokyo, 1976) p.124. Lebra writes on psychotherapy in Japan that 'the self is what is to be forgotten rather than recalled or ruminated on,' *Japanese Patterns*, ibid. p.225.

30. Hisamatsu Sen'ichi, *The Vocabulary of Japanese Literary Aesthetics*, trans. Helen McCullough (Centre for East Asian Cultural Studies, Tokyo, 1963) p.15.

31. Watsuji Tetsurō, '"Mono no aware" ni tsuite', in *Watsuji Tetsurō Zenshū*, 4 (Iwanami Shoten, Tokyo, 1962) pp.144-55.

32. Watsuji, '"Mono no aware" ni tsuite', ibid. pp.149-50.

33. T. Arima, *The Failure of Freedom*, (Harvard University Press, Cambridge, Massachusetts, 1969) p.111.

34. Doi, *'Amae' no kōzō*, ibid. p.91.

35. See S. Matsumoto, *Motoori Norinaga*, (Harvard University Press, Cambridge, Massachusetts, 1970) in an otherwise useful discussion pp.43-67, still glosses *mono* as '"thing" in a broad sense ... added to supply a somewhat broader connotation' (p.43).

36. I. Morris, *The World of the Shining Prince* (Oxford University Press, London, 1964), p.196.

37. R.A. Miller, *Japanese and the Other Altaic Languages*, (University of Chicago Press, Chicago, 1971) p.217.

38. D. Keene, *World Within Walls* (Holt, Rinehart & Winston, New York, 1976) p.329.

39. Watsuji, '"Mono no aware" ni tsuite', ibid. pp.154-5. Maruyama Masao, *Studies In the Intellectual History of Tokugawa Japan*, trans. Mikiso Hane, (Tokyo University Press, 1974) pp.170-3, see Motoori's approach here as involving a depoliticisation of politics through its complete aestheticisation, and *mono no aware*, in this sense, marks a seminal step in the enculturation of what is political discourse in the later *nihonjinron*.

40. Akatsuka, *'Ki' no kōzō*, ibid. p.169. Kuki Shūzō, *'Iki' no kōzō* (1930) (Iwanami reprint, Tokyo, 1967).

41. On Kuki see G. Piovesana, *Recent Japanese Philosophical Thought*, rev. ed. (Enderle, Tokyo, 1973) pp.168-9; Yasuda Takeshi, Tada Michitarō, '"*Iki*" *no kōzō' o yomu* (Asahi Sensho, Tokyo, 1979) esp. pp.16-17. For his supposed anticipation of structuralism, see Isotani Kō, 'Kuki Shūzō ni okeru chisei no shukusai' on *Shisō* (February 1979) pp.1-26, p.4.

42. M. Heidegger, *Unterwegs zur Sprache* (Verlag Günther Neske, Pfullingen, 1959) pp.85-155. Except where specified my quotations are from the English version by Peter Hertz, *On the Way to Language* (Harper and Row, New York, 1971) pp.1-54.

43. Hertz, *Way to Language*, p.12.

44. Hertz, ibid. p.14, *Cf* 'Er (Kuki) sprach vom sinnlichen Scheinen, durch dessen lebhaftes Entzücken übersinnliches hindurchscheint,' *Unterwegs zur Sprache*, p.101. The language is Fichtean, for which see chapter 6, but Heidegger's words uncannily recall Lafcadio Hearn's remark about 'people moving soundlessly through spaces of perfect repose, all bathed in vapoury light', *Japan: An Attempt at Interpretation* (Charles E. Tuttle, Rutland, Vermont & Tokyo, 1955) p.14.

45. Kuki, *'Iki' no kōzō*, p.12. I have given 'existential mode' for *sonzai yōtai*, to convey something of Kuki's style, but perhaps he is drawing on Barbey d'Aurevilly's essay, 'Du Dandysme et de George Brummel' in the same author's *Oeuvres romanesques complètes*, 2 (Bibliothèque de la Pléiade, Gallimard, Paris, 1966) pp.667-733, see the remark, 'Le Dandysme est toute *une manière d'être*'

(p.673). For an excellent exposition of Kuki's book see A. Hosoi, J. Pigeot, '*La Structure d'Iki*', in *Critique*, 29, no.308 (January 1973) pp.40-52.

46. *'Iki' no kōzō*, ibid. p.2.

47. Compare Scaraffia on the Western dandy: 'Declared enemy of repetition and banality, the dandy prefers the uncertainties and instability of fleeting romances to the wearing resignation of the thalamos.' G. Scaraffia, *Dizionario del dandy*, (Laterza, Bari, 1981) p.90. *cf* D'Aurevilly, Du Dandysme, p.686.

48. *'Iki' no kōzō*, ibid. pp.33, 149.

49. *Cf* Sansom, *The Western World and Japan*, pp.219-20: Hisamatsu, *The Vocabulary*, pp.64f. For criticisms of the excessive generality of Kuki's model see Yasuda and Tada, '"*Iki*" *no kōzō' o yomu*, pp.91ff, esp. p. 112. A much more detailed critical survey of love and the *tsūjin* may be found in Tsuda Sōkichi, *Waga kokumin shisō no kenkyū*, 8 pp.187ff.

50. *Culta puella*, Propertius, *Monobiblios*, 2. 26. In general see E.S. Ramage, *Urbanitas: Ancient Sophistication and Refinement*, (University of Oklahoma Press, 1973). On the dandy's femininity see d'Aurevilly, p.710, and Scaraffia pp.109-10.

51. *Bitai* corresponds to d'Aurevilly's *conquetterie* (p.693), *ikuji* to his *vanité*, *orgueil* (pp.669-70), and *akirame* to *désintéressement* (p.686). There are numerous other points of verbal and analytical correspondence.

52. 'Le dandysme est le dernier éclat d'héroïsme dans les décadences' in C. Baudelaire, 'Le Peintre de la vie moderne. IX', in *Oeuvres Complètes de Charles Baudelaire*, 2, ed. J. Crépet (Conard, Paris, 1925) pp.87-92, p.91. Kuki's characterisation of the *tsūjin*, exponent of *iki*, as indifferent to money, and thus different from the dandy of the West (*cf* Hosoi and Pigeot p.50) oversimplifies. See Tsuda's remarks, *Kokumin no shisō*, 8, ibid. pp.237f.

53. For early studies of *iki*, see Minami, *Nihonjinron no keifu*, ibid. pp.88-94. For Kuki's nationalism see Minami, ibid. pp.104-8, and Yasuda, in "*Iki*" *no kōzō' o yomu*, ibid. pp.35ff.

54. 'Baudelaire, 'Le Peintre', ibid. p.89. *cf* D'Aurevilly's 'certaine exquise originalité', 'Du Dandysme', ibid. p.688. On the *tsūjin*'s display of self-superiority, see Tsuda, *Kokumin no shisō*, ibid. pp.200ff, p.236.

55. 'Iki ist das Wehen der Stille des leuchtenden Entzückens', *Unterwegs zur Sprache*, p.141.

56. T. Adorno, *The Jargon of Authenticity*, trans. Knut Tarnowski and Frederic Will (Routledge and Kegan Paul, London, 1973) p.12, in speaking of Heidegger's style. Though *iki* is of foreign provenance, it is treated as a *yamato kotoba*. Kuki's Japanese text, one must admit, is a marvel of style and lucid concision, but, as Hosoi and Pigeot note, 'Là encore, on voit l'influence de la philosophie heideggerienne: interpréter les mots d'après leur sens étymologique (mais étymologie de philosophe plus que philologue)', p.49.

6 THE LINGUISTICS OF SILENCE

'In the world created by these simple *yamato* words, the Japanese can become akin to geniuses. This meaning of the word genius, as it is defined by Kant, denotes the ability to create a symbolic world which is impossible for strangers to follow.'
    Watanabe Shōichi, *Bunka no jidai*, p.110

In the preceding chapter I touched briefly upon the ways in which individual words in the Japanese lexicon are mystified for nationalistic ends. The aim is one of defining concepts elicited from either *gairaigo* or *yamato kotoba* (the latter being a purely subjective category) in such a way as to render them unique, and thus untranslatable. Indeed foreign words imported into Japanese are made to mean exactly the opposite of what their equivalents in Western languages signify ('freedom' entails subordinate dependency, 'public' means private, etc). Here I should like to examine the broader context from which these specific arguments emerge, namely, the putative cultural structure of the language itself, the historically conditioned 'spirit' of the language as a whole.

Any attempt to tease out the ideology of culture attached to the Japanese language does well to start with a representative pre-war text, and there are good grounds for opening the discussion with Tanizaki Jun'ichirō's *Bunshō Tōkuhon*, a manual of prose composition published in 1934. Born in the Meiji era, Tanizaki lived through a period of dramatic social, cultural and linguistic change, and his handbook on style reflects not only problems he encountered as a novelist, but also difficulties he sensed in the Western-inspired attrition of Japanese culture.

Tanizaki opens his work promisingly with some pithy comments on language in general. Gestures may transfer meaning, but finer ideas require that thought be enhoused within speech. Language is a means of transcending isolation, but it does not merely transmit thought, but also actively endows it with those syntactical forms required for coherent expression. Good composition consists in the ability to articulate clearly whatever one wishes to say. The euphuistic prolixity of classical style is outmoded, ill-adapted to the contemporary exigencies of precise and unadorned statement.[1]

The modern style demands a pared-down diction and that minimum economy of words sufficient to enable others to understand the import of one's ideas.

This said, Tanizaki now stops to pose some critical objections and reservations to this general statement. If the modern must strive to get his thoughts over to his audience precisely, yet he must recognise that there are inherent limits to this project. Prolixity in the cause of obtaining an exhaustive understanding is counter-productive. Contemporary style is profligate with words, when proper style should seek a choice and laconic simplicity of diction. To achieve this end, he advocates a return to the spirit of early Japanese classical prose.[2] In effect, Tanizaki objects to the surfeit of Chinese compound words typical not only of Tokugawan style but also of recent works translating Western thought.

This trend towards loquacity is thus linked to the faddish imitation of foreign style, and violates the austere terseness, as he sees it, of early Japanese prose. If such imitation has added some minor advantage in articulate force, he bids us remember that in mimicking extraneous models one risks undermining the sinewy uniqueness of the sparse, indigenous tradition. For, 'There is an eternal barrier between the prose styles of two countries differing radically in their linguistic origins, a barrier which may never be transcended.'[3]

The temptation to indulge in an effusive garrulity derives, he suggests, from a reaction to the limited vocabulary of classical Japanese. But however exiguous its lexical resources may be, this pure language compensated for its diminutive word-stock by a subtle use of context to enlarge the range of meanings any one word may bear (compare the meanings of *aware*, cited in the previous chapter, for example). Foreign languages, by comparison, are rich in words, but, by that very virtue, rather deficient in the use of devices of contextual positioning to elicit the various nuances of a word (table 8).

Table 8: Language

Foreign (China, West)	Native (Japan)
gairaigo *gaikokugo* (denotative) (foreign languages)	*yamato kotoba* (connotative)

Tanizaki is working within the framework of presuppositions we have established for the *nihonjinron* generally. Opposed to the objective, rational discourse of foreign speech (part of which, as borrowed words, is present in contemporary Japanese), he poses the subjective, emotive and situational idiom of his mother tongue in its archaic form (*cf* 26, 26'; 27, 27' and 28, 28' in chapter 4, table 6). This in turn leads him to propose that, 'Our nation's language (*kokugo*) bears an unalienable relationship with our national character (*kokuminsei*), and the fact that Japanese is poor in vocabulary does not necessarily mean that our culture is inferior to that of the West or China. Rather it is proof that chatting (*oshaberi*) is not a part of our national character.'[4]

By implication, foreigners are given to talkativeness, as indeed feature contrast 29, 29' of our paradigm shows (chapter 4, table 6). Tanizaki's choice of illustration for this trait is telling. Though militarily the stronger party, Japan is worsted by China in League of Nations' debates on the Sino-Japanese conflict because the Chinese are past masters of bewitching eloquence.[5] The justice of their case (presumably, the altruistic character of their imperialism) is lost on foreigners because, unlike the Chinese and Westerners with their reliance on the power of language (*gengo no chikara*), the Japanese esteem men whose bearing is distinguished by taciturnity (*kagen chinmoku*). But rather than imitate the foreigner's eloquence, Tanizaki warns his audience against it, since it makes the Japanese uncharacteristically 'forgetful of the efficacy of silence, overly given to chatter, and excessively given to the power of words.'[6]

To make his point, Tanizaki refers us to classical culture, to the Confucian esteem for prudence in speech, to the art of *haragei*, and such idioms as *ishin-denshin* and *kantan aiterasu*, whose very presence in the vocabulary he takes as showing a native preference for silent empathy. We might note that his terms are, for the most part, taken from Chinese culture, and thus the foreign character of his evidence contradicts his thesis of authenticity. Westerners by contrast are brash squanderers of words. The dignity of the self is something they assert rather than demurely convey. In short, unlike the Japanese, the Westerner is not humble before destiny, but defiant. Thus his contrast between linguistic parsimony (Japan), and the exuberant garrulity of outsiders displays a number of dimensions, reflecting on the one hand submission to destiny, society and tradition at the expense of the individual self (*jibun*), and on the other hand, in the West, the individual's challenging of history and society to assert exhaustively his own possibilities (see chapter 4, tables 4 and 5, 10, 10'; 11, 11'; 17, 17'; 18, 18'; 24, 24').[7]

Tanizaki does try to buttress his position by an extended comparison between the succinct, yet ambiguous, style of the Tale of Prince Genji and the padded lucidity of Waley's English version.[8] He argues that what is implicitly understood in the taut but nuanced obliquity of the original, is drawn out and clarified explicitly in the translation. But whereas the aesthetic force of the Japanese text lies in its resident intensity of connotative suggestion, the attraction of the foreign rendering lies rather in the palpable lucidity of its ornate paraphrase.

He hones this argument by recurring to the problem of vocabulary. To compensate for its lexical poverty, Japanese must extend the connotative range of every word by the artful use of contextual placing, and by relying on the reader's imagination to engage in a kind of hermeneutic collaboration with the text to establish the intended sense. Western style, with its wordiness, subverts the resonance of allusiveness by its prosaic surfeit, and thus lucidity vanquishes the poetry of indefinite suggestion. What in fact is being said is that foreign speech is prosaic, and Japanese is poetic. Indeed, Tanizaki is caricaturing in terms of contrast between East and West discursive differences inherent in every language, between prose and poetic style. The rich, allusive economy of Sappho's lyric and the voluble discursiveness of the Platonic dialogues are equally representative of the natural resources of Greek, for example.

In essence, Tanizaki is protesting against the cerebral abstraction of modern speech. His is the cry of the lyrical introvert against the prosaic noisiness of slipshod, everyday language. As a rule, he advocates wherever possible the redeployment of old words for new concepts. Thus instead of *ishiki suru* (to be conscious of), he exhorts us to use the pristine word *shiru* (to know) in an extended sense.[9] Instead of translating Western concepts by means of *kango* one ought, he holds, to extend the meanings of words in the old, native lexicon (*yamato kotoba*) to embrace the new, required sense. Thus the words *shakai* (society), *chōkō* (symptom) and *yokaku* (premonition), for example, should be replaced by old words like *yo no naka* (world), *kizashi* (sign) and *mushi no shirase* (foreboding) respectively.[10]

At first reading, there is something engaging in this critique of the influx of jargon into the modern world, in this advocacy of a lean and nuanced idiom. But read in the sociopolitical context of the times, Tanizaki's thesis takes on rather ominous echoes. At a time of militant aggression in China, antagonisms abroad and vigorous repression on the home front, Tanizaki's extolling of the virtues of circumspection, deference to authority, reverence for the past and accommodation to the established order, conjoined to this fastidious rejection of foreign words, and an attribution of diplomatic failure to the native virtue of diffident reticence, lend sympathy at the level of primarily aesthetic discourse to the dominant rhetoric and values stressed in Japan's emerging fascist order.

The parallel with Germany is instructive. There too, a long tradition of contrasting the pure Teutonic past to the corruptively decadent values of the 'West' was utilised by ideologues to promote the purification of native speech of contaminations from foreign languages. As Adorno pithily remarked, German words of foreign derivation became 'the Jews of language'.[11] As Tanizaki would substitute *yo no naka* for *shakai*, so partisans of Nazism considered *Grünfleck* more *echt deutsch* than *Oase* (borrowed from *oasis*).[12] And Tanizaki's celebration of traditional *junnō* (self-adjustment to the prevailing order) likewise re-echoes the incantatory exhortations of *Selbstgleichschaltung* (self-synchronisation) in Nazi rhetoric.

But, if his advocacy of silence, the dumb language of the intimidated psyche, evokes the politics of self-repression, it is in his attribution to language itself of qualities which inhibit the expressive autonomy of the individual that the most interesting parallel lies. In an ironically rather biblical idiom he asserts that, 'In the beginning there are words, and afterwards ideas are arranged to fit in with these words.'[13]

Language, further, is seen to have an autonomous power of its own, a 'soul' to which the ancients alluded in the word *kotodama*. This is none other than 'the spell-binding lure of the word', and it is this inherent faculty to bewitch the user which leads him to remark that while man is a user of language, it is equally true that 'language uses man' (*kotoba mo ningen o tsukau*).[14] In a less sophisticated, if more lucid, way than his contemporary Heidegger, Tanizaki subscribed to the view that language stands in a 'relationship of domination' (*Herrschaftsverhältnis*) over man.[15] Thought as a tool of social critique and individual reflection is thus doubly constrained in that it comes after, and is determined by, the structure of the language which produces or conveys it, a language which, in the Japanese case, Tanizaki sees as conventionally yielding to the authority of tradition and national character.

Tanizaki was not a professional linguist. He wrote at a time when modern linguistics had not yet gained a firm, widespread foothold on intellectual consciousness. It is all the more strange therefore to observe how his ideas live on, and indeed flourish in elaborate variations, in the works of professional linguists in the postwar period. In the works of a writer like Watanabe Shōichi,[16] for example, we note that not only are his intellectual credentials stronger in linguistics, but that his assumptions about the Japanese language and character are denser, and that the parallels with the linguistic views of German nationalists are both conscious and studied. Indeed what is striking is the way the younger scholar enlists the aid of the classics of German nationalism in order to revitalise these all but moribund clichés of prewar linguistic chauvinism in Japan.

His approach to the analysis of the uniqueness of his mother tongue draws on Fichte's *Reden an die deutsche Nation* (1807-8),[17] where he discerns a 'unique' and invaluable contribution to linguistic theory overlooked by the wrong-headed students of Saussure. What excites him in Fichte is the distinction made between a 'living national language' (*ikeru kokugo*) and a 'dead national language' (*shiseru kokugo*). Following Fichte, he defines a 'living national language' (i.e. *lebendige Sprache*) as one which has been spoken continuously from high antiquity without suffering the deleterious miscegenation of an influx of foreign loan words. In such languages, the relationship between race and speech is neither 'arbitrary' nor 'conventional',[18] as is the case with the 'dead language' spoken by those 'new Latins', Germans who have adopted in time the various vernaculars of Latin, but rather a matter of necessity. That is, peoples who replace their mother tongue with a foreign language lose contact with the suprasensual concepts that are elaborated from within the linguistic roots of a pure language.[19]

That is, on such occasions of linguistic defection, there is no problem in switching for example from saying *Fluss* or *Apfel* to using *rivière* or *pomme*. It is otherwise when it is a matter of concepts. Take the notion of humanitarianism. In German this is expressed by *Menschenfreundlichkeit*, a term built up from knitting together simple words in the native word stock, *Mensch* (man), *Freund* (friend), *-lich*(ly), and *-keit* (abstract suffix, *cf* English *-hood*), that is, 'man-friend-ly-hood'. Thus sophisticated concepts are immediately understandable in such a 'living language' because they are developed directly from the roots of the same language. However, in languages where the abstract terminology of concepts is borrowed, this lucid progression from the simple representation of the real in the root word to the complex reference to suprasensuous abstractions in compound terms is lost. The corresponding French term is *philanthropie*, a word borrowed from Greek (*philos + anthrōpos*), and thus incomprehensible to untutored native speakers. In this sense, French is a 'dead language'.[20]

To understand this point, we must recall that Fichte's theory is a subtle, table-turning polemic against the principles of the Enlightenment, the French revolution and the Napoleonic occupation of Germany. His theory is an astute form of cultural solace for a country deprived of its sovereignty.[21] On occasion, indeed, he betrays a touch of paranoia as when he speaks of the subversive, fifth-column activity of foreign words 'smuggled in' to enfeeble the higher spirituality of the German people. He complains that the French victory was paved by the spread of loan words like *Humanität*, *Popularität* and *Liberalität* which, however seductive to the literati, are merely empty echoes (*cf ein völlig leerer Schall*).[28] Like Tanizaki, he suggests that they be replaced by authentic coinages from the native word stock like *Menschenfreundlichkeit*, *Leutseligkeit* and *Edelmut*. But in this we sense a conservative desire to erase the new democratic current by a traditional language which is either apolitical or subversive of the intended concept (*cf* Liberality, Liberalism are quite distinct from 'noble-mindedness'). His exultant peroration on German 'freedom',[23] with its cunning pseudo-linguistic proof of the condition of higher *intellectual equality* open uniquely to the Germans, betrays the essential point-scoring nature of his analysis, as does his assertion that Germans understand foreign languages better than their native speakers, while at the same time remaining heirs to a profound culture inaccessible to aliens.[24]

We should note finally that Fichte several times repeats his thesis that, 'Man is shaped and informed (*bilden*) more by language, than language by man.'[25]

The human speaker is thus a mere ventriloquist's dummy

through which the autonomous spirit of language declares itself; man does not ideate, but rather, language dictates its thought through man. This deprivation of the speaking subject of his intellectual autonomy is a keynote of the *nihonjinron*. We have observed it in Tanizaki, and there are grounds for believing that, formulated thus, its entry into Japanese thought owes much to German influence. Fichte's theory is a dead letter in linguistic thought (though it is striking that few find it scandalous that Heidegger's philosophy draws in large part on the premises of Fichte's linguistic nationalism[26]) but, revived in Japan by Watanabe, it plays a key role in the revival of certain linguistic tenets of Japanese ultranationalism.

Watanabe's engagement of Fichte's ideas derives from an intuition that the arbitrary distinction between 'living' and 'dead' languages might readily explain certain 'unique' features of Japanese, namely the distinction between *yamato kotoba* and *gairaigo*. The former consist of:

> those words which the Japanese race has continued to use, handed down orally from prehistorical times. To speak in the language of evolutionary theory (though I myself do not believe in evolution), these *yamato kotoba* go straight back to an age when some monkey-like animals first put together coherent sounds as the ancestors of the Japanese. In other words, *yamato kotoba* are words which have their roots set down in the wellsprings of the soul of our race.[27]

That is, to continue with Watanabe's fascist idiom,[28] these pure *yamato* words are 'as old as our blood'.[29] If the philologist protests that large numbers of these words have Altaic or Malayo-Polynesian etymologies, Watanabe would reply that they have been autochthonised to the point that ancient Japanese considered them indigenous.[30] Thus his criteria switch from linguistic to psychological ones at the very juncture where his theory threatens to collapse under the weight of contrary evidence. He cannot see that, in Fichte's schema, in any case, Japanese is a 'dead language', since the suprasensual, conceptual component is constituted by *gairaigo*. *Menschenfreundlichkeit* in Japanese is translated by the Sino-Japanese word *hakuai*.

Watanabe, notwithstanding these difficulties, endorses Fichte because he sees in this theory an occasion for reviving the prewar theory of *kotodama*. As we have seen from Tanizaki, this refers to some latent power, a spell-binding force, resident in Japanese words. The proof of its existence is found in the putative fact that Japanese poems, translated into English, appear as flat doggerel, whereas writers like Shakespeare, when translated into Japanese, retain the austerely moving dignity of the original. This testifies to the existence of *kotodama* uniquely in *yamato kotoba*, and also proves that Japanese is invested with what Kant calls, 'The mental capacity for the formation of genius,' that is the power to form a closed discursive world unintelligible to outsiders.[31] As Miller acutely remarks, Watanabe is taking over into Japanese the nineteenth century German *Shakespearomanie*.[32]

Miller, in an extensive review of the textual sources for Watanabe's quirky thesis, demonstrates that it is rooted in certain interpretations of classical culture popularised in prewar educational propaganda like the *Kokutai no hongi* (1937), in whose drafting Hisamatsu Sen'ichi and Watsuji Tetsurō played a significant role. In that work, the misinterpretation of *kotodama* was employed for the purpose of mass mobilisation and inculcating a spirit of obedient *Selbstgleichschaltung* to the emerging fascist order. By a selective and tendentious use of ancient texts, the idea was promulgated that, given this mysterious power of Japanese words, 'words that are not liable to be put into practice are shunned, and are not uttered'. Since it was held that in Japanese tradition uniquely 'true words most often become true deeds',[33] '(o)nce anything is verbalised, it must necessarily be carried out; consequently, words having reference to anything that cannot be carried out are not lightly uttered'.[34] This philosophy is derived from two passages in the *Man'yōshū* interpreted to mean that Japan is 'a land to which *kotodama* brings good fortune', and 'a land where *kotoage* (word-lifting) is not done.'

This astute cultural rationale for mindless obedience to given orders, and for a culture of silence involving the self-censuring of dissident consciousness builds, as Miller's intensive study proves, on a distorted reading of the original texts, a misreading responsible for the now hackneyed contrast between Japanese silence and Western loquacity in the *nihonjinron* (*cf* feature 29, 29', chapter 4, table 6). Miller shows that both *kotodama* and *kotoage* share a root, ancient *koto* (from *katar-* 'to speak') which was homonymous with another word *koto*, meaning 'thing, matter'. Ancient works considered them to be cognate, and confused the 'thing' in the external world denoted by a 'word' with the word itself.[35] This was connected with the ancient belief that words and things were linked by an inner spiritual force, *tama* (soul, spirit), which was held to embue the thing/word (*koto*) with a resident *mana*-like power (=*kotodama*). The ritual invocation of this power was called *kotoage* (lifting up words/things).[36]

Analysing the appropriate sources, Miller shows that words were 'lifted up' to secure a deed, but that the very power to influence reality by such talismanic[37] invocation rendered it too dangerous to exploit except in the most special circumstances. Thus it came about that the very act of renouncing facile recourse to such magic displayed one's particular fortitude. By not 'raising up words/things', one asserted one's desire to soldier on without depending on supernal agencies. 'Not raising up words' (*kotoage sezu*) thus became a warrior virtue and a fixed epithet for his valiant land of *Yamato* (*cf kotoage senu kuni*).[38]

Further, these expressions occur in poetic *envois* to Japanese diplomatic missions in China. The shock of discovering that, though they had mastered the written script, such ambassadors could not communicate verbally with their hosts, gave rise to a defensive rationalisation among the emissaries that only their native tongue possessed a 'spirit' which instantly communicated itself to other speakers. The *kotodama* myth thus developed to gloss over certain perplexities arising from linguistic contact with foreigners.[39] We might recall that Fichte's theory equally emerged as a defensive rationalisation in response to the shock of cultural encounter with the invading French, and that it was Motoori Norinaga, a rough contemporary of Fichte, who glossed these old terms in a way which was to prove decisive for the modern linguistic ideology of Japan, in writing that 'not to argue (as he takes the sense of *kotoage senu*) means not to expatiate or indulge in much talk, as is the custom in foreign countries.'[40]

This is the origin of Tanizaki's remarks on *oshaberi* (West) and silence (Japan). It lies behind Watanabe's muddle-headed belief that the Fichtean *lebendige Sprache*, implying that the 'word (*koto*) is a variety of the thing (*koto*)',[41] exactly corresponds to the category of *yamato kotoba*, with its parallel insinuation that all foreign languages by contrast are 'dead languages'. In prewar Japan these classical tags became a potent 'documentary' source from 'tradition' to buttress the hand and authority of 'thought policing'. Misunderstood canonically, they served not only as cultural inducements to promote a laconic self-synchronisation of people with the prevailing order, but also, once harnessed to Wang Yang-Ming's concept of the unity of thought and action, were enlisted to propagate unswerving and immediate obedience to any command, and in this sense provided a Japanese version of the Nazi slogan that 'the Leader's words have the force of law' (*Führerworte haben Gesetzeskraft*).[42]

Given this political instrumentalisation of *kotodama*, therefore, it is all the more striking that Watanabe should revive these concepts, in Fichtean garb, in order to demonstrate that *yamato kotoba* not only permit a uniquely Japanese form of educational equality,[43] but also reveal an original Japanese spirit of pacificism. For Watanabe, Japan is militant when consciousness is alienated by the influx of aggressive, abstract foreign words. He revealingly classifies the differences in table 9.

Table 9: Loan Words and Indigenous Words

Kango (Chinese loan words)	Yamato kotoba ('indigenous words')
i Outward-looking (cf. H)	i' Inward-looking (cf. H')
ii Convey aggressive feelings (cf. feature 20)	ii' Placidly homely feelings (cf. 20')
iii Used when the mind works at a distance from objects, intellectually (cf. F,26,27)	iii' Used when the mind brushes up against placid sentiment (cf. F',26',27')
iv Scholarly writing (26)	iv' Poetic writing (26')
v Hard, like the brawny muscles of the father (19,28,G)	v' Soft, like the tender feel of a mother's skin (19',28',G')
vi Language of law, bureaucracy (9,14')	vi' Voice of private lyricism (9',14)

The observations in table 9 merely restate certain key terms in the shorthand list of ideas I have sketched out earlier. Part of Watanabe's formulation draws unconsciously on stereotypes to be found in the writings of the poet Hagiwara Sakutarō.[44] What is striking is the way Watanabe exploits the intellectual clichés of pre-war fascist ideology in the furtherance of his postwar vision of a pacific Japan. Indeed, he invokes the notion of *kokutai* itself, 'the fundamental character of the nation' for the same irenic ends, though quite aware of its danger. Thus he writes that, 'The words "the *kokutai* of Japan" invite misunderstanding, but I make bold to use them nonetheless.'[45] Elsewhere he notes:

> I think there are not a few people for whom the word *kokutai* bears unpleasant associations, but with the reader's indulgence I shall use it as a word which conjoins such concepts as 'national character' (*kunigara*) and 'polity' (*seitai*), since no other words strike me as being appropriate.[46]

It promises to be an interesting age when the idiom of peace draws philological support from the ideological jargon of fascist texts of indoctrination like the *Kokutai no hongi*, when that 'mother lode of philological quackery'[47] is mined by a newer generation of Western-trained linguists for putatively new insights into 'the soul of Japan'. But we should be grateful to Watanabe for inadvertently providing us with a clue to the underlying reasons for this revival. For his antithesis between *kango* and *yamato kotoba* in effect disclose a series of psycholinguistic contrasts between mature, adult usage and the child's chatter, explicitly associated with a rejected paternal image (*kango*, v) on the one hand, and a yearned for maternal image (*yamato kotoba*, v') on the other. To recognise one's unique identity in the character of the latter points once more to an underlying regression to narcissism,[48] under the cultural alias of a return to linguistic origins and purity, whose social logic will be explored in the following chapter.

Our third example comes from Suzuki Takao's 'A closed language — The World of Japanese' which attempts to analyse the so-called Japanese distrust of language. As one sees in the reluctance of Japanese executives abroad to raise their children within the Japanese language, there is a widespread belief that the language is somehow imperfect, illogical and a hindrance to a broader outlook.[49] Suzuki points out that there is indeed a preference among many Japanese writers for imprecision, ambiguous waffle and allusiveness which amounts to 'a kind of mystification through language'.[50] He justly remarks that there is nothing intrinsic to the language itself to warrant such judgements, and suggests that the cause may lie in the national character.

But after a sensible beginning, Suzuki veers off to speak on the natural limitations of language, in a manner that recapitulates strikingly the outset of Tanizaki's book. Backtracking quickly he avers that:

> It is a fact that language has fatal limitations in that it cannot wholly elucidate the objects (*taishō*) it designates, no matter

how much people strive towards that end. We must surely not deny such devices as allusion, ambiguity and lingering resonance (*yoin*). We must also duly recognise that it is precisely these kinds of basic elements which serve as effective ways to both transcend the essential limitations of language, and to bear down on objects (*taishō ni semaru*), particularly in those arts which exploit the resources of language. However, I do not think that when an author is arguing and presenting a point of view, where bringing others to understand and agree with one's assertions is the case, there is any sense in avoiding clarity. This would be tantamount to ignoring the existence of the other person, and is equivalent to communicative suicide.[51]

Suzuki's concession to traditional views is, after all, only tactical. In some ways indeed he gives us an advance on Tanizaki's position since devices like allusion are here not seen as uniquely Japanese, but rather supplementary means that abet the descriptive power of language used rationally. He illustrates his point by citing a recalcitrantly vague passage which only begins to yield some sense, and its mysterious power (*myō na chikara*), after several rereadings. The reader is somehow drawn on and into the text by the secret pleasure he feels in torment, anguish or pain, as provoked by such difficult writing.[52] It follows that, for Suzuki:

There is a tendency among Japanese readers to value ambiguity (*kaijūsa*) highly, and one could say that the idea that clarity is to be disdained as vapid and lacking in depth is not altogether without foundation. To parody Rivarol, it would seem that 'What is clear is not Japanese'.[53]

In essence, Suzuki is paraphrasing Tanizaki's views in sociolinguistic terms. Thus the latter's definition of *kotodama* as the 'spell-binding lure of words' becomes in the former a 'mysterious power'. In both, an initial stress on language as a means of communication is reversed by a passionate defence of the evasive communicatory style they associate with their mother tongue.

What is extraordinary about the argument which follows, in which Suzuki tries to demonstrate the analytical superiority of Japanese over Western languages and thus the intellectual and educational edge gained by Japanese students, is that Suzuki arrives at this conclusion using precisely the evidence which

Watanabe excludes in arriving at the same conclusion. Where for Watanabe the advantage stems from the character of *yamato kotoba*, for Suzuki it derives from *kango* which, though loan words, are here treated as authentic elements of the Japanese glossary. Rather, for Suzuki, it is the newer *gairaigo*, Western loan words, which are to be regarded as alien to the Japanese way. The argument is familiar, namely, that the *kokutai* endogenises the alien culture in such a way that it may carry the Japanese spirit. Suzuki writes that,

> *Kanji* (Chinese characters) have already dovetailed deeply into the basic constitutional disposition of the Japanese language, and it is no longer possible to exclude them as foreign elements of an heterogeneous kind.[54]

For Suzuki, the genius of the Japanese language lies in the way each character in its Chinese script has a Chinese reading (*on-yomi*) and a native Japanese reading (*kun-yomi*). This device enables the Japanese to translate difficult concepts into simple language instinctively. What in effect Suzuki has done is to borrow Fichtean ideas from Watanabe's exposition, and use the *on-yomi/kun-yomi* device to restore to Japanese (in strict Fichtean terms a 'dead language') the Fichtean relationship between sensuous word and suprasensuous concept in 'living languages'. This allows him to assert that Japanese have unique access to sophisticated ideas that are understandable in the West only to the educated élite.

Take the word for anthropology, *jinruigaku*. Suzuki argues that an English typist would have difficulty understanding this word literally (being composed of Greek roots), whereas her Japanese equivalent may immediately determine its sense by glossing each component Chinese lexis with its Japanese reading. That is *jin* is read *hito* (man), *rui* as *tagui* (category) and *gaku*, study. This specious instance[55] allows him to praise the system as having 'an advantage unparalleled in any other language in that it links together high-class vocabulary and the vocabulary of everyday speech.'[56] That there must be something gravely wrong with two arguments which arrive at the same conclusion via mutually exclusive premises is of little consequence, since both authors are concerned purely with questions of linguistic 'face'; they exploit Fichtean ideas in order to turn on its head the *nihonjinron* stereotype of an egalitarian West contrasted to an hierarchical Japan by asserting that, linguistically, the Japanese have a unique form of equality in educational terms.

A large part of the book is devoted to providing a socio-cultural explanation for what Miller has called 'The Law of Inverse Returns', according to which the more fluent a foreigner becomes in Japanese the less he is praised. Suzuki invokes the notion of mental instability to account in part for this phenomenon, since foreigners speaking Japanese break that 'natural' law which correlates the language with race.[57] His account amounts to a handy compendium of the clichés of Japaneseness linked for once in something like a coherent order of causes and consequences.

Suzuki begins by contrasting the '*absolute* self-expression' of Western languages to the '*relative* self-expression' of Japanese (*cf* principle C, C', chapter 4, table 7).[58] That is occidental speech has one, invariant term (*I, ich, je, ya*) for the first person pronoun whereas Japanese has a large variety indicating status situations. He takes this as proof that the Western ego is stable, and the Japanese unstable (22, 22', reversed). From this he deduces that the Japanese have a *situational* mentality as opposed to the *rigid* outlook of Westerners (28, 28'). He is again imitating Tanizaki here, but his choice of terms provides us with a classic *lapsus calami*. For in attributing to Westerners the trait of a 'rigidity in arbitrarily acting on one's own authority' (*dokudan senkōteki na kōchokusa*), his language betrays an unconcious association of Western behaviour with the defiant bellicosity characteristic of the Kwantung army in Manchuria.[59] Such evasive projections onto foreign countries of unseemly aspects of one's past history is a characteristic of *nihonjinron* discourse and tells us much about its motivation.

To corroborate the view that Japanese display acute sensitivity to situations compared to Westerners, he cites a series of Japanese expressions which are supposed to resist easy translation into foreign languages, phrases that simply refer to being quick on the uptake, tactful or empathetic. His curious belief that they are untranslatable derives from his equally odd notion that 'In non-Japanese cultures, it is the norm not to make inferences about the feelings of the other person when that person does not express his opinions and wishes in words.'[60]

The Japanese have what he calls 'anticipatory perception' which enables them, apparently, to 'tune in to other people's wavelength'. This capacity derives from being a 'unitary race' (5', table 2) in an ideal 'island country' (1', table 7), which an 'homogeneous culture of high purity' (B', table 7), devoid of those tensions and violence characteristic of mixed pastoral-agricultural societies (6, 6'; 20, 20', tables 3 and 5), of antagonisms between monotheism and pantheism (21, 21', tables 5) and in short, which lacks all polarising conflict (25', D', tables 6 and 7). Given the unheralded 'homogeneity of (Japanese) existence' (*dōshitsuteki sonzai*, the postwar euphemism for racial purity), the Japanese have developed an innate capacity over millenia for intuiting exactly what all other Japanese are thinking.

> Naturally enough in human relationships of this kind, one can get by with very few words (*cf* 29'). From the very nature of language itself, it is impossible to convey the facts as they are (*jijitsu sono mama*) and, in this sense, language is a very imperfect thing. Consequently, where understanding is possible simply at the level of facts, it is not only unnecessary to varnish such comprehension by (the addition of) inadequate words, but indeed thoughtlessly using the imperfect medium of words may often result in merely pouring cold water (*mizu o sasu* = alienating) a unified understanding that has been obtained only with great difficulty. (In Japan) saying nothing is the most apt and suitable thing to do.[61]

Suzuki at this point has collapsed and reversed all of the sensible ideas which occupied the first chapter of his book, and has convinced himself into an ideological self-synchronisation with the standard *kokutai* myths. He displays an equal fidelity to the stereotypes of the West, which is depicted in a model which inverts systematically the features he deems unique to Japanese culture.

Given the polyracial makeup of the Eurasian continent, conflict at a racial cultural, religious and social level was endemic. Originally, the tribes there each interpreted reality in a different way. Such diversity eventually entailed a need for an agreement on reality to allow a *modus vivendi*, and 'self assertion via language and verbal persuasion'[62] came to the fore as the only means of narrowing, by however small a margin, the differences separating parties, and for transcending those differences which lie between oneself and people of a different kind. Westerners, like the Japanese, understood that language was imperfect but had to stress its importance as the only means of guaranteeing security. Thus the arts of rhetoric, and persuasion, and the practice of adhering tenaciously to contracts written in words established themselves in

China, India and the West.

> Indeed, it would be no exaggeration to say that everything related to courts, politics, education and foreign diplomacy reveals a vehement clash of words. This enthusiasm for words, passionate to such a degree that one might well say that they consider that what cannot be verbalised is virtually non-existent, is far removed from how we Japanese feel, in that we think that the more important and vital a matter is, the less it may be expressed in words.[63]

Suzuki's exposition, of which I have given but a brief résumé here, runs through the gamut of every cliché in the paradigm of contrasts, showing by a logic of associations how, from the assumption of an insular pure-blooded tribe one arrives at a culture of peacefully silent consensus. Conversely, the intellectual world of the West, with its apparent preference for "arguments over proof", is deduced from the multiracial character of continental existence.

The keynote of all this is his linguistically-derived theory of personality, which contradicts what he tells us about the antithesis between verbose Westerners and laconic or taciturn Japanese. For Suzuki, whereas Westerners never disclose their inner selves to others, the Japanese have a compulsive desire to 'pour out their hearts' to one another (18′, 26′, tables 4 and 6). Given that their self-definition depends on the other, their tendency to identify their own standpoint with others, and the 'other-directed type of principle of accommodation to the general drift of society',[64] the sense of ego individuality is consequently weak.[65] In compensation, they develop a quasi telepathic ability to read the thoughts and feelings of the other. Dialogue obtains only among people with strong egos (a defensive mechanism arising from racial conflict), among whom it functions as a means of coordinating antagonistic interests and *Weltanschauungen.*

This ego-theory is riddled with contradictions of a highly revealing nature. Suzuki speaks of a Japanese need to discover others with whom they can unburden their souls, a desire which, if unrequited, may lead to suicide:

> It would appear that we Japanese unceasingly require that some suitable person understand what we are thinking and what our true feelings are. The wish to gain the assent and approbation of

others, to savour their sympathy in one way or another, appears in every kind of our behaviour in contexts of interpersonal relationships.[66]

Such a voluble self-centered ego-type is precisely the opposite of the silent, empathising type he speaks of elsewhere. We are given a weak ego-type that is unstable unless it manages to align itself with some sympathetic other,[67] and an ego-type that demands of the other a patient empathy with one's own true feelings. His construction demands self-abnegation and conformity (hiding the self) and self-exposure and revelation to the other. If the Japanese are so empathetic that words are not needed, why are we told at the same time that they are all desperate to unbosom their real feelings (presumably verbally)? In short, the Japanese are reserved and outgoing, reticent and prone to garrulous psychobabble, egotistic and conformist. If all aspire to fuse their identity with others, why is an 'understanding that mutually unites'[68] people achieved only with great difficulty? An attempt will presently be made to untangle these paradoxes, but it is clear that in these diametrically opposed images of the ego, inner desire is in contrast with social reality.

Suzuki has refrained from explicitly using the *kotodama/ kotoage* jargon, unlike the other writers (whose texts he otherwise tacitly plays on). Yet he has managed to insinuate the doctrine, with its earlier *kokutai* associations of racial and cultural uniqueness, in the form of his linguistic analysis of the Japanese ego. In affirming that the Japanese ego is characterised by 'the assimilation of the self with external objects'[69] and 'the alignment of oneself with the other' to achieve 'the unity of self and other' (*jita gōitsu*),[70] he is redeploying the *kotodama* theory of the unity of word and thing in the sphere of psychosocial relationships. It naturally follows that when ego and alter are fused, homogenised, and conflated, dialogue or recourse to language, which presupposes the existence of individual interlocutors, is preempted by the harmonious complicity of silent empathisers. The resonance of such ideas, for all of their vaunted originality, is ominously familiar. For such a view makes of the Japanese people 'a clustering of individuals bound to each other by an intimate affinity of conscience, by a fundamental unity in the way of thinking and feeling'[71] while denying them what even Italian fascist thinkers conceded, namely individual personality and language.

Notes

1. Tanizaki Jun'ichirō, *Bunshō Tokuhon*, in *Tanizaki Jun'ichirō Zenshū* 21 (Chūō Kōronsha, Tokyo, 1974) pp.87-246, pp.91-7.
2. Tanizaki, *Bunshō Tokuhon*, ibid. pp.100ff.
3. Tanizaki, *Bunshō Tokuhon*, ibid. p.116.
4. Tanizaki, *Bunshō Tokuhon*, ibid. pp.118, 223.
5. Tanizaki, *Bunshō Tokuhon*, ibid. p.118.
6. Tanizaki, *Bunshō Tokuhon*, ibid. p.118.
7. Tanizaki, *Bunshō Tokuhon*, ibid. pp.119-20, 219-223.
8. Tanizaki, *Bunshō Tokuhon*, ibid. pp.124ff. See also R.A. Miller, 'Levels of Speech (*keigo*) and the Japanese Response to Modernization' in Donald H. Shively (ed.), *Tradition and Modernization in Japanese Culture*, (Princeton University Press, Princeton New Jersey, 1971) pp.601-67, esp. pp.614f, 651ff; Watanabe Shōichi, *Kokugo no ideorogii*, (Chūō Kōronsha, Tokyo, 1977) pp.49-80.
9. Tanizaki, *Bunshō Tokuhon*, ibid. pp.151ff, 160-1.
10. Tanizaki, *Bunshō Tokuhon*, ibid. p.166. B. Karlgren, *Philology and Ancient China*, (Goteburg, 1926) pp.149ff, makes a similar proposal *to reduce ambiguity*.
11. T. Adorno, *Minima Moralia*, ibid. p.110.
12. *cf* R. Grünberger, *A Social History of the Third Reich*, (Penguin, Harmondsworth 1974) p.416. On the German view of the decadent West, see L. Poliakov, *The Aryan Myth*, (Meridian, New York 1977) pp.72ff.
13. Tanizaki, *Bunshō Tokuhon*, ibid. p.154. W. Betz, *Verändert Sprache die Welt?* (Edition Interfrom, A.G., Zurich, 1977) pp.38-9, arguing against the nationalist conflation of *Wortschatz*, *Weltbild* and *Wirklichkeit*, remarks that, 'eine neu beobachtete Empfindung sucht sich einen neuen sprachlichen Ausdruck'.
14. Tanizaki, *Bunshō Tokuhon* ibid. p.156. Compare the view of the philosopher of Italian fascism Giovanni Gentile, *Genesi e struttura della società*, 1943 (Biblioteca Sansoni, Florence, 1975) p.15 that the individual's language is that of his fathers, his tribe, and thus when 'I speak' the community or 'we' at the base of his spiritual existence speaks through him.
15. See the prefatory citation to G. Steiner, *After Babel* (Oxford University Press paper, 1977). Tanizaki's contrast between *oshaberi* (chat) and prudent care against garrulousness (*jōzetsu o tsutsushimu koto*) is a precise equivalent, as a West-East contrast, to Heidegger's contrast between *Gerede* (chat) and *Rede* (speech), for which see G. Steiner, *Heidegger*, (Fontana Modern Masters, Glasgow, 1978) pp.92-3.
16. Watanabe Shōichi, 'Nihongo ni tsuite' in *Shokun!* (August 1974) trans, in edited form in *Japan Echo*, 1:2 (winter 1974) pp.9-20. The article is available in Watanabe, *Bunka no jidai*, (Bunshun Bunko, Tokyo, 1978) pp.83-128, and in an expanded version in his *Nihongo no kokoro* (Kōdansha Gendai Shinsho, 1974) esp. pp.156ff.
17. I use the edition, J.G. Fichte, *Ausgewälte Werke in Sechs Bänden*, hrsg. F. Medicus, Bd. 5 (Wissenschaftliche Buchgesellschaft, Darmstadt, 1962). Watanabe draws on the fourth speech, here pp.422-38.
18. Watanabe, *Bunka no jidai*, ibid. p.86. Watanabe distorts Fichte. It is not the relationship of race and language, which is neither arbitrary (*shiiteki kettei*) nor conventional (*yakusoku*), but that between words and objects. *cf* 'Die Sprache überhaupt, und besonders die Bezeichnung der Gegenstände in derselben durch das Lautwerden der Sprachwerkzeuge, hängt keineswegs von *willkürlichen Beschlüssen* und *Verabredungen* ab,' (Fichte, ibid. p.425).

19. Fichte held that objects are represented in language by necessary sounds, and that the primary word-stock of a language embodies a direct perception of the sensuous reality denoted. It is by building on these sensuous words that a race develops the power of pure cognition of suprasensual realities. Such a language '*gibt ein sinnliches Bild des Übersinnlichen*', and it is this formulation which underlies Heidegger's 'etymologising realism' (as Steiner puts it, *Heidegger*, ibid. p.30), and thus the work of Japanese philosophers like Kuki and Watsuji influenced by Heidegger. Compare the language of p.69, and chapter 5, note 44. Fichte's theory of a 'living language' itself derives from Hamann's theory of the Edenic language in which 'everything that man heard or saw with his eyes, or touched with his hands, was in the beginning *a living word*', as R. Pascal puts it, *The German Sturm und Drang*, (Manchester University Press, Manchester, (2nd edition) 1959) pp.176-7. For Fichte, when foreign words enter such a language, thought is cut off from its living roots in the sensuous, primary word-stock.

20. Watanabe, *Bunka no jidai*, ibid. pp.87-8; *Nihongo no kokoro*, ibid. pp.159-63. Compare Fichte, *Vierte Rede*, ibid. pp.431-2. For an incisive corrective analysis of the popular contrast between concrete and abstract languages see R. Brown, *Words and Things*, (Free Press, New York, 1958) pp.264ff.

21. For Fichte's nationalism, see Poliakov, *Aryan Myth*, pp.99ff. The situation was reversed in the Franco-Prussian war. Daudet in his *La dernière classe* has the schoolmaster exhort his pupils in Alsace to hold fast to their French mother tongue during the German occupation since it is 'la plus belle langue du monde, la plus claire, la plus solide'. See L.C. Harmer, *The French Language Today*, (Hutchinson's University Library, London, 1954) pp.13f.

22. Fichte, *Vierte Rede*, ibid. p.432.

23. A very peculiar philosophy of freedom (not unlike Doi's in substance) since it made it possible 'to proclaim the police state as the incarnation of liberty'. *Cf.* L. Kolakowski, *Main Currents of Marxism* trans. P.S. Falla (Oxford University Press paper, 1981) vol. 1 p.55.

24. Fichte, *Vierte Rede*, ibid. pp.437-8.

25. Fichte, *Vierte Rede*, ibid. p.425 ('... mehr die Menschen von der Sprache gebildet werden, denn die Sprache von den Menschen'), p.426 ('Nict eigentlich redet der Mensch, sondern in ihm redet die menschliche Natur,') *cf* Heidegger's view that, 'It is *language that speaks* not, or not primordially, man', as Steiner puts it, *Heidegger*, ibid. p.27.

26. The puzzle is that no linguist (other than perhaps Watanabe) treats Fichte's theory of language seriously today, after Saussure's revolution. But it is altogether another matter with Heidegger's thought which draws implicitly on the linguistic premises enunciated by Fichte. Compare Steiner's presentation of Heidegger's views, *Heidegger*, ibid. pp.14-16, 27-30, 49ff.

27. Watanabe, *Nihongo no kokoro*, ibid. pp.11-12. For the full reverberation of this to Japanese ears, see chapter 11.

28. Watanabe, *Gengo to minzoku*, ibid. p.142 specifically refers to a pro-Nazi writer's celebration of Fichte's theory. Given his clearly deep familiarity with German books of the 1930s, one wonders whether he is familiar with Lothar Tirala's *Geist und Seele* (1935) where separate races are seen to derive from distinct primate families.

29. Watanabe, *Nihongo no kokoro*, ibid. p.8.

30. Watanabe, *Bunka no jidai*, ibid. p.104; *Seigi no jidai*, ibid. p.94.

31. Watanabe, *Bunka no jidai*, ibid. p.110, referring apparently to Kant's *Kritik der Urteilskraft*, 2, sects. 44-50. *More suo*, he gets his sources wrong. Genius for Kant was the talent for original creation, not amenable to imitation because ruleless, as opposed to the imitative learning by which we can *follow logically* the productions of science. See *Kant's Critique of Aesthetic Judgement*, trans. and ed.

with annotations James Creed Meredith (Oxford University Press, 1911) pp.168-83. The closest thing in Kant to Watanabe's reading of *Genie* is the remark 'genius can produce original nonsense' (p.168).

32. R.A. Miller, 'The "Spirit" of the Japanese Language', in *Journal of Japanese Studies*, 3:2 (summer 1977) pp.251-98, p.255 n.5.

33. Miller, ibid. p.259 compares '*shingen wa yoku shinkō to naru*' of the *Kokutai no hongi* to '*das schöne Wort erzeuge die schöne Tat*' in Thomas Mann's *Der Zauberberg*, and it may thus be an unacknowledged borrowing from Western literature. We should not forget however Carlyle's oration on Cromwell, 'what this man speaks comes out of him to pass as a fact' (cited H. Trevor-Roper, *Times Literary Supplement*, 26 June 1981, p.733). Mann, in his novel Lotte in Weimar has Goethe say '*Ein reines Wort erreget schöne Taten*' (T. Mann, *Gesammelte Werke*, (S. Fischer Verlag) Bd. 2, 1960, pp.444, 678) and this with Carlyle's remark, points to a source in German romanticism. Compare the immediate realisation of the Emperor's spoken word in Faust II, lines 10,252-57. But it equally plays off the Confucian *Analects*, esp. *yen chih pi k'o hsing yeh*, at *Lun Yü*, 13. 3, and the *cheng ming* (rectification of names) tradition in Chinese thought. A keynote in Japanese philosophical nationalism is the use of Western idioms to express traditional oriental ideas. See chapter 12, p.216.

34. As translated in Miller, 'The "Spirit" of the Japanese Language', ibid. p.259.

35. Miller, 'The "Spirit" of the Japanese Language', ibid. pp.263-4. Heidegger, with the advantage of not knowing Japanese, defines *koto* as '*das Ereignis der lichtenden Botschaft der hervorbringenden Huld*' (*Unterwegs zur Sprache*, ibid. p.144) which may mean something in German, but has no relevance whatsoever to the word *koto* it presumes to define.

36. Miller, 'The "Spirit" of the Japanese Language', ibid. pp.276-7.

37. On amuletic language in Japan see Tsurumi Shunsuke, *Nichijōteki shisō no kanōsei*, (Chikuma Shobō, Tokyo, 1976) pp.32-56.

38. Miller, 'The "Spirit" of the Japanese Language', ibid. pp.276-7. A rough parallel is Hektor's rejoinder to Polydamas who wishes to fight according to the portents: 'To defend one's fatherland is the best and only omen (*oiōnos*)', *Iliad*, 12.243.

39. Miller, 'The "Spirit" of the Japanese Language', ibid. pp.281.

40. Motoori, *Naobi no mitama*, as cited in Nakamura, *Ways of Thinking*, ibid. p.539. See also *Motoori Norinaga Zenshū* 5 (Chikuma Shobō, 1970) pp.375ff, esp. p.388.

41. Watanabe, *Gengo to minzoku*, ibid. p.144. We should not forget the force of this idea in traditional Chinese linguistics and philosophy. See for example, J.J.L. Duyvendak, 'Hsün-tzŭ on the Rectification of Names', in *T'oung Pao* 25 (1924) pp.221-54.

42. Nazi usage changed the early term *Befehlsempfänger* (receiver of orders) to *Befehlsträger* (bearer of orders) for this very reason. Compare the expression *shōshō hikkin* in Japanese, for which see Maruyama, *Thought and Behaviour*, ibid. p.69. The *hsing ming* variant on the *cheng ming* which held that performance should correspond to title, demanding a supine acquiescence in orders from superiors, may have influenced the Fascist conceptualisations. On *hsing ming* see H.G. Creel, 'The Meaning of Hsing Ming' in *Studia Serica Bernhard Karlgren Dedicata*, S. Egerod and E. Glahn (eds.) (Ejnar Munkgaard, Copenhagen, 1959) pp.199-222, esp. p.210.

43. Watanabe, *Bunka no jidai*, ibid. pp.94ff; *Nihongo no kokoro*, ibid. pp.48ff. The idea is borrowed from Fichte, *Vierte Rede*, ibid. pp.437-8.

44. See Miller, *Japan's Modern Myth*, ibid. p.114, for Hagiwara's views. Watanabe's contrasts are in *Nihongo no kokoro*, ibid. pp.24-5. On militarism and Chinese words see also Maruya Saiichi, *Nihongo no tame ni* (Shinchō Bunko,

98 *The Linguistics of Silence*

Tokyo, 1978) pp.112ff, and Kindaichi Haruhiko, *Nihonjin no gengo hyōgen* (Kōdansha Gendai Shinsho, Tokyo, 1975) p.240.
    45. Watanabe, *Kokugo no ideorogii*, ibid. p.88.
    46. Watanabe, *Bunka no jidai*, ibid. p.67.
    47. Miller, *Japan's Modern Myth*, ibid. p.203.
    48. As does the primitive insistence on the unity of the word and reality. It is not mere coincidence that the same view is maintained by the radical prophets and harbingers of a schizo-culture in the West, like Guatteri and Deleuze who celebrate the fact that, '(f)or the schizophrenic, word and deed are one, saying is doing'. See Turkle, *Psychoanalytic Politics*, ibid. p.84.
    49. Suzuki Takao, *Tozasareta gengo*, ibid. pp.9-19.
    50. Suzuki, *Tozasareta gengo*, ibid. p.32. Suzuki's expression plays off the words *kotoba ni yoru komyunikēshon*, introduced in Japan from Western sociolinguistics.
    51. Suzuki, *Tozasareta gengo*, ibid. p.32.
    52. Suzuki, *Tozasareta gengo* ibid. p.35. Not so much 'sociolinguistic *Schadenfreude*' (Miller, *The Japanese Language in Contemporary Japan*, ibid. p.38) as much as masochism (as Miller later notes, *Japan's Modern Myth*, ibid. pp.123ff). A precise parallel is Shimomura's remark, *Nishida Kitarō*, ibid. p.244, that readers of Nishida's dense, if not incomprehensible philosophy, are seized by this style of writing, and sense its sympathetic appeal.
    53. Suzuki, *Tozasareta gengo*, p.35. Had he read Rivarol, he would have understood that his words are not a parody. For Rivarol not only says 'Ce qui n'est pas clair n'est pas français' but also 'ce qui n'est pas clair est encore anglais, italien, grec ou latin', and by implication Japanese. See Harmer, *The French Language*, ibid. p.51.
    54. Suzuki, *Tozasareta gengo*, ibid. p.50.
    55. Suzuki, *Tozasareta gengo*, ibid. pp.79ff, esp. pp.86ff. There are two sources underlying Suzuki's example. One is the Fichtean approach, illustrated through Watanabe's example of *Menschenfreundlichkeit*; the other is Watsuji Tetsurō's neo-Heideggerian analysis of the Confucian ethical vocabulary (*cf ningen*, a component of *ningengaku*, anthropology) in terms of *kun-yomi* readings. See below, chapter 12. Etymology is no guide to meaning, as Miller, *The Japanese Language in Contemporary Japan*, ibid. pp.57-8 notes. Anthropologists like E. Leach, *Social Anthropology*, (Fontana Master Guides, London, 1982) pp.13ff, strongly question the view that anthropology is simply 'the study of mankind'.
    56. Suzuki, *Tozasareta gengo*, ibid. p.95. The view is Fichtean, compare his *Vierte Rede*, ibid. pp.437ff, and thus the genius of German as Fichte sees it has become, transposed, a feature of Japanese uniqueness.
    57. Suzuki, *Tozasareta gengo*, ibid. pp.165ff, esp. pp.174ff; Miller, *The Japanese Language in Contemporary Japan*, ibid. pp.77ff, *Japan's Modern Myth*, pp.156ff. Suzuki's expression *gaijin kyōfushō* (xenophobia, p.174) puns on the expression *taijin kyōfushō* (anthropophobia) current in Japanese psychiatry for an ostensibly peculiar Japanese condition of pathological shyness. See on this Kasahara Yomishi, 'Fear of Eye-to-Eye Confrontation among Neurotic Patients in Japan' in T.S. Lebra, W.P. Lebra (eds.) *Japanese Culture and Behaviour: Selected Readings*, (University Press of Hawaii, Honolulu, 1974) pp.396-406.
    58. Suzuki, *Tozasereta gengo*, ibid. pp.181-8, esp. p.185. An earlier version may be found in his *Kotoba to bunka*, ibid. pp.146ff. Miura Tsutomu, *Nihongo no bunpō*, (Keisō Shobō, Tokyo, 1975) pp.54ff, challenges Suzuki's analysis.
    59. Suzuki, *Tozasareta gengo*, ibid. p.186. On *dokudan senkō*, as 'field initiative' among the Japanese forces in Manchuria see M. Peattie, *Ishiwara Kanji and Japan's Confrontation with the West*, (Princeton University Press, Princeton and London, 1975) p.119.

The Linguistics of Silence   99

60. Suzuki, *Tozasareta gengo*, ibid. p.188. The cliché of sympathy (Japan) versus rationality (West) overlooks the fact that the former requires the latter. See Andreski, *The Uses of Comparative Sociology*, ibid. p.186.

61. Suzuki, *Tozasareta gengo*, ibid. p.89. Here Suzuki unconsciously destroys his prior argument for clarity in discussion. Thus whether in terms of silence or ambiguity, his position is now one of 'communicative suicide'.

62. Suzuki, *Tozasareta gengo*, ibid. p.190. The phrase *kotoba ni yoru settoku* here forms a contrast with Japanese *kotoba ni yoru misuteifuikēshon.*

63. Suzuki, *Tozasareta gengo*, ibid. p.191. The point about 'what cannot be expressed in language is tantamount to (being considered) non-existent' plays on Wittgenstein's famous dictum that 'Whereof one cannot speak, thereof one must be silent', and is copied by Kimura Shōsaburō, *Seiyō no kao, Nihon no kokoro*, ibid. p.95.

64. Suzuki, *Tozasareta gengo*, ibid. p.186. The expression unites Suzuki's misunderstanding of Riesman's 'other-directed' concept with Tanizaki's *junnō.*

65. Suzuki, *Tozasareta gengo*, ibid. pp.182-7, esp. p.187 (*yowai jiga*).

66. Suzuki, *Tozasareta gengo*, ibid. p.182.

67. Suzuki, *Tozasareta gengo*, ibid. p.187.

68. Suzuki, *Tozasareta gengo*, ibid. p.189 (*gōitsuteki na rikai*).

69. Suzuki, *Kotoba to bunka*, ibid. p.202.

70. Suzuki, *Kotoba to bunka*, ibid. p.204. For *jita gōitsu*, see *Tozasareta gengo*, ibid. p.183. Suzuki is drawing on Doi's idea of *amae*. See chapters 8 and 9.

71. B. Giuliano, *Elementi di Cultura Fascista*, (Zanichelli, Bologna, 1932) p.9.

7 SILENCE AND ELUSION

'Elusion is a way of getting round conflict without direct confrontation, or its resolution.'
Ronald Laing, *Self and Other*, 1972 p.47

'From long monologues to short dialogues: this is the evolution of conversation.'
Ōsugi Sakae, cited T.A. Stanley, *Ōsugi Sakae. Anarchist in Taishō Japan*, 1982, p.120

Underlying the ideology of the Japanese language surveyed in the previous chapters we may discern beneath the specious variety of illustrative detail a united set of principles. The linguistic *nihonjinron*, in effect, posit three points of antithesis between Japanese and all other languages (table 10).

A moment's reflection suggests that the antic discrimination between the prosaic character of foreign languages and the poetic nature of Japanese disguises a sentimental revolt against the language of critical thinking and a concomitant nostalgic reevocation of the infant's world of cognition and speech. The *kotodama* doctrine is used to substantiate the view that uniquely for the Japanese, 'name and reality coincide' (*meijitsu ittai*), which in turn leads to a 'concurrence of word and deed' (*genkō itchi*) in behaviour, and 'the unity of self and other' (*jita gōitsu*) in interpersonal relationships.[1] Thus the national character (*kokuminsei*) derived from such a *mother* tongue by its very nature is said to

Table 10: Characteristics of Japanese and Other Languages

West (earlier China)	Japan
Miscegenated language, *cf* B, table 7	Pure language — *yamato kotoba*, B', table 7
1 Elaborately expressive (rhetoric favoured, *cf* table 6, 29)	1' Allusively laconic (reticence prized, *cf* table 6, 29')
2. Rational, impersonal (adapted to logic, *cf* table 6, 26)	2' Emotive and personal (a vehicle of sentiment, *cf* table 6, 26')
3 An idiom of intellectual abstraction, *cf* table 6, 27 and table 7, F)	3' A voice of immediate subjective response to palpable reality (*cf* table 6, 27 and table 7, F)

resist individualising consciousness, which sets man against himself, opposed to the world, and alienated from others. There seems to be sedimented in such an interpretation a nurtured historical resentment against those languages, Chinese and Western, whose culture of learning was twice utilised to pull Japan out of a primitive, then a village feudal world into the bureaucratic, industrial mainstream of world history.[2]

Topping all this is the curious celebration of silence as a unique mode of communication. As a recent writer puts it, the Japanese 'don't understand when something is spoken, but understand when nothing is said.'[3] Clearly, communicative fluency in this linguistics of telepathic silence represents an imposing bulwark against foreign students of Japanese! We have already remarked on how this myth was diffused in modernising Japan by official spokesmen for culture to ensure a supine taciturnity and reflexive obedience to orders from above. What remains is to unmask the covert realities which such rhetorical mythopoeia camouflages and to explain why this patently absurd notion exercises such widespread appeal.

The deductions about a putative tendency towards reticence among the Japanese are made from reflections on certain expressions in the language, such as *ishin denshin, kantan aiterasu, kotoage sezu, kagen chinmoku* and *haragei* which comprehensively allude to non-verbal interaction. The *kotoage sezu* element is, as we have seen, based on a faulty philological analysis. Three of the other terms derive from Chinese and thus are irrelevant to discussions of Japanese uniqueness. *Ishin denshin* properly refers to the transmission of the *dharma* from one Buddha to another, for example, and thus has as much relevance to national traits as would the quietistic phrase of occidental mysticism *cor ad cor loquitur* to some discussion of Western reticence.[4]

This leaves *haragei*, often translated as 'belly art', a term used in reference to the idea of acting on the strength of one's personality, rather than on argument, to achieve a difficult consensus. Yet even here we are informed that this 'last bastion of Japanese uniqueness' is understood by politicians but is an enigma to the Japanese at large.[5] It behooves us to look at this *haragei* in context, specifically in the *locus classicus* of Suzuki Kantarō's use of the art in the last stages of World War Two.

Appointed Prime Minister after the fall of the Koiso Cabinet, Suzuki was required to form a plan for the cessation of hostilities acceptable to both the 'peace' faction and the diehard militarists.

Where one false step might have involved a breakdown in talks or assassination, Suzuki had to show empathy for both the military's desire for fighting to the end, and the moderates' demand for some progress towards a peaceful conclusion. He adopted the posture of *haragei* as a negotiating style. That both parties found his 'art of the abdomen' bewildering, and that it virtually torpedoed the initiatives because it involved a fencing double-play with irreconcilable factions, testifies that each side considered him deceitful and hypocritical.[6]

Far from being a unique means of achieving consensus by a delicate manipulation of symbiotic feelings, in which 'I'm OK' is melded to 'You're OK' to arrive at a 'We're OK' situation, as Matsumoto puts it in the borrowed jargon of pop psychobabble, *haragei* simply testifies to the existence of an atmosphere in which sober compromise via open debate is impossible, where bitter factional intransigence and mutually distrustful rivalries call for innuendo, ambiguity, tactful and tactical expressions of false sympathy for antagonistic views, in order to get basically hostile groups on the same side.

Haragei is only non-verbal because open declaration of intent is explosive. This suggests an outlook marked by intolerance and suspicion rather than cosy symbiosis, and 'harmony' here is a very tenuous, fragile matter. *Haragei* is the last recourse when the usual channels of negotiation have broken down, and far from suggesting some unique mood of empathy, points towards antipathy. Conducted by wary reticence and feinting sympathy, it breeds misunderstanding rather than comprehension precisely because the negotiator, in necessarily playing his cards close to his chest, must appear to both sides to be hiding something, and thus deceptive. *Haragei* is the sort of behaviour we refer to when we speak of 'sounding someone out', 'putting out feelers', 'testing the water', 'reading between the lines', and of a 'winning personality'.

The espoused trait of silence therefore appears more an idiom of cautious, defensive reticence between mutually antipathetic groups than an instrument of telepathic exchange between harmonious people. Marx, in a letter, refers us to a ruler who, having difficulties in controlling his talkative subjects, pined for a return to the ossified state wherein, 'The slave serves in silence and the owner of the land and the people rules as silently as possible, ... Neither can say what he wishes, the one that he wishes to be human, the other that he has no use for human beings in his territory. Silence is therefore the only means of communication.'[7] We have abundant evidence from the prewar period that the myth of silence was instrumentalised precisely by ruling élites in this sense, so it is strange to observe that ostensibly empirical modern studies of the Japanese insistently recur to this fiction as if it were an ethnological datum.

Lebra, for example, in a work which claims to be an anthropological account of typical behaviour, writes:

> Inward communication of unity and solidarity stems from the notion that in perfect intimacy Ego does not have to express himself verbally or in conspicuous action because what is going on inside him should be immediately detected by Alter. The Japanese glorify silent communication, *ishin denshin* ('heart to heart communication'), and mutual 'vibrations', implying the possibility of semi-telepathic communication. Words are paltry against the significance of reading subtle signs and signals and the intuitive grasp of each other's feelings. The ultimate form of such communication is *ittaikan* ('feeling of oneness'), a sense of fusion between Ego and Alter.[8]

To substantiate this myth, reference is frequently made to the clipped laconic exchanges between boss and employee, husband and wife, or intimates.[9] But such abbreviated discourse is nothing other than what in Western linguistics is described as 'exophoric or context-dependent speech', and is hardly unique.[10] Indeed, many celebrations of the *sui generis* silence of the Japanese versus the verbose rhetoric of Westerners tend to remind one of Basil Bernstein's classification of working-class speech style and middle-class language in the United Kingdom.

For Bernstein, a 'public' language is one structured by brief commands and statements, where the references are 'tangible concrete and visual and of a low order of generality' (28', F', in tables 6 and 7). Learnt from the mother, it is more emotive than logical (19', 26', in tables 5 and 6 and Watanabe's definition *v'*, table 9), and is devoid of the individuality of personalised verbal exchange in that it is first and foremost the idiom used between peer-group members (10', table 4). Stylised primarily to promote social identity, its idiomatic standardisation affirms relational solidarity at the expense of private sentiment and logical communication.[11]

To this he contrasts the 'formal language' of middle-class children, richly individual and expressive of private thoughts and sentiment. The subtle use of complex arrangements of words facilitates not only the exploration of inner feelings but also sensitivity to role and status. A critical difference is that where 'formal' language enables one to articulate subjective intentions, 'public' language has inner constraints which militate against the explicit saying of individual experiences which, if expressed, would threaten the overall allegiance and solidarity of the peer group.[12]

At one level, then, Bernstein's categories roughly coincide with the mythic values attributed to *yamato kotoba* ('public' in the sense of embodying an homogeneous race spirit, *cf* 5', 14', in tables 2 and 4), and, by contrast, to *gairaigo/kango*, (foreign 'formal' languages expressive of abstract intellectual values). An apparent divergence appears in the definition of *yamato kotoba* as vehicles of personal or private feeling but, in the *nihonjinron* it is precisely inner sentiment which is seen to synchronise with corporate spirit, and thus the distinction still holds. In short, the 'unique' identity of the Japanese sociolinguistic codes as means for achieving *ittaikan* and *jita gōitsu*, fusion of self with the other or peer group, strangely corresponds to a mode of expression typical of the impoverished, impersonal speech style of a kind of Western, close-knit lower class community.

A caution however is needed, and one which may prove instructive. Traditional sociolinguistic conventions militated against the use of what Bernstein calls 'formal language' in social encounters, and both components of Japanese, the two (linguistically inexact) categories of *gairaigo* and *yamato kotoba*, are circumscribed by the 'public' code. Authoritarian custom dictates reticence precisely at that juncture where the individual's inner sentiment comes into conflict with the peer group's constrictive code of social conformity. What the myth of silence discloses is that there is little public leeway conceded for the expression of private thought and feeling. The expression of the latter sphere is left to literary genres like the diary and the 'I novel', of which Tanizaki Jun'ichirō's *Kagi* (The Key, 1956) is an outstanding example.

To clarify more precisely the underlying reality to which the myth refers we must return to the problem of *public/private* discussed earlier. In the *nihonjinron*, a major series of overlapping distinctions is made between outer and inner spheres of life which highlights a fundamental tension between desire and social reality, inner feeling and the censorious pressure to conform taciturnly to 'public' roles and conventions. We must recall that what passes linguistically for 'public' and 'private' has nothing to do with what we normally understand by these terms. Where in the West they are mutually enhancing, tandem concepts, in Japanese usage they are diametrically opposed in antagonistic hostility (table 11).

The literature manipulating the public–private binary oppositions over the whole range of Japanese culture and experience (in a pseudoanalytic, 'amuletic' fashion) is vast.[13] The reiterative intensity of their use in the *nihonjinron* suggests that 'the discrepancy between the formal and the actual, between the ideal and the normative functioning'[14] of institutional and social life is profound. In the absence of public institutions mediating the relationship between State and private citizen, we find a direct confrontation here between the overwhelming force and rigidity of the formal codes governing the individual in society, and the hidden inner reality of personal existence with its aspiration for autonomy. Bernstein's 'formal' language, so akin to what the *nihonjinron* derogate as occidental, inauthentic language, lacks a real equivalent because the emergence of what is loosely called the Japanese 'middle class'[15] was unaccompanied by the construction of public institutions and values to defend collective private interests in the manner of the Western bourgeoisie.

The problem emerges in clearer focus when we examine the cultural mythology surrounding the major corporations that drive the so-called 'economic miracle', those private firms which though constituting less than 0.2 percent of Japanese enterprises hold roughly 65 percent of the paid-up capital (and therefore are highly unrepresentative).[16] The *nihonjinron* view, widely reflected and praised by Western economic studies, highlights the unique, beneficent structure of corporate paternalism and managerial

Table 11: 'Public' or 'Private'?

Kōteki ('public')	—	*shikteki* ('private')
soto (outside)	—	*uchi* (inside)
omote (front)	—	*ura* (behind)
tatemae (overt principle)	—	*honne* (real intent)
giri (obligation)	—	*ninjō* (human feeling)

familyism, with its integral expropriation for productive efficiency of the individual employee's private life.

The distinction this approach makes between the individualism of Western capitalism and the 'group-oriented' paternalism (*onjōshugi*) of Japanese industrial organisation (10, 10', table 4) dates from Suzuki Bunji's synthesis of Prussian concepts of 'socialism from above (*cf* the *Verein für Sozialpolitik*) and Ninomiya Sontoku's neo-Confucian ethics as the ideological framework for Japan's largest labour union in Taishō times, the Yūaikai.[17] In reaction to the growing power of local labour movements, he promoted the analysis of economics in terms of national characteristics, insisting that the Japanese worker had a unique psychology which grew out of the paternal family structure of his society, which had no parallel in the alienated Western labourer of classical economics.

Suzuki held that collective progress required 'harmony' between capital and labour, and that the employer was not an exploiter but rather a beneficent father who tended to his workers' welfare as if they were his own children. It followed that in Japan there was no need to imitate Western legislation for legal minimums of pay and basic working conditions since the cordial spirit of the paternal corporation prized moral obligation (*giri*) over legal obligation (*gimu*), humaneness (*ninjō*) over rights (*kenri*). This approach neatly manipulated the familiar elements in the contrastive paradigm (9,9'; 10,10'; 17,17'; 26,26' and principle D,D', tables 4-7) to strengthen the leverage of Japanese business against labour by an ideological appeal to fidelity to authentic national traditions. Arbitration between corporations and employees was placed beyond neutral, legal forms of mediation between equal and *contracting* parties, and thus naturally weighed in favour of corporate power, with its paternalist idiom of a uniquely *kintractual* (13,13', table 4) structure of workplace relationships.

A parallel in the West, contemporary with this movement, may be found in the syndicalist thought of such Marxist heretics as Panunzio, Olivetti and Michels, the founding fathers of that corporative ideology which paved the way for the revolutionary mass mobilisation of another late-developer, Italy, under fascism. They emphasised the importance of creating the elaborate symbolic formulae of national and communal myths to reinsert the subaltern working classes back into a compliant subordination to the collective national interest as determined by élites under a charismatic leader. The difference was that Western syndicalism's animosity towards plutocracy led to a tendency to invest the organs of the State with directive control of the economy and social life, whereas in Japan these functions were left in charge of the key corporations and cartels (*zaibatsu*).

The compromise enacted between unions and business interests, in interpreting employer–employee relationships in terms of the quasi-feudal, patriarchal idiom of *oyabun* (parent-role) and *kobun* (child-role),[18] not only suggested a rhetorical infantilisation of the working class image, but also transformed the reality of class conflict and business–labour antagonism into a collusive struggle against foreign trading nations as the real agents of exploitation.

Internally, however, this collusion significantly inhibited the modernisation of social structures, given this syndicalist acquiescence in the cartel-guided industrial modernisation as the key to the improvement of working class conditions. State investment in the bettering of social conditions was replaced by the enhanced role of private companies in the public sphere of social security, and in assuming this function the business sector enormously increased its power over the worker. Once the company itself became the source of social improvement the worker's life was subsumed wholly within the sphere of the individual company's interests, since '(e)mployers do not employ only a man's labour but really employ the total man, as is shown in the expression *marugakae* (completely enveloped)'.[19] Such 'incorporation' (scarcely dreamed of by fascist syndicalists) became a vaunted model for a 'Japanese type' of productive structure, though it involves the cost of a concomitant desocialisation of the working class and a valuable subversion of emerging bourgeois capacities.

It is doubly ironical that not only is the postwar variant of this model an object of admiring study by the foreign worshippers of 'Japan as Number One', but also that this 'traditional' structure draws off Japanese images of paternalistic capitalism in the very West from which its later ideologists wished to distinguish their programme. Early Japanese travellers of the Meiji period expressed their surprise for the paternal character of Western enterprise (and this in the heyday of Marx), with its detailed planning, its optimisation of productivity, its social engineering and the close collaboration of business with government. The prosperity of Western companies was seen to depend upon smooth relations between management and labour in which, '(t)he worker's physical wellbeing is provided for. He is given practical education, and he is inculcated with the value of thrift and hard work. Enticing fringe benefits — company housing, educational facilities, saving arrangements — keep workers content with their lot and strikes to a minimum.'[20] This is very much the image of Japanese corporate structure (one, we ought note, hardly valid for a vast number of companies in Japan's 'dual-structure' economy) purveyed to the West as being uniquely rooted in indigenous Japanese traditions. Admiring Japan as 'Number One' belies a nostalgia for the idealised world of nineteenth century capitalism, minus the encumbrance of bourgeois institutions and civil rights.

Haragei, the myth of silence, and the problem of translating Western concepts of 'public' and 'private' cannot be understood without taking into account this institutional subversion of the individual, and the drastic narrowing of public space in which he might socially express and develop his personality, resulting from this total incorporation of the employee within a formally alien productive structure. The notion of the corporation as a 'family' implies the personalisation of impersonal relationships that in fact harbour the coercions of semi-feudal codes of 'face', 'status' and obligation, and therefore lack that indispensable depersonalisation of personal relationships which, in demystifying the power and authority of the old code, enables modern man to reactivate personal relations with strangers, employers and fellow citizens without compromising his essential autonomy.[21]

It follows that the contrast between the estranged individualism of the West and the cosily symbiotic groupism of Japanese life, as celebrated endlessly in the *nihonjinron*, betrays an ideological personalisation of what are essentially impersonal relations and a concomitant depersonalisation of what are personal relationships in the West. We discern this from the contradictions which emerge from the way such texts describe personal interactions. The argument that silence goes hand in hand with an interpersonal ideal of the fusion of the self with the other relates to conventions which regulate the interaction of lower status subjects with their superiors. Tension and vigilance increase in interaction with higher status subjects, and the mistake is made of confusing this tension (*kinchō*) with emotional (*cf kanjō*) empathy, in confusing mutual vigilance with mutual sympathy. Ambiguity as a discursive habit functions not only to protectively camouflage one's real thinking, but also to preserve a relationship that is so fragile that it will not sustain open expression of diversity and conflict. Hence the celebration of the idea that the Japanese read each other's thoughts, and hone their sensibility to any ticks of behaviour or clipped nuances of speech that might enable them to read between the lines to uncover those traces of ulterior intent repressed by the abrupt, formal and ambiguous language of interpersonal discourse.

You cannot have it both ways. Were the myth of silence true, then the corollary myth of empathetic human relationships, intimate and unestranged, must collapse, and vice versa. We detect as much in the inadvertent contradictions made by many writers in describing these interactive encounters. Suzuki says that, 'thoughtlessly using the imperfect medium of words may often end up in pouring cold water on a unified understanding that has been attained only with great difficulty.'[22] Hamaguchi equally informs us that Japanese taciturnity does not imply that they lack private opinions but rather that, 'It only means that people fear that self assertion may possibly open up cracks in a friendly relationship with those people who form the very basis of one's own subsistence.'[23]

In short we are back with Marx's parable of the lord and his subjects, in which the parties in any relationship cannot sustain frank expression of private opinion, and thus reveal themselves as neither friendly nor harmonious but rather intolerant and tense, as the instance of *haragei* amply illustrates, and as certain projective interpretations made by Japanese scholars on Western behaviour tend to suggest. For example Kimura Shōsaburō, on the thin evidence of observing a Frenchman in a Marseilles restaurant profusely thank a waitress, leads himself to deduce that:

> Leaving aside male–female relationships, if two Europeans were to keep quiet while facing one another, it would signify that they were either thinking up murderous designs against each other, or that they were expressing unconditional surrender. Europeans, who are, as it were, instinctively combative and self-defensive (*cf* 5,20,29 in tables 2, 5 and 6), always have to express clearly in their day-to-day life that they intend no violence to each other.[24]

The myths of personal relations in a 'family' company and of the skinship[25] (another tellingly infantile metaphor) nature of interpersonal relations in general are used to sustain the defensive thesis that words are needed to meld interactions only when relations, as in the mythical West, are alienated. But if social relationships in the workplace and elsewhere are tendentiously interpreted in terms of some *ie* principle in Japanese civilisation, it is also true that the *nihonjinron* anchor this myth of social intercourse in the ostensibly 'unique' type of mother–child nurture of Japanese rearing patterns.

In Lebra's picture, stress is laid on the constant physical closeness of child to mother, of sleeping *en famille*, of always appeasing the child with the breast. This pattern is apparently reinforced by overt socialisation which emphasises the need to empathise with others, of sensitivising oneself to their needs, and subordinating one's whims to the exigencies of community order. This dual structure of nurtured dependence and socialising discipline is held to provide the affective base for 'groupishness', empathy, silence and self-synchronisation with others.

Another interpretation is possible which would bring out the double-bind character of such rearing. The breast is proffered to the crying child, but at weaning his demands are met with a peppered nipple (and demons tattooed on the breast, we might add). The child is soothed when discomforted, and toilet training is not strict, but then he is taught to sit rigidly, and to control his bowel movements. His tantrums are appeased by cuddling, but in his temper tantrums he is allowed to beat his mother. Envy towards peers is prohibited, but he is constantly disciplined by being told about the exemplary behaviour of other children. He is told to understand his mother's feelings, but not stopped if he beats her. He is conditioned to be placid, yet insistently impressed with the importance of achieving. He is related to more in a physical than a verbal way (Japanese mothers respond to a child's 'unhappy vocals', while American mothers respond to their children's 'happy vocals'), and yet every sign of language acquisition is heartily praised and complimented.[26]

The pattern described here is one of early, mother-fixated dependence followed by social discipline; a nurturing of narcissistic identity topped off by a training which accentuates the submission of the self to others. We understand why Suzuki's ego theory is contradictory, for there is a self which feels suicidal if it cannot find a sympathetic other to whom it may unbosom itself, and yet fears to speak because words might imperil the unity of self and other. The contrast in the nature of these twin, primary vectors of nurture also helps us to understand the effective basis underlying the conflict between outside norm (*kōteki*) and internal feeling (*shiteki*).

Socialisation is here characterised as a series of reversals of that mother-bonded sense of uniqueness encouraged at the outset of childhood. The myths of skinship, *jita gōitsu*, silent empathy and *yamato kotoba*, in addition to the idea of the company as a 'family', imaginatively revive in the context of what are impersonal social relations the repressed structure of the primary phase of childhood. The *nihonjinron* description of mature Japanese interaction projects as a regressive fantasy the child's ideal of pre-linguistic symbiosis with the mother onto what are precisely orders of impersonal relationship in a patriarchal structure which is otherwise hostile to the individual's sense of his own uniqueness. The contrast between the cosy warmth of tactile Japanese life and the alienated individuality of verbose Westerners is all the more strange if we are to believe Barnlund's study which, on the basis of empirical surveys, concluded in defiant contrast to the *nihonjinron* picture that:

> In nearly every category, whether one focuses on an area of the body or a communicative partner, the amount of physical contact reported by Americans is nearly twice that reported by Japanese. As a channel of interpersonal communication, touch appears to be nearly twice as important within one culture as within the other.[27]

and that indeed, non-verbal contact is greater with the least attractive associate among Americans than it is with the most attractive associate among the Japanese.[28]

Barnlund records the shock of self-revelation among the Japanese students filling out his test-forms, the shock of realising the extreme degree of their physical isolation, especially from their parents. Of particular note is the evidence suggesting that the average American youth's communication with an absolute stranger is only marginally lower than the average verbal communication of Japanese youth with their fathers.[29] It is hard to reconcile this provisory work with the myth that extols the 'intimate behaviour ... characterised by expression and confirmation of unity, oneness, or solidarity, based on mutual liking and emotional attachment.'[30]

The tradition of arranged marriage, as social contract rather than inner emotional choice, hints again at the ascendency of the 'outside' world of socially stipulated norms over the volitional and emotional sphere of the individual. This primary alienation from the wife is compounded when a company is formed on paternalistic lines. For if the company exacts fidelity from its employees on the grounds that the employees and bosses all form one 'family', then a tension emerges between this situation and the worker's real family, in which the latter is inevitably worsted. If the firm 'completely envelops' (*cf marugakae*) not only the man's labour but his personal life, then the husband must absent himself from his real family, and the wife's role diminishes as her role as mother increases. This alienation of couples leads to the mother's exclusive presence before the child as socialiser in an attitude marked by passive domination, total control and silent suffering as a means of inducing guilt as a motivating agent.[31]

The initial enchanted world of maternal conviviality is then, again with the mother as agent, broken and reversed by a disciplined subordination of the child to the outside world of the alienated father where the patriarchal code predominates. In such a milieu, all relationships tend to assume surrogate forms: the male child is ersatz husband, and grown to maturity, will treat his wife as a secondhand mother, while the *nihonjinron* endlessly convince him, notwithstanding, that the hard social world of the patriarchs in which he works somehow recreates the lost Eden of the mother-bond.[32]

It is here that Bernstein's analysis assumes renewed pertinence. For his distinction between 'public' and 'formal' languages draws on disparate forms of family life, the 'positional' family of the lower class and the 'personal' family of the middle class. The one focuses on general attributes in children, endowing them with a sense of their age, sex and status standing, while the other cultivates the individual attributes of the child. Given that this Japanese kind of 'positional' family lacks two of the three elements which underlie the bourgeois family's sentimental formation (courtship, and closing off the family from the surrounding society), while retaining only the mother–child bond in exacerbated form,[33] we are not surprised to see the relevance of Bernstein's conclusions in terms of the thesis that an inverse relationship exists between role segregation and verbal self-expression.

In positional families, he finds a 'weak or closed communication system',[34] whereas in personal families individual psychological orientations, rather than social criteria of status, form the basis of judgements. That is, personal growth is handled by discussion rather than interdiction, which in turn proves conducive to the development of an 'open', fully individualised power of communication. Relevant here is the fact that Italian and middle class American families attempt to bring out a sense of self-direction in the child, whereas working class families stress his conformity to external, social prescriptions in a way reminiscent of Japan.[35]

The myth of silence then, at another level, mystifies the problematical aspects of family structure in Japan, and of social communication in a 'family-structured' society. None of the prolix writers who, in defiance of the very code they celebrate, repetitively descant on this fiction face the obvious fact that the Japanese are no more taciturn than any other national group. The difference, if there is one, lies more in a conditioned reticence with regard to personal disclosure not only in what we regard as public contexts, but also within intimate relations. Westerners, likewise, are not more garrulous, as Tanizaki, Watanabe, Suzuki and so many others assert, for what we are discussing 'is not just a question of more talk but of talk of a particular kind',[36] an open discourse. To parody Wittgenstein, these writers appear to hold that 'whereof one can speak, thereof one must be silent,' and if this is the case we must examine the socio-historical reasons for such verbal constraint. The irony remains that far from being 'unique', the reticent anti-discourse ascribed to the Japanese by the *nihonjinron* appears akin to a speech style that, in Western terms, is associated with the cultural consequences of poverty and intellectual deprivation. Writers in the *nihonjinron* genre assume the right to gabble endlessly in this void, 'public' jargon of authenticity while arrogately refusing voice to the silent majority whose reticence they so profitably exploit.

Notes

1. For *meijitsu ittai*, see Toyoda, *Nihonjin no kotodama shisō*, (Kōdansha Gakujutsu Bunko Tokyo, 1980), p.15. For *genkō itchi*, see Okonogi, *Moratoriamu ningen no jidai*, pp.146ff.
2. A frequent complaint is that philosophical works translated into Japanese become almost incomprehensible. See Ōno Susumu, *Nihongo no bunpō o kangaeru* (Iwanami Sensho, Tokyo, 1978) p.66; Tanizaki, *Bunshō tokuhon*, p.128.

114 Silence and Elusion

3. Hamaguchi, *'Nihonrashisa'no saihakken*, ibid, p.126, citing the views of Katō Hidetoshi.

4. Also frequently cited in this context is *Lun Yü*, I. 3, and *Tao Te Ching*, ch. 56. Relevant also here is Nakamura's exposition of Dōgen's interpretation of the phrase *kyōge betsuden* in Nakamura, *Ways of Thinking*, ibid., p.463.

5. Matsumoto Michihiro, *Asahi Evening News*, 9 October, 1978 p.8. For wife-beating as a *haragei* strategy to make one's mother accept one's wife, see his article in the same newspaper, 9 January 1979, p.22.

6. See J. Toland's account, *The Rising Sun*, (Bantam Books, New York, 1971) pp.787-8, 840, 846, 912. An excellent treatment may be found in R. Butow, *Japan's Decision to Surrender* (Stanford University Press, Stanford, California, 1967 paper.) pp.70ff.

7. Letter to Ruge, May 1843, in *Karl Marx — Early Writings*, trans. R. Livingstone and C. Benton, (Penguin, 1975) p.205.

8. Lebra, *Japanese Patterns*, ibid., p.115.

9. Aida Yūji, *Nihonjin no wasuremono*, (Kadokawa Bunko, Tokyo, 1974) pp.231-2. A perfect parallel may be found in E.T. Hall, *The Silent Language*, (Premier books, New York, 1961) p.94.

10. R. Hasan's term. See B. Bernstein, *Class, Codes and Control* (Paladin Books ed., England 1973) pp.30-2.

11. Bernstein, ibid. pp.49-62ff. His analysis has been contested but many find his categories useful in stylistic analysis. *Cf* R. Fowler, *Linguistics and the Novel*, (Methuen, London and New York, 1979) pp.115-22, and P. Violi, *I giornali dell'estrema sinistra*, (Garzanti, Milan, 1977) pp.7ff.

12. Bernstein, *Class, Codes and Control*, ibid., pp.49, 64-9.

13. For some popular expositions see Minamoto Ryōen, *Giri to ninjō* (Chūkō Shinsho, Tokyo, 1969); Aida Yūji, *Omote no ronri. Ura no ronri* (PHP, Tokyo, 1977); Lebra, *Japanese Patterns*, pp.111ff., (on *soto-uchi, ura-omote*). Nieda Rokusaburō, *Tatemae to Honne* (Daiyamondosha, Tokyo, 1973). Ōno Susumu, *Nihongo no bunpō o kangaeru*, pp.73ff. In general see Minami Hiroshi, *Nihonjin no ningen kankei jiten* (Kōdansha, Tokyo, 1980) pp.62, 94ff, 102ff, 122ff. Watsuji Tetsurō, *Fūdō. Ningenteki Kōsatsu* in *Watsuji Tetsurō Zenshū*, vol. 8, pp.144ff, remarks that the *soto-uchi* distinction does not exist in the family because traditional house design, with its lack of private space, impeded the growth of individual consciousness. Conjugal intimacy and the idea of privacy in Europe arose with the diversion of rising income into the functional separation of household activities and the family, by contrast. See E. Shorter, *The Making of the Modern Family* (Fontana, London, 1979) pp.47-52.

14. *Cf* The important paper by Chalmers Johnston, '*Omote* (Explicit) and *Ura* (Implicit): Translating Japanese Political Terms', in *Journal of Japanese Studies*, 6:1 (winter 1980) pp.85-115, p.91.

15. Subjectively 90% of the Japanese perceive themselves as 'middle class', but rephrased in terms of property-owning class, 70% define themselves as working class. See T. Fukutake, *The Japanese Social Structure*, trans R.P. Dore (University of Tokyo Press, 1982) pp.152-7.

16. Fukutake, ibid. p.153.

17. K. Pyle, 'Advantages of Followership: German Economics and Japanese Bureaucrats: 1890-1925' in *Journal of Japanese Studies*, 1:1 (1974) pp.127-64, esp. pp.146ff. B. Marshall, *Capitalism and Nationalism in Prewar Japan* (Stanford University Press, Stanford, California, 1967) passim, esp. pp.78ff, 85ff.

18. On *oyabun-kobun* (with a striking structural parallel in *mamluk* society in Ottoman Egypt) see J.W. Bennett, I. Ishino, *Paternalism in the Japanese Economy* (University of Minnesota Press, Minneapolis, 1963) ch. 3, p.293 n.5. The tactical blocking of modern legislation for social conflict is now explained in terms of an

emotional resistance in the cultural consciousness of the Japanese to Western-style conflict resolution in the works of Kawashima Takeyoshi. See his *Nihonjin no hōishiki* (Iwanami Shinsho, Tokyo, 1967) pp.15-60, 125ff, and his article, 'Nihonjin no gengo ishiki to hōritsu' in *Sekai*, no. 399 (February 1979) pp.249-62 (where Tanizaki's influence is strong) and his remarks in '*Amae*' *to shakai kagaku*, pp.126ff, on conflict resolution and *kotoage*.

19. Nakane, *Japanese Society*, ibid. p.15.
20. E. Soviak, 'On the Nature of Western Progress: The Journal of the Iwakura Embassy' in *Tradition and Modernization in Japanese Culture*, pp.7-34, p.22.
21. Maruyama, *Thought and Behaviour*, ibid. pp.257-8.
22. Suzuki, *Tozasareta gengo*, ibid. p.189.
23. Hamaguchi, '*Nihonrashisa*' *no saihakken*, ibid. pp.127-8.
24. Kimura, *Seiyō no kao. Nihon no kokoro*, ibid. p.96.
25. Kimura, ibid. pp.90-2. On the word *skinship* see Mori Jōji, *Nihonjin — 'kara-nashi tamago' no jigazō*, (Kōdansha Gendai Shinsho, Tokyo, 1977) pp.10-22 who considers it a Japanese formation, and Suzuki, *Tozasareta gengo*, ibid. pp.146-7, who considers it as foreign, and protests at its use in Japanese since there is a natural *yamato kotoba* term *hada no fureai*.
26. Lebra, *Japanese Patterns*, pp.137ff. Compare Benedict, *The Chrysanthemum and the Sword*, (Riverside Press, Cambridge, Massachusetts), 1946, pp.253ff, who however perceives rightly a conflict between a 'shameless' childhood of indulged gratification and an adult life meticulously conditioned by fear of violating strict social sanctions (pp.286ff).
27. D. Barnlund, *Public and Private Self in Japan and the United States*, (Simul Press, Tokyo, 1975) p.105.
28. Barnlund, *Public and Private Self*, ibid. p.106.
29. Barnlund, *Public and Private Self*, ibid. p.86.
30. Lebra, *Japanese Patterns*, ibid. p.115.
31. On the mechanism see G. de Vos, *Socialization for Achievement* (University of California Press, Berkeley and Los Angeles, 1973), pp.144-61. Tolerance of the child's aggression against the mother (forbidden against the father) was a central theme of wartime research, for which see Benedict, ibid. pp.263-4, and G. Gorer, 'Themes in Japanese Culture' reprinted in Bernard S. Silberman (ed.) *Japanese Character and Culture: Selected Readings*, (University of Arizona Press, Tucson, 1962) pp.308-24. Lebra simply compares this to the storm god's tantrums in traditional mythology, *Japanese Patterns*, p.144.
32. Fromm, *The Anatomy of Human Destructiveness*, ibid. p.494 relates the sense of uniqueness to overindulgence and pampering by the mother. If later group socialisation reverses this pattern, then the narcissistic feeling would only find a legitimate expression in a self-identification with the sense of corporate, or national uniqueness and this would explain the appeal of the *nihonjinron*.
33. E. Shorter, *The Making of the Modern Family*, ibid. pp.14-5; on 'positional' and 'personal' families, see Bernstein, *Class, Codes and Control*, ibid. pp.176-89.
34. Bernstein, *Class, Codes and Control*, ibid. pp.176-7.
35. W. Caudill, H. Weinstein, 'Maternal Care and Infant Behavior in Japan and America', in Lebra and Lebra (eds.) *Japanese Culture and Behavior*, pp. 225-76; p. 265 n. 1.
36. Bernstein, *Class, Codes and Control*, ibid. p. 177.

8 OMNIA VINCIT AMAE

'The abstract intellectual discussions and speculations in which young people delight are not genuine attempts at solving the tasks set by reality. Their mental activity is rather an indication of a tense alertness for the instinctual processes and the translation into thought of that which they perceive.'
Anna Freud, *The Ego and the Mechanisms of Defence*, revised edn (The Hogarth Press, London, 1968), p.162

In the previous chapter we detected hints that many of the sociolinguistic myths in the *nihonjinron* are intimately related to aspects of a kind of Japanese socialisation, to certain structures of worker incorporation in larger Japanese businesses and residual forms of disindividualisation in public life. The myths that celebrate the ostensibly unique emotional symbiosis of social relations in these spheres are highly self-contradictory, and it behooves us, at this juncture, to examine Japanese theories of psychology by shifting our focus from linguistics to psychoanalysis in order to discover other clues to unravel the affective structure underpinning the myths of identity in Japan.

Psychoanalysis provides us with a particularly congenial locus for such an approach, in that its very logic is hostile to the corruptions of nationalising thought. The great power of that system lies in its stern programmatic intent to unmask the deceptions practised on the self, in its assiduous personalisation, as interior conflict, of displacing styles of discursive argument. As Lasch remarks, 'It is precisely the subjection of individuals to the group that psychoanalytic theory, through a study of its psychic repercussions, promises to clarify.'[1] The neurotic self-evasion typical of nationalistic, group-centered rhetoric would, one think, have small chance of dissembling itself where the discipline of psychoanalysis took root. And yet, intriguingly, the Japanese case gives stubborn witness to the contrary.

Here I will be concerned with the exposure of those cultural theses used by a 'Japanified' psychoanalysis to legitimate and justify the 'endogenisation' of Freudian ideas to the Japanese context,[2] and secondly, the way such attempts to harmonise

Freudian concepts with 'unique' aspects of the 'national psyche' inadvertently betray evidence as to the reasons behind these consistent mystifications. Given that a distinctively Japanese psychoanalysis must nationalise what is, in its inherent character and essence, a purely personal mode of analysis, we have every grounds for expecting a vigorously defensive confrontation. The exceptional stress on ideological palliatives of cultural uniqueness to soften the human costs of modernisation could scarcely have provided a climate conducive to the induction of a body of rigorously iconoclastic thought so dedicated, as was psychoanalysis, to the stripping of cultural pretensions, to a system that equates individual 'enlightenment' with civilised disillusion.

Though rudimentary knowledge of psychoanalysis was circulating in Japan as early as 1912, real attention only became focused in the 1930s, with the return of Marui Kiyoyasu and Kosawa Heisaku from Vienna. While many historians emphasise the importance of their contact with the Viennese circle, we should note that Marui was only analysed for a month (by Paul Federn), while Kosawa's analysis lasted no more than three months (under Richard Sterba).[3] The unusual briefness of these analyses is crucial for understanding what followed, since Freud repeatedly remarks that experience of a thorough analysis is a prerequisite for competent theoretical work, especially in understanding the nature of transference in the patient-analyst relationship.[4]

Of the two, it is Kosawa Heisaku (1897-1968) who exercised the greater influence on the formation of a 'Japanese style of psychoanalysis.' His disciples openly acknowledge the influence of prewar trends of 'orientism' (*tōyōshugi*) on his thought, but claim that this does not essentially undermine the epochal importance of his theoretical revisionism. We are told that his clinical work 'exceeded international standards' by 1950, and that his theory was a 'unique' achievement in that it anticipated the later course of postwar Western psychoanalytic thought itself.[5]

During his Viennese sojourn, Kosawa is said to have delivered to Freud a treatise entitled 'The Ajātasattu Complex — Two Varieties of Guilt Consciousness', in which a critical distinction is made between Oriental guilt and Western guilt. The former is analysed from the data provided by a Buddhist tale. In this Queen Vaidehi, wife of King Bimbisāra of Magadhā, ageing and childless, fears that her failure to bear a son to the throne might occasion the loss of her spouse's love. When a seer informs her that she will conceive and give birth to a child on the demise of a holy man, she has the ascetic killed and in due course finds herself pregnant. Yet fearing the child's wrath (as the embodiment of the murdered seer's spirit), she attempts to do away with it, only to halt at the last moment from her intended infanticide. When this child, Ajātasattu, grows up, he usurps his father's kingdom and tries to murder his mother. But before he can, a vile sickness overcomes him, and it is only the patient nursing of his mother which restores him to health. Their mutual enmity dispelled, mother and son are thus finally reconciled to one another.[6]

The 'uniquely Japanese psychological complex' elicited from this Indic contrast to the Sophoclean myth of Oedipus is that this Buddhist tale is believed to show how a child's primal sense of identity wih the mother (*ittaikan*), once found to be illusory, gives rise to a sense of resentment (*urami*) in the child. The mother by enduring the child's hatred silently induces in him guilt feelings by her forbearing and forgiving attitude, and these in turn restore his sense of unity with the mother. This guilt is a 'being forgiven type of guilt consciousness' (*yurusare-gata no zaiishiki*), which Okonogi calls 'autonomous guilt' or 'self-developed guilt' (*jihatsuteki zaiishiki*) and is 'superior' to Western guilt in that it is forgiving instead of punitive, matriarchal instead of patriarchal, leading to reconciliation ('harmony') rather than continual anxiety over possible chastisement.[7]

Despite its pretensions this is clearly in no way a psychoanalytic reading of the myth presented since it (tellingly) overlooks the most important elements in the narrative (the mother's passion for her husband, her fear of the child, etc), and merely restates the hackneyed contrasts of a punitive patriarchal West to a harmonious matriarchal Japan (*cf* 20,20'; 19,19'; D,D' in tables 5 and 7) in terms of ostensible differences in guilt-consciousness. More subtle is the way it reverses to Japanese advantage contrast 18,18' (table 4) by presenting Western guilt as dependent on punitive others in opposition to the ostensible inner-directed guilt of the Japanese variety. It is not explained how such a distinction can be made when guilt by definition is the consequence of reparative trends towards the parental object against which the initial sadistic impulses (now introjected) were directed.[8] As we shall see, in addition, the critique of 'Western guilt' is invalidated by certain misunderstandings arising from the word in Japanese taken to correspond to the notion of guilt (*cf tsumi*).

Kosawa's use of this myth to counterpoise to the Oedipus complex an oriental, and specifically Japanese, matricidal complex provides us with another outstanding example of a purely personal problem masquerading within an overtly nationalistic interpretation. Kosawa's reading ignores variants to the Vinaya account, such as the Dīgha tradition in which Ajātasattu is said to have murdered his father[9] (which would confirm a classic Freudian analysis). This evasive dismissal of parricide as occidental does betray not only the superficial character of his own analysis, but also a profound political concession, for in a patriarchal society centered on the Emperor, the notion of parricide would have been an explosive challenge to the imperial ideology. As Moloney acutely noted, the Oedipal theory may have been supplanted by a matricidal one in a culture suffused with an ethic of filial piety,[10] whose ultimate source was the reconstructed mythic authority of the Emperor himself.

A key to the nature of the resistance underlying Kosawa's modification of Freud may be found in his theory that neurosis in Japan is a result of Westernisation, in that modernisation destroyed the matriarchal culture of the country by repressing the racial need *to presume upon the mother's indulgence*. His therapeutical technique consisted in trying to restore a sense of primal unity in the patient with his mother by 'dissolving the repression of dependent attachment to the mother' through a releasing of the analysand's estranging attachment to the newer values of rational individualism.[11] What in effect this implies, in classical Freudian terms, is a fictive attempt to reinstate, regressively, a pre-Oedipal condition with its 'fusion of object libido and ego libido',[12] and valorising this recursion to a state preceding the child's encounter with the reality principle (society and the father) as 'uniquely Japanese'. This reading of the Ajātasattu myth thus not only betrays the superficial character of Kosawa's analysis (which rationalises his own homoerotic fixation and oral cannibalism[13] arising from his experience of severe maternal neglect as a child), but also explains the nature of his evasion of parricidal themes.

In revolt against the 'public' (*cf kōteki*), desexualising and authoritarian world of a patriarchal, Emperor-centered society, Kosawa simply flees back unconsciously to a mythical reaffirmation of primal identity with the mother, associating the former with 'Westernisation' and the latter with 'Japan'. This tack is suggestively emblematic of the *nihonjinron* themselves which, in this light, may be seen to constitute an ideological attempt to equate the reality principle (the social symbols of fatherhood in Japan, especially the austere and unbending forms of social authority and structure in the modern period) with something ontologically alien to the Japanese, namely China or the West as cultural and modernising influences. Tellingly, *nihonjinron* are concerned with the male world of Japan, women barely figure in them. The male world there described is however, revealingly feminised, and brute masculinity in its varied forms is palmed off as distinctively characteristic of the 'West'. It is only the woman as 'mother' who occasionally obtrudes, and the tendency is stronger the deeper the reference is to the historical past, especially in that bystream of pseudo-historical literature (a branch of the *nihonjinron*) concerned with archaic origins. There we encounter a fascinated search for the real nature of such mythically ancestral figures as the sun goddess *Amaterasu Ōmikami* and that hazy 'She' figure of prehistorical *Yamatai,* popularly identified with a certain *Himiko* (the linguistic reconstruction of the name involves great difficulties).[14]

Under its founding father Kosawa, Japanese psychoanalysis, in melding ill-digested Viennese ideas with Buddhist fables and the *kokutai* ideology,[15] sacrificed its essence from the very outset. Outlawed in Hitler's Germany, it was readily accepted in Japan in this matricidal form. Military uniforms are amply evident in the Association's early photos, and a prince of the imperial house actually became a member of the Tokyo chapter.[16] Moloney's survey of these early writings reveals a consistently symptomatic character underlying the ostensibly diagnostic intent of its naive practitioners. The terminological shell of the psychoanalytic lexicon was retained and exploited for ends diametrically opposed to their original purposes in a way that is paradigmatic for the history of incorporation of many key terms in the Western conceptual vocabulary into Japanese. The Emperor was conceived as the super-ego, the individual ego seen as a splintered fragment of the vast mosaical ego of the *kokutai* body politic, while the *id* was conflated with the immutable essence of the 'Nipponese race'.[17]

This amuletic use of psychoanalytic jargon, amalgamated with the sociologese of Japaneseness developed in the postwar period, renders any reading of the texts of this tradition arduous. Thus, for example, Okonogi, in expounding the Ajātasattu complex of mother-fixated guilt, argues that this is repressed into the unconscious as *honne*, while 'imported Western guilt', which provokes children to acts of violence against their parents, is a superficial value (*cf tatemae*) which is productive of alienation that resists therapy because it occludes a Japanese kind of forgiveness.[18] Little wonder that Moloney concluded in his early postwar review with the prediction that psychoanalysis, in the Western sense, would not take root because, 'The Japanese political, spiritual, and cultural programmes are such that each system would have to give too much for there ever to be a satisfactory wedding of the Japanese and Western psychoanalytic movements.'[19]

Yet Moloney's pessimism seemed to have received a brilliant rebuff with the publication of Doi Takeo's 'psychoanalytic' study of Japanese personality in the early seventies. Running through well over 100 editions, his work had a profound influence on the *nihonjinron* and received enthusiastic accolades from such foreign specialists as Ezra Vogel and Robert Lifton. Indeed his terminology became part and parcel of educated slang and highbrow jargon. Abroad it was hailed as an epochal oriental contribution to psychoanalytic thought.

Doi's theory arose from the 'culture shock' he experienced while doing postgraduate study in the United States, from his frustration in being unable to express an emotion (*amae*) in Western company. On examination, it appeared that no term existed in occidental languages to translate this word, and thus it struck the author that he had stumbled upon a 'key word' whose analysis might unlock the secrets of the Japanese psyche. Armed with his linguistic weapon of *amae*, as a unique psychoanalytic value and affect, Doi sought to explain the whole structure of Japanese historical culture, finding the tireless working of this emotion in such disparate phenomena as student riots and the Emperor system, terrorist adventurism and docile obedience to authority.

Having unriddled the sphinx of Japaneseness in this audaciously singleminded fashion, Doi then ventured to uncover the repressed traces of *amae* in European civilisation, where it had apparently escaped the lynx-eyed gaze of Freud himself. For, lacking a linguistic synonym for the uniquely Japanese word *amae*, the founder of the psychoanalytic art could not detect the emotional complex it represented. This emboldened Doi to embark on a rewriting of psychoanalysis itself from an explicitly Japanese focus. Such extraordinary claims clearly demand our keenest attention. The analysis of his central theses which follows may strike the reader as obvious. But the fact that it is precisely the self-evident which escapes the scrutiny of so many professional students of Japan requires that we exercise particular care in raking through the ashes of this apparent senselessness.

Doi's thesis is constructed on the basis of certain linguistic assumptions about the uniqueness of the Japanese language, which we have briefly sketched in the preceeding chapters. It had been standard practice in Japanese medicine to describe a patient's symptoms by recourse to technical terms in German, and Doi is only following Tanizaki's advice in suggesting that such complex technical terms from abroad should be replaced by simple Japanese words, if only to discover symptoms that cannot be described adequately within the terms of occidental classification and nomenclature. As he puts it:

> 'I gradually came round to the view that, if one were to accept that there were singular elements in the psychological makeup of the Japanese, then there would also have to be an intimate relationship between these, and the peculiar nature of the Japanese language.'[20]

Breaking with convention, Doi began to analyse his patients in Japanese and soon obtained striking results, in that they appeared to behave as if their *amae* were being frustrated, in a way not dissimilar from his experiences as a Japanese in foreign company. To follow him here, we must examine his key word, bearing in mind that, according to a linguistic principle of the *nihonjinron*, *amae*, as a *yamato kotoba* cannot (or perhaps more properly, should not) be translated into foreign languages, being like all words in this subjective category expressive of a uniquely ineffable race experience. *Amae* is a deverbal noun formed from *amaeru*, a word which, until Doi's intervention, was innocently translated into English by such words as 'coaxing', 'fawning', 'wheedling' etc. In short, *amaeru* is the word habitually used to describe the behaviour of spoilt children when they play up to their parents to gain their indulgent attention.

The transitive form of *amaeru* is *amayakasu*, 'to pamper', 'spoil', 'blandish', or 'mollycoddle'. Doi apparently believes that it is the intransitive form which cannot be translated,[21] though his foreign commentators refer to its sense as something like 'seeking indulgence'. Doi himself, in his foreign publications, renders it as 'presuming upon another's indulgence', and it is this which gives us another clue as to Doi's confusion. For a Western doctor, in observing a wheedling child coax the mother to obtain her pampering, might well simply speak of the child's wheedling or coaxing. But, he could equally speak more abstractly, in professional jargon, of the child's presuming on his mother's indulgence. In line with *nihonjinron* assumptions, Doi interprets the contrast between abstract terminology and colloquial expression in terms of the antithesis between *gairaigo* and *yamato kotoba* (table 12). Doi's Japanese critics have often remarked on his cavalier mode of defining words, and on his tendency to embue simple terms like *amae* with so many varied meanings that his concepts become blurred to the point of irretrievable ambiguity.[22]

It is in his moving back to psychoanalytic language that Doi enables us to gather further hints as to the real nature of this *amae*. It is, he tells us, the feeling aroused in the suckling child, and thus pre-oedipal and roughly cognate with what Freud called 'the child's primary object choice'.[23] For Doi, Freud came close to discovering *amae* but was distracted from it by his pursuit of the theme of narcissism. In fact, Doi inadvertently here provides us with independent evidence for the notion advanced earlier as to the pre-oedipal character of the *nihonjinron* images of Japanese identity. And we might add that it is Doi's distraction with the pseudo-concept of *amae* which blocks him from pursuing the theme of narcissism which underlies the literature on Japanese uniqueness.

Further light is shed on this mysterious category when Doi informs us that *amae* refers to what Balint understood by his notion of 'passive object-love'.[24] Balint indeed argued that 'all European languages cannot distinguish between the two kinds of object love, active and passive',[25] and Doi leaps at this misleading statement in order to declare that precisely such a distinction does exist in Japanese. Again, what Doi is actually doing is simply

Table 12: Abstract *v.* colloquial

Foreign languages, including Sino–Japanese terms	Japanese, in its 'authentic' *yamato kotoba* form
dependency, izon	*amae*

referring to an abstract concept by a colloquial word, to 'passive object love' by 'coaxing'. To understand with greater precision what this trick of identification between vernacular Japanese and psychoanalytic jargon involves we do well to examine Balint's own writings.

Balint's work aimed at reconciling divergences in theory between the British and Viennese schools of psychoanalysis concerning infant states of feeling. The former held that the infant was subject to primary narcissism, while the latter held that this period was marked by a state of passive tranquillity. Both views arose from the interpretation of patient behaviour under regressive analysis. Balint considered that the apparent narcissism of the regressed patient was provoked by the analyst's posture of unresponsive neutrality, which induced a sense of frustration in the analysand. When, conversely, the analyst broke with this convention and gratified the whimsical needs of the patient, the latter showed himself to be blissfully happy.

From this Balint concluded that infants had a drive towards objects which was essentially passive in character, that the child desired the satisfaction of being loved, without feeling a responsive need to reciprocate these attentions. It followed that Freud's view of primary narcissism was a direct result of his clinical interdiction against appeasing the patient's desire for symbolic gratification. But we should note that while rejecting the thesis of primary narcissism, Balint and his wife stressed that object relations of an active kind existed from the outset of infancy, as could be deduced from the so-called 'clinging' reflex.[26] This led them to reject their initial formulation of 'passive object love' in favour of 'archaic' or 'primary' object relation on the grounds that, 'The term *passive* was not a suitable description of a relation in which such markedly active tendencies as the instinct to cling play a paramount role.'[27]

We can now close in on what Doi understands by *amae*. It corresponds to the first formulation of an idea of the passive need for gratification which was however later modified by Balint himself as being inadequate and misleading. Doi's concept of 'coaxing' (*amae*) denotes the emotional behaviour of regressed patients, their seeking after gratifications, when the analyst breaks his rule of neutrality and responds to his patient's capricious requests. To clarify this still further we must recall that Freud insisted that the analyst temper his solicitude with a posture of diffidence in order to overcome problems involved at the stage of transference. For

Freud, were the analyst to gratify his patient, a personal relationship would set in which might block the release of more deeply repressed material.

The attempt to involve the therapist constituted an evasion, or a misdirection of emotions in the patient from their primary, historical locus. The analyst was to resist these emotive explorations because they were not signs of a genuine and novel attachment of the patient to his analyst but rather unconscious subterfuges that aimed at deflecting the problem, at evading the resolution of the underlying, primary conflict. Therefore the therapist was bidden to be neutral before such behaviour, and to simply clarify to the patient the original object of such displaced affections and needs, and to illustrate thereby how this transferred desire for gratification merely revealed a 'new edition of an old disorder.'[28]

The identification of *amae* with Balint's 'passive object love' (a term which, Doi fails to inform us, was later rejected by Balint himself) must therefore relate to Doi's difficulties as an analyst in coping with the phenomenon of transference. His remarks on the obtuseness of Americans in social interaction, and his criticism of the icyness of American clinical practice, though explained in terms of the standard clichés of the *nihonjinron* paradigm (*cf* 10,18,26, etc in chapter 4), actually points to his own incomprehension of the fact that Freud's advocacy of neutrality in the analyst, by blocking the evasive mechanisms of transference in the patient, embodied a 'new kind of human relationship'.[29] Doi's theory of *amae* as an explanation of the image of emotional, group-dependent relations among the Japanese thus stems from his personal failure to see that his patients' coaxing of attention arises and persists because of his own difficulties in handling the transference problem.

Indeed Okonogi, who is otherwise another great offender in what passes for 'a Japanese kind of psychoanalysis', provides us with a decisive piece of evidence to corroborate the deductions we have made here. In an early address in 1953, Doi apparently confessed his failure to cope with counter-transference in treating a young man's anxiety neurosis in the following terms:

> I failed to evaluate correctly the positive transference which had sprouted after so many difficulties. My response to this (transference) was one of feeling flattered or, to put it more bluntly, I thought to myself: 'Well, here's a fine change! Up to now

you've been mercilessly mouthing off at me, and now at this late stage you're singing my praises! What sycophancy!' My feelings were one of complete resistance to the transference and, as a result, I gave the patient an incorrect interpretation. That is, I explained the appearance of these positive feelings in him by recourse to such words as *amaeru* (coaxing, fawning) and *suneru* (sulking) words which naturally imply something which one ought not to do (*ikenai koto*). As a consequence, the patient's positive emotions, which had been elicited with so much difficulty, were nipped in the bud. This in turn provoked negative feelings, which appeared in the form of an explosion of dissatisfaction with the treatment.'[30]

Doi reveals here, in himself, a distaste for 'coaxing' behaviour (*amae*) as something 'not done' which some 20 years on he then attributes to Westerners. It is the kind of slip which reminds us that the *nihonjinron* discourse on Western characteristics is very much an evasive projection of inner resistances.

Balint's method was developed by such analysts as Winnicott, who advocated occasional gratification of patients afflicted by a deeply unhappy relationship with their mother. But in Japan these tentative modifications of analytical neutrality have been deployed to justify the approach of analysts who have not been themselves sufficiently analysed. The modification is there taken as a necessary adaptation of foreign theory to some uniquely Japanese sentiment (*cf amae*). The result is that Doi can characterise the analyst-patient relationship in Japan as one of 'collusion' (*nareai*).[31] This is another unconscious and revealing slip on his part, since it is borrowed from existential psychoanalysis where it denotes the mutual self-deception of members in group analysis, or to a kind of gentleman's agreement to avoid any exposure of the underlying neurosis. The 'endogenisation' of psychoanalysis embodied in the theory of 'coaxing' thus involves that very collusion between therapist's phantasy-system and patient's phantasy-system against which the trained psychoanalyst must constantly guard.[32]

The rest of Doi's system, once this is understood, is easily deciphered. When he tells us that the patient's *toraware* (captiveness = neurotic self-absorption) leads to *kodawari* (obstructiveness) and recedes only when he becomes aware of his *amae* (desire to coax gratifications),[33] Doi is only rewriting in *yamato kotoba*, that mystified patois of uniqueness, the commonplace form of the onset of transference. Lebra hints as much in her attempt to modify Doi's thesis by arguing that his one-sided emphasis on the intransitive nature of *amaeru* to the exclusion of its transitive form *amayakasu* (to spoil) overlooks the fact of role complementarity in Japan, 'Perhaps because of the role assymetry in the therapeutic relationship, where the therapist is inhibited from indulging the *amae* wish of the patient.'[34]

That the pseudo-hypothesis of *amae* thus rests on the twin poles of verbal equivocation and psychoanalytic misapprehension is now self-evident. We are not dealing with the 'unique', but with a clinical commonplace. Freud relates of his young patient Little Hans that he woke one morning weeping because, as the child put it, 'When I was asleep I thought you (= mother) were gone and I had no mummy *to coax with*'.[35] The word *schmeicheln* (to coax, fawn) used here, which Freud glosses with the verb *liebkosen* (cuddle up to) undoubtedly expresses that *amae* which Doi stubbornly considers to be unique to the Japanese.

Doi proceeds to explore the world of Japanese emotions in terms of *amae*, citing many words which he thinks reveal, as heteromorphic variations or transformations, certain aspects of this unique 'coaxing'.[36] One sulks (*suneru*) when coaxing (*amae*) is not indulged. If this need is further unappeased, the person becomes spiteful or disaffected (*futekusareru*) and despairing (*yakekuso ni naru*). If this failure to gratify coaxing continues, then eventually it leads to jaundiced feelings (*higamu*) and a delusion of maltreatment arising from the thorough thwarting of one's desire to be indulged (*cf amae*).

Such a person will then turn his back on the world by refusing to expose to view his need for indulgence; he becomes warped (*hinekureru*), and then resentful and bitter (*uramu*), showing the hostility of one to whom coaxing is denied. Our interest is gripped by this grim progress of *amae* from blissful dependence to sullen autonomy. But a contrary facet exists when one seeks to satisfy the need to coax. In order to solicit a favour (*tanomu*), one may humour others by indulging them in order to obtain an egotistic self-gratification as the word *toriiru* (ingratiate oneself, curry favour) shows. However one may scruple (*kodawaru*) when one fears to depend on (*cf amae*) others and denies to others the right to presume upon (*amae*) oneself. In this case, a person will show self-constraint (*kigane*) by becoming standoffish, in the fear that others may not be as indulgent as one would desire them to be. This in turn may lead to *wadakamari* (vexatious brooding) in which one displays an air of indifference while in fact resenting others, or it may lead to *tereru* (to be shy, bashful), when the ability to express one's desire to be pampered is obstructed by shame.

In thus mapping the contours of that linguistic terrain whose sentimental capital is *amae* (understood variously as being indulged, gratified, pampered, dependent, allowed to presume, etc), Doi imparts the impression that he has surveyed the peculiar geography of a uniquely Japanese type of psychomental structure. But if we sum up his little excursus here, stripping it of the contrived exoticism of *yamato kotoba*, what we see is merely an oriental portrait of that society of types like the fop, the toady and the man of spleen which parades through the literature of the eighteenth century.

For, in effect, we are being told that one who is not gratified becomes pouty and then splenetically disaffected to the point of being warped by a sense of resentment. Such a testy outlook may lead to obstructive scrupulosity which in turn engenders bad blood. Being unable to presume one becomes bound by restraints and afflicted by timid abashment. More sanguinely one may on the other hand seek gratification by soliciting the indulgence of others, by stooping to flatter, by insinuating oneself into another's good graces, and thus, through such sycophantic fawning secretly gratify one's self. In short, Doi's work sounds original because he consistently tethers his theory to a vocabulary that rings with unfamiliar echoes of the exotic for his foreign readership. In a review of the English edition of his work Douglas Price-Williams remarked that, 'The evaluation of *The Anatomy of Dependence* really depends upon one's degree of acceptance of semantic analysis as a legitimate method for understanding psychological processes.'[37] To the contrary, semantic analysis is an indisputably valid and indispensable tool, but in Doi's work linguistic ideologies have supplanted philological common sense. He entrusts himself not so much to the guidance of speech as much as to the rhetorical valencies of *yamato kotoba* (an ideological, not a linguistic category) as the grammatical images of a uniquely Japanese structure of identity. After his lexicographical sortie, the confident intimation that, 'Japanese is extraordinarily useful not only for naming mental disorders but also for conveying the minutiae of psychopathology,'[38] is only to be expected. We shall presently have occasion to see precisely how the *nihonjinron* premise juxtaposing the abstract alienated speech of all foreign languages to the concrete, emotive and direct nature of *yamato kotoba*, conditions all of Doi's judgements, and contaminates his exposition with the usual resonances of nationalistic upstaging.

It is this conventional assumption underlying Doi's practice of translating the technical language of occidental psychoanalysis into colloquial Japanese which enables him to regard his 'new', 'Japanised' text as closer to experience than the Freudian original. We have already seen that Freud's 'primary object choice' and Balint's 'primary object love' are translated equally as '*amae*' or coaxing. In dealing with anxiety in interpersonal relationships (*taijin-kyōfu*), he cites *hitomishiri* (shyness) as another 'unique word with no correspondence in Western languages', and argues that it gives us a new insight into the phenomenon of infant bashfulness.

He reasons as follows. René Spitz's work is cited to prove that Westerners have, until recently, been wholly unfamiliar with the fact that babies, at a certain age, begin to evince shyness towards strangers. Spitz had given this phenomenon a technical label, 'eight-month anxiety' or 'stranger anxiety'. From this, Doi deduces that, 'It is a fact worthy of note that a phenomenon first observed in the West by a scholar has been noticed from time immemorial in Japan by mothers with no special upbringing as shyness (*hitomishiri*).'[39]

Now Spitz nowhere claims that he was the first to notice this. His originality lay in the way he interpreted the significance of this universal stage in infant growth. 'Eight-month anxiety' was, he argued, merely the third and last stage in the genesis of anxiety. The first stage began with the trauma of delivery, and the second with the arousal of percepts associated with prior unpleasure, around the fourth month. 'Stranger anxiety' merely indicated the child's negative response to someone with whom it had never experienced an unpleasurable sensation. Spitz suggested that this final stage was not a matter of 'getting to know (other) people' (the strict sense of *hitomishiri*) but rather an apprehension, provoked by the sight of an unfamiliar, strange face, that the mother was absent. The presence of alien features indicated the absence of the known mother.[40]

There is no clue in the Japanese word to this interpretation. Doi is confused by Spitz's recourse to jargon, by his technical term 'eight-month anxiety' (instead of a term like shyness or bashfulness). When Doi says that *hitomishiri* marks the onset of *amae* he is simply rendering into *yamato kotoba* Spitz's remark that 'stranger anxiety' marks the beginning of a child's identification with the mother as libidinal object.[41] Doi's argument that ignorant mothers in Japan from time immemorial have always understood what only sophisticated scientists have discovered recently in the West parallels the conclusions of both Watanabe and Suzuki concerning the greater advantages, in terms of educational level and democratic sentiment, of Japanese as a mother tongue compared to foreign languages. Doi's particular example of cultural point-scoring could have been avoided had he read Tolstoy's moving description of *hitomishiri* in Anna Karenina.[42]

Doi's linguistic assumptions are further clarified in his analysis of the word *ki* (pneuma, temper, mood, feeling). A word of Chinese provenance, it took on, Doi maintains, 'peculiar' connotations in the Japanese language. Using this endogenised word, he proceeds to advocate that it be used to substitute for the standard technical terms (expressed in Sino–Japanese) coined to describe mental illness in Japan (table 13). By this simple operation of substitution, Doi thinks that we may gain a more incisive understanding of psychological breakdown. That is, 'These words (i.e. *ki no yamai, kichigai*) clearly express the essence of these psychological disorders much better than the translating terms (*shinkeishō, seishinbyō*) or indeed the original Western terms.'[43] Aside from the fact that it is not words that explain the nature of an illness but theory, we might note that all Doi is doing here is substituting simple for complex words. We might equally prefer to speak in English or German of 'mind-sickness' or *Geistesverwirrung* in preference to the Greek-derived technical term psychopathology. *Kichigai* in Japanese means 'loony', 'crackpot' and Doi's recourse to the slangy argot of everyday abuse in preference to the technical nomenclature of psychiatry tends, as he elsewhere admits, to upset

Table 13: *Ki* Equivalences

Foreign abstract word		Indigenous sense word
English	Sino--Japanese	'naturalised' *yamato kotoba*
neurosis	*shinkeishō* (nerve disease)	*ki no yamai* (an ailing of *ki*)
psychosis	*seishinbyō* (mental sickness)	*ki-chigai* (a crazed *ki*)

his patients.[44] However, his constant recursion to 'indigenous words' enables him to retravel the well-trod paths of psychoanalysis and, by blazing over once familiar signs with the exotic badges of *yamato kotoba*, contrive the specious impression for those who hazard to venture in his footsteps that such colloquial retracings mark out a pathfinding reconnoitre of the human spirit.

Some of the more obvious aspects of Doi's crypto-linguistic one-upmanship escape the foreign reader because his translator seems to have diligently excised his sillier blunderings from the English version. Take his discussion of *ki ga sumanai* (to be dissatisfied).[45] In this idiom he discerns something which succinctly anatomises the 'Japanese' tendency towards compulsiveness, and he gives us the following illustrative example. This habit of punctiliousness becomes neurotic when one feels compelled to return time and again to check if one has switched off the gas, even though one may be sure that one has done so. Doi continues:

> In Western languages, this kind of pathological dissatisfaction is expressed by the words 'compulsive' and *zwangshaft*. But these words belong to technical nomenclature and are hardly ever used in everyday conversation, since they are not even listed in ordinary dictionaries. Moreover, if we take these two Western words and translate them into Japanese, we come up with *kyōhakuteki*.[46] Now this is a technical term also, and ordinary (Japanese) people would probably not understand its meaning. On the contrary, there is a risk that in using this *kyōhakuteki* (強迫的) it might be confused with its homophone *kyōhakuteki* (脅迫的) (meaning, 'threatening, intimidating').

Now, if one looks up in a standard English dictionary of psychiatry a Western word to fit this (first) *kyōhakuteki*, one generally finds the following sort of statement: '(Compulsion) is a repetitive, ordinary and often trivial action of a man who, even when he doesn't feel inclined to do something, somehow cannot help but do it. The anxiety increases while he leaves it undone, and his tension is only momentarily relieved when he finally gets round to doing it'.

Now, objectively, this is a very precise description, and yet, since it is troublesomely complicated, it is perhaps difficult for the general layman unacquainted with psychiatry to call to mind what is meant by such a condition. However, if one were to say to just such a person, 'By the word *kyōhaku* (compulsion) is meant an action of the kind in which one feels dissatisfied (*ki ga sumanai*) unless one does it', then undoubtedly any Japanese would instantly comprehend the meaning. Thus there is a convenient way of saying things in Japanese, and I consider it a fact of extraordinary linguistic importance that there is nothing comparable to this expression in European languages.[47]

Doi clearly not only has a poor grasp of 'European languages', but also appears to be working out of skimpy pocket dictionaries. This whole passage has been solicitously excerpted from the official translation, and understandably so, since the logic is so circuitous that, were it included, Doi's whole programme, with its semantic juggling, would have been exposed to withering ridicule. The gesture of discreet erasure indicates that something is dreadfully askew. It is the same error we have consistently exposed above (cf. table 14). Yet the detailed description of how Doi obtains these results clues the reader in to the confusion of his expository technique. However the foreigner is denied access to this passage, and is not even averted to the censorious intervention of the editor, and so by this suppression is deprived of the one lead which might have exploded Doi's linguo-gymnastic enterprise in the rewriting of psychoanalytic theory.

Doi's belief that Japanese uniquely opens up a readily accessible linguistic pathway to the primordial wellsprings of the human psyche, in a way ineffably more incisive than foreign technical language, underwrites every passage in his oeuvre. His discussion of *higaisha-ishiki* (the feeling of being victimised) is equally instructive, though again it has run foul of the translator's censorious scissors.[48]

This term gained popular currency with its appearance in Maruyama Masao's excellent book on 'Japanese Thought', where the author noted that Japan's élite sees itself as a victim despite the fact that it holds the reins of monopoly power. He related this to

Table 14: Interpretations of 'Compulsive'

Foreign abstract word		Indigenous sense word
English–German	Sino--Japanese	*yamato kotoba*
compulsive *zwangshaft*	kyōhakuteki	ki ga sumanai

what he called the 'octopus trap' (*takotsubo*) structure of Japanese society in contrast to the bamboo whisk (*sasara*) structure of occidental societies.[49] In such a society, groups are organised into vertical, mutually competing hierarchies rather than into horizontally stratified classes. Thus the public integument binding together class interest groups in Western 'bamboo whisk societies' (that is, joined at the base in one stem and only fissuring at the top) is wholly lacking. This conceptualisation easily lends itself to a *nihonjinron*-type formulation.

For Maruyama, each group thus composed senses itself more and more isolated as society's complexity increases, breeding a defensive sense of *higaisha-ishiki* or victimisation. Now Doi traces the term back to the Meiji period, when *higaisha* was coined to denote the injured party in litigation, as a Sino–Japanese equivalent for the Western concept. Now in Japanese psychiatry *higai* (literally, receiving harm) is used in the compound term *higai-mōsō* (delusion of being harmed) to translate the notion of paranoia, specifically in the German term *Beeinträchtigungswahn* (literally, delusion of being hurt, encroached upon). The passage, which Doi's translator inexplicably omits to reproduce, runs as follows:

> What is interesting here is that in the German word *Beeinträchtigungswahn* which is the original that *higai-mōsō* serves to translate, the meaning of being harmed (*higai*) is not literally contained. If we translate it directly, it simply becomes *shingai-mōsō* (literally, delusion of being infringed, encroached upon). But since its true meaning is one of having been infringed, the (Japanese) word *higai-mōsō* which translates it is clearly more precise than the original German expression.[50]

Japanese words are thus seen as being more faithful to the original sense of the foreign texts they serve to translate than the language of the original itself. Doi here attributes to *kango* a power that he elsewhere associates with *yamato kotoba*, moving momentarily from Watanabe's position to Suzuki's. Widely seen as a depletion or sub-version of the original, translation here becomes a positive advance or improvement. As Watanabe redeployed the ideas of *Shakespearomanie*, so Doi inadvertently revives, in a modern Japanese form, the theory of German hermetic linguistics, with its belief in an Adamic vernacular in which the languages of

Babel are restored to their original sense.[51] Once more we observe how congenial affinities are discovered between contemporary 'Japanese thought' and nineteenth century German ideologies in the heyday of nationalism.

Doi now subjugates Maruyama's concept to his ubiquitous *amae*. A child coaxes indulgence from its mother, and any diversion of her attention from him is seen as an hindrance (*jama*). Any frustration of his monopoly over her affections leads to a sense of grievance which prepares the way for a feeling of being a victim (*higaisha-ishiki*) in 'normal people' (*seijōnin*) and paranoia (*higai-mōsō*) in 'abnormal people'. That is:

> A person who embraces this kind of paranoid delusion is conscious solely of himself as a victim. Where this differs from the sense of victimisation of normal people is that, while the latter do not regard their victimisation as personal, but rather share it with the community to which they belong, the person with delusions of persecution feels himself to be helplessly and completely isolated within society.[52]

In short, what distinguishes paranoia from a sense of victimisation is, for Doi, the *private* character of the former, and the *public* character of the latter. The myth of Japanese social cohesion (groupism) is so strong that even assemblies with a sense of victimised grievance are differentiated, by virtue of their normal 'harmonious' alienation, from the 'pathological' cases of the individually estranged.[53] His theory at this point thus naturalises entrenched moralities of sanity in collectivism, which leads him to the remarkable judgement that:

> Many of these people (paranoids) grew up without experiencing the indulgence of others (that is, without exercising *amae*). This could be considered to be chiefly due to their environment. However, in not a few cases one may consider that it is the environment itself which is thus formed by the patient's congenital hypersensitivity.[54]

Thus the mad are justly shut up in asylums because their condition is contagious, tempting into madness the very people who concern themselves with their therapy and cure.[55] Diffidence in conceding environmental causes in the etiology of neuroses is typical of highly authoritarian, conservative societies dominated by an ideology of social solidarity (*cf* the USSR), since this would imply the existence of pathogenic elements or flaws in the idealised social structure of the state. But Doi goes one step further in considering the individual neurotic a danger, a destabilising presence, in a society dominated by a salubriously social, groupist sense of persecution.

Since coaxing is a basic need of the Japanese, they become prone to anything that hinders them, and Doi sees the student riots as symptomatic of the blocking of dependency.[56] This modern *anomie* is rooted in the fact, he believes, that we live in a 'fatherless society',[57] and thus, after two hundred pages of rampant, matriarchal *amae*, we are finally averted to the perils ensuing on the absence or retreat of that *deus otiosus* of modernity, patriarchal authority, particularly as exemplified in the Emperor system, whose ideology (defined as 'the conceptual backbone supporting the character of the society')[58] he links with the desire to coax, to presume upon another's indulgence.

He adduces the case of a student patient who, in analysis, declared that he 'wanted someone to serve and assist him in the execution of his duties' (*hohitsu*).[59] *Hohitsu* is a rare term denoting the counsel proferred to the throne by a minister of state, and Doi rightly deduces that the student unconsciously identified himself with the Emperor. From this he argued that while pre-eminent in status, the Emperor had nonetheless to depend or rely upon others (*cf amae*), and thus was in fact a mere babe-in-arms.

> This fact does not only apply to the Emperor; all people with positions of authority in Japan, in a sense, need to be rallied up and fostered by those around them ... In other words, it is precisely the person who is able to embody infantile dependence in its purest form (*cf amae*) who is most qualified to stand at the top of Japanese society.[60]

We have come a long way here from Maruyama's study of the 'transference of oppression' (*yokuatsu no ijō*) as a mechanism of hierarchical equilibrium from higher to lower authority.[61] For Doi there is a transference of coaxing dependence from below to above, from ruled to ruler. The desire to presume that he sees as flooding contemporary Japan is an outcome of the dismantling of this imperial system in the postwar period.

So long as concepts like 'obligation and emotion' (*giri-ninjō*) the duty of 'repaying a debt incurred by another's benevolence' (*hōon*), and the 'spirit of Yamato' (*yamato-damashii*) performed their role in the regulation of society, as I have analysed above, it was impossible to take cognisance of the fact that their essence resided in the psychology of coaxing (*amae*). It was only when the Emperor himself denied his divine status, and became the symbol of Japan, that it became possible for the first time to bring out into the open the dependence (*amae*) latent in the inmost heart of every Japanese.

The present age has born witness to the destruction of the imperial system, and in its place, as it were, an unregulated seeking for gratification (*amae*) has run rampant, giving rise to 'little emperors' everywhere one turns.[62]

Doi's remarks here are tellingly contradictory, since he makes *amae* the lynchpin of the repressive imperial system's values of constraint, and equally the basis of the more open society which followed its dismantlement. As we have seen earlier in his confession to his colleagues, cringing servility and unctuous flattery of the kind which emerges during regressive analysis were alien to the 'samurai' ethics of prewar Japan.[63] What is evident underneath this contradiction is that double socialisation explored in the previous chapter, in which the mother's exclusive and indulgent nurture is quickly replaced, after an initial reinforcing of narcissism, by the opposite, rigid self-synchronisation of the child with external peer group norms. The *coaxing* psychology of the first phase is not the formative basis for the second, but rather something which wider socialisation represses and denies.

In a sense, Doi is here restating the old view of his mentor Kosawa, which identifies Westernisation (here in its second, postwar phase) with neurosis, in that the Occupation loosened the bonds that held in coercive thrall this ostensible urge for infantile gratification in the Japanese. He elsewhere says that the transition from rural community (*Gemeinschaft*) to urban society (*Gesellschaft*) rendered the instinctive recourse to dependent coaxing much more difficult, leading to an upsurge in shyness (*hitomishiri*) in consequence of this frustration of *amae*.[64] This equation of neurotic symptoms like anthropophobia and nervosity with Western-style modernisation is not far from the prewar view linking the subversion of the *kokutai* by 'thought criminals' to the spread of foreign ideas. The political judgement is replaced by a psychiatric one.

In discounting social influences in psychological formation (although he tacitly recognises them when mental dysfunction is identified with the social impact of 'Westernisation'), Doi must view the social structure of Japan itself as a necessary precipitate of an inherent tendency to coax in Japanese character. In line with his customary practice of subordinating all other *nihonjinron* theses to that of his master concept of *amae*, he writes of Nakane's *tate-shakai* or 'warp society' thesis (which itself plays off Maruyama's *takotsubo* idea), that:

> Recently, the social anthropologist Nakane Chie has stipulated the importance of hierarchical (*tate*) relations as the distinctive characteristic of Japanese social structure. However, one could probably define this also as, in fact, an emphasis on the emotion of presuming on others (*amae*). Or rather, one is perhaps justified in saying that the predilective susceptibility of the Japanese for having their desire for dependence indulged is the cause for the importance attached to hierarchical relations in Japanese society.[65]

That is to say:

> The indulgence (*amae*) a child seeks from its parents, a student from his teachers, company personal from their superiors and junior colleagues from their superiors, is considered to be totally natural in Japanese society.[66]

Here again, a social system which blocks the gratification of desires nurtured in primary socialisation by the mother is interpreted as growing out of the same, although it is itself patriarchal. On the one hand, the Emperor must presume upon his subordinates, and on the other hand, as here, it is the other way round; the rulers must allow their inferiors to presume upon their indulgence. The concept of *amae* is so elastic that it may explain, and simultaneously mystify, everything Japanese. For Doi it is indeed the relentless affective demiurge of Japaneseness whose primordial energy shapes the forms of all native experience and reality.

At this point we ask ourselves how Doi reconciles this view with the Freudian thesis of the 'reality principle', that stern agent of self-restraint which compels man to sublimate his search for immediate gratification. And, not to our surprise, we find that here Doi can find no equivalent in the native glossary of *yamato kotoba*. Discussing the word *ki* he expresses the view that:

> If one observes the other workings of this word *ki*, one may conclude that it usually denotes pleasure-intentionality (*kairaku-shikōteki*). And it is precisely this which is the principle of mental activity expressed in the drift of the word *ki*. Thus it roughly corresponds to what Freud called the pleasure principle, differing only in that Freud established a reality principle alongside the pleasure principle, and regarded the two as acting in concert in the regulating of mental activity. In the Japanese instance, no thought was ever given on the contrary to a principle controlling mental activity other than that of the pleasure principle of *ki*.[67]

This is at the same time the most jejune and most instructive of Doi's remarks. Doi has once more ensnared himself in the deceptive traps of language in his reading of the pleasure principle (though his misreading is common and may derive from Marcuse). For belying its apparent meaning, the expression actually refers to a psychic tendency to diminish mental sensitivity to external stimuli. It denotes, properly, the evasion of unpleasure,[68] and is thus the antithesis of that appetitive principle Doi constructs on the basis of the word *ki*.

We might note that integral to Doi's attempt to rebuild the ill-fabricated edifice of Western psychoanalysis with the solid masonry of the Japanese tongue is the assumption that the greater 'concreteness' of *yamato kotoba* allows for a sensuous articulation of concepts that are only obliquely framed in the cerebral language of the West. But when his expeditions for native synonyms in these *yamato kotoba* for occidental nomenclature fail to come up with an adequate corresponding term, as here with the reality principle, then he is forced to conclude that the phenomenon in question must not exist in Japan, that the reality designated by the alien word is wholly absent from the indigenous cultural system.[69]

It is not clear whether Doi himself appreciates the significance of his disavowal of the existence of a reality principle in Japanese socialisation, apart from the fact that this declaration effectively destroys any residual claims he might make to be practising psychoanalysis. The denial is perhaps necessary if his thesis that Japanese society is a pure product of pre-Oedipal drives for motherly nurture is to hold, but this leaves in the air an explanation of how in such a climate could such repressive norms as *giri, hōon* and self-adaptation to the other (*cf junnō*), which are all hostile to individuality, arise in the first place. Indeed, his position here abrogates any need for a developmental psychology, and controverts the very possibility in the formation of Japanese personality of such crucial mechanisms as repression, sublimation, inhibition and displacement during socialisation. It implies that the instinctual *id* in the Japanese mind not only cannot accommodate itself to the inflexible constraints of external reality, but that this objective world itself is somehow conditioned by the *id*. That is, Doi is saying in effect that the Japanese jump from infantile dependency to indulged maturity with the whole integument of nurturant dispositions intact. Doi thus inverts the adultomorphic fallacy of some aspects of Western psychoanalysis with an infantomorphic fallacy, whereby all phases and aspects of social comportment and behaviour are reductively analysed in terms of the archaic patterns of nurturance of the child at breast.[70]

Freud took the striving for pleasure to be an instrumental device for diminishing external stimuli. Whereas the sexual instincts were seen to work towards a direct, economic discharge of tensions, the ego instincts were considered to modify this 'pleasure principle' by yielding to the inexorable constraints of that social reality external to the child's mind. Here the principle of avoiding unpleasure predominates, a tactic of strategic deferral which ensured the eventual attainment of pleasure by postponing immediate gratification. The ego became 'reasonable', and the transition from the 'pleasure' to the 'reality' principle was seen as crucial to the development of a socialised ego.[71] By his own admission, Doi is thus denying that any Japanese has 'a capacity to observe reality and a tendency to protect (himself) from the damage which the unchecked satisfaction of the instincts could inflict on one.'[72]

One cannot but be impressed by the ideological tenacity of educational indoctrination in the prewar school system, under which many of the writers presented in this book were taught. While splashing the pronoun 'I' about with great liberality in their books, they insist on telling their anonymous readership in Japan that they lack a sense of the self. Doi's denial of the ego, implicit in his discarding of the reality principle, aligns itself with Suzuki's remarks on the 'weak-ego' (*yowai jiga*), Mori Jōji's pseudo-theory of a Japanese '"shell-less egg" ego',[73] and Nakane's enigmatic judgement that 'the Japanese have no ego, but they like to talk about their selfs (*jibun*)'.[74] Of this *jibun*, Doi tells us that:

> Actually, not only is it impossible for the individual to get his own way (*wagamama o tōsu*), but it causes him to feel great distress in his inmost heart. That is to say, for him the group is a fundamentally great mental prop, and to isolate himself by defecting from the group would render void his self (*jibun*) completely, in a way he would feel unbearable. He therefore tries to choose the path of aligning himself with the group even if inevitably he must efface for a time his selfhood (*jiko*).[75]

We are not far from the prewar definition of the ego as a mere fragment in the mosaical body of the *kokutai*. But even foreigners free of the unconscious grip over intellect exercised by such prewar disindividualising doctrines can marvel, in admiring the selfless style of Japanese corporate life, how in Japan, unlike the West, 'each person is believed to possess a unique spirit ... — but his self (or "self-concept") is seen as an impediment to growth'.[76] Such a mindless parroting of 'emic' views only makes sense if we presume that the growth referred to is economic and not spiritual.

But if we think back through the disparately uncovered evidences of this book, we can begin to make sense of the function of these ideological mendacities. The analysis of the *kō/shi* distinction points to the lack of an institutional framework for the neat separation of public and private spheres. It follows that the individual is conceived as engaged continually in a direct facing off or confrontation with social power, and the collectivity.

Secondly, in the home, the indulgent nurture of the mother is followed up by a type of socialisation which reverses the previous vector of self-interest by subjugating the sense of individuality in peer group identity. As Doi would put it, 'The individual desires where possible to make the group's interests coincide with his own'.[77] That is, primary narcissism is nurtured, then abruptly effaced, only to be reconstituted in the egotism of the group. The soft idiom of *yamato kotoba* learnt from the mother (*cf* Watanabe) is replaced by a school curriculum drilling the child to an arduous mastery of the intricacies of the Sino–Japanese script. The *nihonjinron* evocation of these *yamato kotoba* as the archaic wellsprings of authentic sensual existence (in contrast to 'foreign', 'abstract' *kango/gairaigo*) is thus, psychoanalytically, a nostalgic recursion via linguistic myth to the edenic world of pre-peer group socialisation.

As Doi now indirectly confirms, the myth of *amae* or pre-Oedipal mother-fixated sentiment as the binding batter of social relations in Japan wherein the child's primal sense of unity with the mother (*ittaikan*) is reproduced interpersonally as a social striving for *jita-gōitsu* (unity of self and other), constitutes a bungled attempt to reclaim the lost ground of that infantile phase of primary socialisation by analysing the repressive socialisation which follows and reverses it, as in fact its natural outgrowth or consequence. The denial of both the ego and the reality principle are thus evasive disrecognitions of the patriarchal structure of the uncompromising social world external to the individual.

Properly speaking, this radical penetration of social authority in which self-synchronisation subverts the initial maternal presence as confirming agent in the child's narcissism, leads to the diffuse sedimentation of the other in the self. The initial hostile penetration of society causes the ego to sublimate that indulged sense of uniqueness nurtured in the mother–child relationship and reconstitute it by an identification of the self with the group. The fact that it is the mother again who oversees this behavioural backflip makes her tacit presence felt ambivalently throughout the double-bind realities of adult life. One is taught to 'pretend oneself away from one's original self' in a way that the more one is conditioned to hide the self within society, the more the self becomes hidden from oneself, so that every discreet return to that residually latent sense of personal identity carries with it the newly assumed, covert baggage of an inexpungible 'group identity'.[78]

It is here then that we discern an effective basis for the perennial, enthusiastic boom of interest in the *nihonjinron* discussions of Japanese uniqueness, in which the tabooed sense of individuality finds its narcissistic expression only through the socially sanctioned idiom of an evoked racial, disindividualised national uniqueness as defined against the monolithic 'otherness' of the alien, of China or the West. And it is here that we may understand how this 'West' is unconsciously constructed, being a penetrative element of foreign, disauthenticating culture, to bear the resentments engendered by the narcissist against that arduous secondary socialisation which his own post-feudal world stamps upon him. It is this which underlies the dialectic of antagonism between a primordially intact 'Japan' and a relentlessly maturing 'West' (patriarchalism, meat diet, rationalism, abstraction, alienation and violence) in the *nihonjinron*'s paradigm of fictive cultural contrasts.

Doi's work provides us with an exemplary number of inadvertently revealing slips and misunderstandings to confirm such a reading, and in this he has tacitly or unconsciously rendered us a signal service. But in its own terms his work is an outstanding instance of that conceptual misappropriation which I have elsewhere called the *gekokujō* principle. For his technique of linguistic erasure, of reconstituting Japanese words over the palimpsest of Western psychoanalysis effectively expropriates a system of foreign thought to service the self-esteem of Japanese nationalism. If by his method of semantic substitutions the key concepts of psychoanalysis can be improved upon and finessed in a Japanese idiom, uniquely, then it follows that what we have hitherto taken to be the singular creation of a nineteenth century Viennese genius turns out to be merely the abstract, reified expression of what has always been, unknown to the rest of the world, the archaic collective patrimony of the commonsense of the Japanese race.[79] *In occidente tenebrae, ex oriente lux.*

Notes

1. C. Lasch, *The Culture of Narcissism*, pp.33-4. *Cf* 'The discoveries of psychoanalysis are diametrically opposed to the nationalistic ideology and threaten its existence', Wilhelm Reich, *Reich Speaks of Freud*, M. Higgens and C.M. Raphael (eds.) (Pelican, London, 1975) p.139.

2. If we are to believe Nakamura when he remarks that the misinterpretation of Chinese sources and originals is 'one of the most significant phenomena in the history of Japanese thought' (*Ways of Thinking*, p.348) then the fate of psychoanalysis in Japan is merely a recent instance of a very long tradition.

3. J.M. Moloney, *Understanding the Japanese Mind*, (C. Tuttle reprint, Rutland Vermont and Tokyo, 1975) pp.129-30.

4. C. Rycroft, *A Critical Dictionary of Psychoanalysis* (Penguin ed. 1977) pp.xxf. *cf* S. Freud, *New Introductory Lectures on Psychoanalysis*, trans. J. Strachey (Pelican ed. 1973) p.101. Moloney, ibid., p.135.

5. Okonogi Keigo, *Gendai seishin bunseki*, I (Seishin Shobō, Tokyo, 1974) pp.117.

6. I follow the account in Okonogi, *Gendai seishin bunseki*, ibid., pp.127ff., and *Moratoriamu ningen no jidai*, ibid., pp.193-258. A version of Okonogi's presentation may be found in *Japan Echo*, 5:4 (1978) pp.88-105 and 6:1 (1979) pp.104-118. See also Moloney, *Understanding the Japanese Mind*, pp.53ff.

7. Okonogi, *Moratoriamu ningen*, p.206.
8. M. Klein, *The Psychoanalysis of Children*, rev. ed. (Delta Books, 1976) p.5, n.1; p.171, n.2.
9. cf E.J. Thomas, *Life of the Buddha*, 2nd ed. (Routledge and Kegan Paul, London, 1949) p.138.
10. Moloney, *Understanding the Japanese Mind*, ibid., p.165.
11. Okonogi, *Gendai seishin bunseki*, ibid., pp.144.
12. Murphy, *The Dialectics of Social Life*, ibid., p.123.
13. Okonogi, *Gendai seishin bunseki*, p.121.
14. *Fimika/Pimika? See Ledyard, 'Galloping Along with the Horseriders', ibid., p.222 and note 13.
15. Moloney, *Understanding the Japanese Mind*, pp.126-218, esp. pp.135ff, 153ff.
16. Moloney, *Understanding the Japanese Mind*, ibid., p.201. Iwakura Tomohide apparently played a key role in assimilating psychoanalysis to the Imperial ideology (pp.170-1).
17. Moloney, *Understanding the Japanese Mind*, ibid., p.151.
18. Okonogi, *Moratoriamu ningen*, ibid., p.220.
19. Moloney, *Understanding the Japanese Mind*, ibid., p.211. Miyamoto Tadao, 'The Japanese and Psychoanalysis', in *The Japanese Interpreter*, 8:3 (autumn, 1973) pp.387-89, p.387 notes that of the 4,400-odd psychiatrists in Japan less than 40 had any use for psychoanalysis and less than a dozen were registered with the International Psychoanalytic Movement of London. Psychiatric treatment in Japan is basically organic.
20. Doi Takeo, *'Amae' no kōzō*, p.6. The book is translated by John Bester as *The Anatomy of Dependence* (Kodansha International, Tokyo, 1973).
21. Doi Takeo, *Seishin bunseki* (Sōgen Igaku Shinsho, Ōsaka 1977) pp.180-1.
22. See Okonogi, *Gendai seishin bunseki*, ibid., p.149; Kimura Bin, *Hito to hito to no aida*, pp.148ff. Kawashima in *'Amae' to shakai kagaku*, pp.27ff. Doi's etymological linking (*'Amae' no kōzō*, pp.78-80) of *amae* via *amai, umai* (sweet, tasty) to the *ama* (heaven) of the ancestral goddess's name Amaterasu Ōmikami is pure fantasy. On the origins and Altaic etymology of the word see Murayama Shichirō, *Nihongo no gogen*, (Kōbundō, Tokyo, 1974), pp.112-14.
23. Doi, *'Amae' no kōzō*, ibid., p.13.
24. Doi, *'Amae' no kōzō*, ibid., p.14. The concept is actually Ferenczi's. See M. Balint, *Primary Love and Psychoanalytic Technique* (Tavistock, London, 1965). For a review of theoretical developments on the mother–child bond see J. Bowlby, *Attachment and Loss: I, Attachment*, (Penguin Harmondsworth, 1978 reprint) pp.424-43.
25. Doi, *'Amae' no kōzō*, p.14; Balint, *Primary Love*, ibid., p.56.
26. Balint, *Primary Love*, ibid. pp.74ff, 85. Bowlby, *Attachment*, ibid. pp.435-6. This explains Doi's otherwise strange remark that Westerners, lacking a word for *amaeru*, describe it by an 'objective word' like 'to cling to' (*sugaritsuku*). cf Doi, *Seishin Bunseki*, ibid., p.181.
27. Alice Balint, 'Love for the Mother and Mother Love', in M. Balint, *Primary Love*, ibid., pp.91-108, at p.108.
28. S. Freud, *Introductory Lectures on Psychoanalysis*, trans. J. Strachey (Pelican ed., 1973) pp.491ff, p.496.
29. Rycroft, *A Critical Dictionary*, ibid., pp.xxf. On 'thick-skinned' (*donkan*) Americans see Doi, *'Amae' no kōzō*, ibid., p.16.
30. Cited in Okonogi, *Gendai seishin bunseki*, ibid., p.153.
31. W. Caudill, T. Doi, 'Psychiatry and Culture in Japan' in Henry P. David, (ed.) *International Trends in Mental Health*, (McGraw Hill, New York, 1966) pp.129-46, 133-4.

32. R.D. Laing, *Self and Others* (Pelican ed. 1971) pp.108ff; E. Fromm, *The Crisis in Psychoanalysis*, (Pelican ed. 1978) pp.11-12.

33. Doi, *'Amae' no kōzō*, ibid., p.119.

34. Lebra, *Japanese Patterns of Behaviour*, ibid., p.54. Doi admits as much in his technical treatise *Seishin bunseki*, ibid., p.16.

35. S. Freud, *Case Histories I. 'Dora' and 'Little Hans'*, trans. Alix and James Strachey (Penguin ed. 1979) p.189. The German text runs, 'Wie ich geschlafen hab', hab' ich gedacht, du bist fort und ich hab' keine Mammi zum schmeicheln.' S. Freud, *Gesammelte Werke*, Bd. 7 (Imago reprint, London, 1955) p.257. See also J. Bowlby, *Attachment and Loss: 2, Separation* (Penguin ed. 1978) p.327.

36. Doi, *Seishin bunseki*, ibid. p.181, 198. *cf* Doi, *'Amae' zakkō*, (Kōbundō, Tokyo, 1975) p.123 likewise speaks of *dada o koneru* (to fret) as a 'variation of *amae*'. The exposition of these variations on the theme of *amae* I give here follows Doi, *'Amae' no kōzō*, ibid., pp.24ff.

37. D. Price-Williams, 'Culture and Passive Love' in *Contemporary Psychology*, 19:6 (June 1974) pp.445-6.

38. Doi, *'Amae' no kōzō*, ibid. p.116.

39. Doi, *'Amae' no kōzō*, ibid., p.123.

40. R. Spitz, *The First Year of Life*, (International Universities Press, New York, 1965) pp.150ff.

41. Spitz, *The First Year*, ibid., p.155. Doi, *'Amae' no kōzō*, ibid., p.124. Doi performs the same operation on the concept of ambivalence (which he mistakenly attributes to Freud, who in fact got it from Bleuler). Fashionable among Western intellectuals, ambivalence was, according to Doi, already known to the Japanese in antiquity in terms of the *honne tatemae* contrast'. See Doi, *'Amae' zakkō*, ibid., pp.67-9, 182-3.

42. *Anna Karenina*, Part 8, 18.

43. Doi, *'Amae' no kōzō*, ibid., p.115.

44. Doi, *Seishin bunseki*, ibid., p.194 records that his patients are upset if they are told they are 'mentally sick' (*ki no yamai*), but not too worried if told they have a neurosis (*shinkeishō*), since the latter term suggests the possibility that the malady is scientifically curable.

45. Doi, *'Amae' no kōzō*, ibid. pp.128ff, and Bester's translation, *The Anatomy of Dependence*, pp.109ff.

46. In the compound form *kyōhaku-shinkeishō*, it is the standard technical term in Japanese psychiatry for 'obsessional neurosis'.

47. Doi, *'Amae' no kōzō*, ibid. pp.128-9. Compare Rycroft on 'compulsive'; 'referring to the *conscious* thoughts and actions which the subject feels compelled to think or carry out and which he cannot prevent (or, at least, the omission of which leads to *anxiety*)'. *A Critical Dictionary*, ibid., p.20.

48. Doi, *'Amae' no kōzō*, ibid., pp.153ff. *The Anatomy of Dependence*, ibid., pp.127ff.

49. Maruyama Masao, *Nihon no shisō*, (Iwanami Shinsho, Tokyo, 1961) pp.127ff.

50. Doi, *'Amae' no kōzō*, ibid., p.153. He concludes, typically, that, 'Thus, in languages other than Japanese one cannot observe such a convenient and nuanced mode of expression for manifesting the psychology of being harmed (*higai*)' p.154. Writers like Araki Hiroyuki, *Nihonjin no shinjō ronri*, ibid. pp.172-5, esp. p.173 now assert that *higaisha-ishiki*, though a Sino-Japanese calque on Western words, is unique to Japanese and untranslatable into Western languages!

51. G. Steiner, *After Babel*, ibid., p.58. Pierre Coste, Locke's French translator, made a similar boast in arguing that the French version restored 'lucidity' to Locke's obscure original. See P. Hazard, *The European Mind*, (Penguin, Harmondsworth, 1964) pp.94-5.

52. Doi, *'Amae' no kōzō*, ibid., p.157.
53. Compare the similar value judgement made by Aida Yūji, *Nihonjin no Wasuremono*, ibid., p.172, on Japanese alienation (*sogai*) as diametrically opposed to Western alienation. In contrast see T. Adorno, *Minima Moralia*, ibid., p.163; E. Fromm, *The Anatomy of Human Destructiveness*, ibid., p.473.
54. Doi, *'Amae' no kōzō*, ibid., pp.157-8.
55. Doi Takeo, 'Folie, dépendance et maladie' in *La folie dans la psychanalyse*, ed. Armando Verdiglione (Payot, Paris, 1977) pp.78-82, p.82.
56. Doi, *'Amae' no kōzō*, ibid., pp.173ff, *'Amae' zakkō*, ibid., pp.102ff.
57. Doi, *'Amae' no kōzō*, pp.187ff. The term is that of Paul Federn. Kitagawa Masakuni, *Nihonjin no shinwateki shikō* (Kōdansha Gendai Shinsho, 1979) pp.171ff, rightly argues against Doi that the postwar system, while it has weakened the father's authority within the home, has strengthened patriarchal authority by integrating the father within the family corporation. However, his attempt to develop a non-oedipal, Japanese Susanowo complex, although formally more sophisticated than Doi's work, (*cf* pp.130ff) tends to amount to the same thing.
58. Doi, *'Amae' no kōzō*, ibid., p.60.
59. Doi, *'Amae' no kōzō*, ibid., p.61. The case cited is not unlike that of the hero of Frederik Rolfe's *Hadrian the Seventh*, a novelistic depiction of the author's fantasy of being elevated to the papacy. No one, however, would cite such slender evidence, as provided by this 'misanthropic altruist', as proof that all Westerners have a 'pope-complex'.
60. Doi, *'Amae' no kōzō*, ibid., p.62.
61. Maruyama Masao, *Thought and Behaviour*, ibid., p.18.
62. Doi, *'Amae' no kōzō*, ibid., pp.64-5.
63. Both Kawashima and Ōtsuka rightly argue against Doi (*'Amae' to shakai kagaku*, ibid., pp.111ff, 177ff, 190ff) that expression of what Doi takes, as *amae*, to be the lynchpin of traditional society was strictly forbidden in samurai families.
64. Doi, *'Amae' no kōzō*, ibid., p.126.
65. Doi, *'Amae' no kōzō*, ibid., p.23.
66. Doi, *'Amae' no kōzō*, ibid., p.141. Interestingly, Doi here considers that this *coaxing* sentiment, underpinning all social relationships in Japanese society, to be homosexual in its nature.
67. Doi, *'Amae' no kōzō*, ibid., p. 113.
68. Rycroft, *A Critical Dictionary*, ibid., p. 121; E. Fromm, *The Crisis in Psychoanalysis*, ibid., pp. 28ff.
69. Note that while his inability to find a *yamato kotoba* for 'reality principle' leads Doi to deny the existence of the same in Japan, the converse is not true. That is, though he says no word exists for *amae* in Western languages (of which he knows roughly two), this allows him to conclude that coaxing must be deeply repressed from Western consciousness (*cf* Doi, *'Amae' zakkō*, ibid., p. 19). The contradiction in logic stems from his ambition to reformulate psychoanalysis in Japanese, and then re-export it back Westwards as something new.
70. Tellingly, Miyamoto in his article 'The Japanese and Psychoanalysis', ibid., p. 388, argues that the Japanese *id* is not clearly demarcated from the ego, since *amae* (understood this time as instinctual gratification) while repressed in the West is expressed in Japan. Where the *id* was identified with *ninjō* in prewar Japan, now it is conflated with *amae*. It must be emphasised that the *id* according to Freud's formulation can be described mainly as 'a contrast to the ego', *cf* S. Freud, *New Introductory Lectures*, ibid., p. 105.
71. S. Freud, *Introductory Lectures*, ibid., pp. 401-3.
72. E. Fromm, *The Crisis of Psychoanalysis*, ibid., pp. 28-9. S. Freud, *New Introductory Lectures*, ibid., p. 108 writes that the ego '(takes) on the task of representing the external world to the *id* — fortunately for the *id*, which would not

escape destruction if, in its blind efforts for the satisfaction of its instincts, it disregarded that supreme external power.'

73. Mori Jōji, *Nihonjin* = *'kara-nashi tamago' no jigazō*, ibid., pp. 27ff.
74. Nakane, in Egami Namio et al. *Nihonjin to wa nani ka: Minzoku no kigen o motomete* (Shōgakukan, Tokyo, 1980) p. 266.
75. Doi, *'Amae' no kōzō*, ibid., p. 163.
76. R.T. Pasquale, A.G. Athos, *The Art of Japanese Management*, (Penguin, 1982) p. 121.
77. Doi, *'Amae' no kōzō*, ibid., p. 163.
78. R.D. Laing, *Self and Other*, ibid., p. 45.
79. Doi's outlook is neatly summed up by Goethe's couplet:
'Mein Kind, ich hab' es klug gemacht:
Ich habe nie über das Denken gedacht.' (*Zahme Xenian*)

9 THE COMPLEX OF JAPANESE PSYCHOANALYSIS

'No one whose language is Japanese needs to be psychoanalysed.'
J. Lacan, cited Miyamoto, *The Japanese and Psychoanalysis* p.389.

'When one examines Japanese interpersonal relationships, what in the West are described as highly pathological features, appear, frankly, among the elements of everyday Japanese relationships.'
Okonogi Keigo, in 'Nihonjin no kokoro to kotoba' with Suzuki Takao, Kitayama Osamu, *Eureka*: 2 (1981) pp.104-32, p.120.

The publication of Doi's work witnessed an enormous critical and popular success not only within Japan, but also within Western Japanology. The blurb to the English edition cites Ezra Vogel's view that Doi offers 'profound insights' and Robert Lifton's appraisal of its 'penetrating' thought. William P. Lebra is also mentioned on the jacket as considering *The Anatomy of Dependence* as 'a major contribution to the science of human behaviour in general'. For Robert Shaplen, Doi is a 'brilliant clinical psychiatrist' whose book is considered 'throughout the world as one of the best analyses of the Japanese character'.[1] Doi himself is on record as saying that it was foreigners rather than his own fellow countrymen who first showed an encouraging interest in his ideas.[2]

Amae thus entered into the mainstream of Japanese studies. Frank Gibney deploys it to 'explain' how subordinates controlled their superiors in the putsches and rebellions of the thirties, and why they were docile once captured, and concludes that:

> At least in an emotional sense, Japan's society has realised quite naturally the Marxist slogan so vainly preached to the Russians and other assorted peoples. From each according to his abilities, to each according to his *amae* needs.[3]

If you produce, you may presume upon your superior's indulgence! Charlotte Carr-Gregg finds the desire to coax of 'great explanatory value' for understanding the revolt of the Japanese prisoners in Cowra in Australia. They rebelled not so much to preserve their good name by an honourable death, but rather because of their need to be loved (*cf amae*) by their leaders.[4] Gibney uses *amae* to explain why Japanese were model prisoners, while Carr-Gregg employs it to establish why they revolted in captivity. For Gregory Clark this is not inconsistent. *Amae*, he tells us, holds the clue as to why, puzzlingly, such an outwardly submissive people can manifest violent behaviour marked by such defiant emotionalism.[5]

Japanese politics and law are now wholly explained down to the minutest detail in terms of coaxing by Douglas Mitchell,[6] while Robert Marsh apparently interpreted the breakdown in the sugar-trade talks as due to the failure of Australian negotiators to understand this ineffable sentiment of coaxing, *amae*. CSR, in keeping the Japanese strictly to the letter of their legal contract (*cf* 13), 'rode roughshod over the Japanese cultural norm known as *amae*'.[7] Thus non-theory becomes social norm, incoherent hypothesis the reality it fails to explain. Indeed, so potent is the explanatory power of the concept that it is used to explain the relationship between Japanese spirits and mediums in possession cults.[8] Third World psychiatrists have been quick to seize on Doi's theory of collusion in the analytical relationship. The argument of Wen Shing Tseng is that in countries where the people are accustomed to depend upon (*amaeru*) autocratic authority, it is best, in the patients' own interests, for the analyst to present himself as a 'very confident, powerful, authoritative figure'.[9]

That *amae* is useful in tactically discrediting Western-style analyses of structures of power and authority in Japan is evident from Fr Maurice Bairy's proposal that the feudal heritage of loyalty, hierarchy and discipline 'necessitates' the psychology of dependence adumbrated by 'the great Japanese psychiatrist Takeo Doi'. We are warned against making eurocentric value-judgements about this 'great organism of interdependency', for Japan is not a class society but an 'organism', a 'totality' wherein each man is linked 'biologically' to the source of life which is his country of Japan.[10] *Amae* thus serves to read and valorise Japan in terms that, if not totalitarian, certainly ring with the latent resonances of the political theory of the Catholic Middle Ages. An advantage of using Japanese idioms is that they permit one to revalorise one's own transcended, feudal past under the foreign conceptual alias of an 'alternative' contemporary culture.

Doi in the meantime has published a number of smaller works which attempt to sketch out a more general theory, but these are of a very tentative kind, perhaps because it is difficult to apply universally an idea consciously developed to account for 'uniqueness'. But the wish to do so remains, as when he writes that:

> Japanese patterns of thought have the advantage of using the surpassing concept of coaxing (*amae*) as a common denominator for critically dissecting all kinds of human relationship ... By borrowing Japanese patterns of thought one can deepen psychoanalytic insight into the essential character of man.[11]

Since for Doi *amae* is one of the most universal of needs, he expresses his intention to use the theory of coaxing to open up new paths in the understanding of human psychology, and yet nothing of the kind has been forthcoming other than elusive hints at an eventual grand theory. For example, he has suggested obliquely that children's games may provide us with a hypothetical model to elucidate all psychotherapy, and he finds, as a starting point, the Japanese game of *inai-inai bah* to be the earliest prototype of the universal game of peek-a-boo.[12] In this game, the mother covers her face saying 'not here!', and then, reappearing, shouts 'Boo!' The assertion that this is both distinctive and somehow more fundamental than similar nursery games in the West is in keeping with Doi's oneupmanship, though there, as in the West, peek-a-boo starts from five to seven months after the child's birth.[13] The importance of this game for theory lies in the way it clues us in to the beginning of object relations in the child.

Doi's ostensible point of departure is Freud's famous discussion, in *Beyond the Pleasure Principle*, of a child playing with an object to make it disappear, cooing *fort* (away) then pulling it into view and exclaiming *da!* (here). For Doi, this provides us with a metaphor of a principle of 'hide and seek' underlying the psychotherapeutical relationship itself, the patient being induced to bring to light the hidden shapes of his covert neurotic complex. The presumption that this Japanese game thus gives us an essential clue for a unified general theory of psychoanalysis, Oriental and occidental, which is 'deceptively simple', shows that Doi is still playing his game of upstaging his authorities by tacitly counterfeiting his sources, in this case the ideas of Jacques Lacan, whose *Discours de Rome* gave great prominence to the *fort-da* case.

For Lacan, in this game the child as absolute subject discovers for himself the existence of independent objects by contriving their absence. The ensuing disappearance of the object stimulates the desire for a reunified identity with the object, and in this toying way, infantile narcissism actively transcends its subjectivity by a recognition of difference.[14] Doi, in drawing on the cottonreel incident ignores the point made here about object-relations (the game being a symbolic means of mastering the anxiety caused by the mother's successive appearance and disappearance),[15] whose analysis was central to the innovative work of the fifties on the genesis of anxiety (Spitz), the function of transitional objects and the 'false self' (Winnicott) and infantile epistemology (Lacan). He merely uses these ideas, superficially, to rescore his by now worn point that simple Japanese mothers from time immemorial have understood what Western scientists are only now discovering. The golden ideas mined deep in the conceptual ore-bodies of occidental thought are all visible alluvium in Japan.

The grand theory cannot be constructed precisely because, as we may readily appreciate from the absence in his work of any notion of a reality principle, Doi's basic hypothesis excludes any awareness or consideration of the indispensable centrality for psychoanalytic thought of a coherent theory of object relations. Despite an enormous initial impact upon the conceptualisations of the *nihonjinron*, precisely because Doi seemed to provide for the first time an independently original Japanese analytical method, his work, now absorbed, is considered to require further modification, and is challenged as being defective for its excessive leaning towards occidental value-judgements.

This critique is disconcerting, indeed, bewildering because our reading of his work cannot but impress us with the thoroughness with which his approach is permeated by the frail assumptions of the Japanese tradition of intellectual nationalism. Yet Okonogi, another pupil of Kosawa, writes that:

> The fact that Doi Takeo's book *'Amae' no kōzō*, which severely criticised the coaxing for an indulged dependency (*amae*) of the Japanese from the perspective of Western individualism, became a bestseller in Japan speaks volumes for the masochistic

anguish afflicting the contemporary Japanese over their separation from their mothers.[16]

Among Kosawa's epigones, it would appear, Doi baulked at his teacher's advocacy that the analyst should respond maternally to his patient, and instead suggested that the Japanese remain fixed in a state of dangerous infantility throughout their adult life. In fact, Doi is ambivalent about this *amae*; internally, within Japan, it has proved to be very effective, he maintains, but in Japan's intercourse with the outside world it will not do to behave in a presumptuously dependent manner. He clarifies his expression that the Japanese 'must overcome their need to presume on relationships of indulgence' (*amae o kokufuku suru*)[17] by stressing that such coaxing is not so much to be overcome as much as brought into awareness as a determining element in Japanese behaviour.

Those who follow after Doi want to rid this otherwise very nationalistic thesis of what they hold to be residual elements of Western value-judgements by rendering psychoanalytic theory in Japan completely free of foreign traces. Indifferent to the occasional critique of Doi's work as completely lacking in methodological coherence,[18] they build upon it in various attempts to claim, each for himself, the mantle of fathering a truly endogenous psychoanalysis. Okonogi, who wishes to revive and develop Kosawa's original line, takes issue with Doi's apparent 'individualism' and occidental 'rationalism'. But he does not wish to throw the baby out with the bathwater. Rather, he adapts the *amae* theory by arguing that there are two types of coaxing, a healthy type which underlies all interpersonal relations in Japan, and a pathological type which arises from the inhibition of the drive for *dependence*.

> That is to say, the *amae* used by Doi as a concept of psychoanalytical pathology is not the same *amae* which the Japanese in general understand by that word. It is rather the *amae* of neurotic attachment which arises as a consequence of the failure of these dependency desires (that accompany the separation of mother and child) to receive egotisation as healthy *amae* in relationships of basic trust.[19]

This adds another complication, for the word 'basic trust' indicates that Okonogi is moulding together Kosawa and Doi's ideas with the glue of a concept derived from Erik Erikson.[20] Besides the fact that *amae* can hardly be egotised if the traditional view denies the idea of ego to the Japanese, Okonogi's criticism is supererogatory. Had he read his colleague's book more closely he would have found that Doi himself makes precisely this distinction between healthy and pathological *amae*.[21]

Even more confusing is the use to which Kimura Bin puts Doi's ideas, since he tries to adjust them to the bewilderingly eclectic amalgam of chauvinism, phenomenology, Buddhism and Watsuji's 'contextualist' theory of social climate that constitutes his own erratic work. Kimura praises Doi's ideas as a 'contribution of epochal importance' for its encouragement of native psychoanalysts to think things through in Japanese,[22] but challenges Doi's misleading use of the word *amae*, which he doubts can be made to refer to an idea of passive love. *Amaeru*, he reminds us, means getting one's own way by playing on the affection of others. But having thus half-torpedoed the linguistic raft on which the shaky conceptual shipwreck of *amae* rests, he then attempts a salvage operation.

Kimura distinguishes a difference between Kantō and Kansai with respect to *amae*. In his native Kansai dialect, he tells us, there is a specific character type referred to by the form *amaeta*, denoting someone adept in finding people with whom he can indulge himself. Reserved with many people, such a person excels in selecting specific friends to presume on and spoil. In Kantō, on the other hand (where Doi hails from), Kimura argues that the dominant type is the *amaembō*, the spoilt brat who unilaterally seeks a dependent relationship with all and sundry.[23] From being a national trait, *amae* now bifurcates and loses itself in the provinces. Kimura's point is little more than a regionalisation of that habit of point-scoring which Doi himself deploys against the West.

Hamaguchi Eshun takes all of this one step further, in a work which constitutes a sort of *summa ideologica* of uniqueness theories in the so-called sciences of behaviour in Japan. He attempts to reconcile Doi's theory with Kimura's critique in arguing that where for the former, coaxing is a 'functional prerequisite' for the establishment of interpersonal relationships, for the latter *amae* is an 'intrinsic attribute' of already established interpersonal relationships.[24] Explaining the difference in emphasis in terms of the respective regional origins of these two writers, he maintains that:

> To sum up, by *amaembō* is meant nothing more or less than a person who shows directly how the Japanese set up relationships by means of those mutual desires of dependence and expectation which we call coaxing (*amae*). By *amaeta*, we mean people who show a thorough familiarity from experience with the basic attribute inherent in relationships of human sympathy (*ninjō*) so characteristic of the Japanese. Together, both could be said to be exemplary embodiments of that coaxing (*amae*) which is the distinctive hallmark of the Japanese.[25]

The two views are thus made out to be complementary, in that Doi's interpretation stresses a state of high passive dependency deriving from the difficulties in ego formation during the oral stage, while Kimura's analysis is directed at mature dependence, in which both seeking indulgence (*amaeru*) and spoiling (*amayakasu*) are integrated into the mature adult ego.

Thus successfully conflating these two non-theories, Hamaguchi then adds to the pile by inducting into the discussion the 'Sino–centric' concept of psycho-social homeostasis. That is, he tries eclectically to subordinate these twin aspects of *amae* theory into Francis Hsu's model of homeostasis, which he himself modifies in turn by setting these melded models into the context of his own version of Watsuji's fascist theory of Japanese personality. The result is that:

> It is surely better to analyse 'coaxing' (*amae*) phenomena as the expressive configurations (*hatsugen keitai*) of a Japanese kind of psychosocial homeostasis, rather than to describe them in terms of an unique word *amae* which is not to be found in any other language than Japanese.[26]

I have all too briefly summarised these veerings, readjustments and theoretical mergers in order to illustrate the enormous difficulties facing the outsider in studying such Japanese texts. They adapt, embroider, redevelop and conflate ideas that, in the first place, have no status whatsoever as viable concepts because they arise from a profound incomprehension of original sources, and a disturbing absence of critical consciousness in the ideological mainstream. Here Doi's erroneously constructed theory of 'coaxing', which arose out of his critique of Kosawa's abortive theory of Oriental guilt and the matricidal complex (wherein, however, each radically misunderstands Freud), has in turn been reabsorbed back into Kosawa's position, as modified by Okonogi (under the influence of Klein and Erikson), then subject to a pseudo-phenomenological critique by a scholar influenced by Dōgen's Buddhism and Watsuji's fascism, namely Kimura. This conceptual farrago is then reharmonised once again by Hamaguchi by means of Francis Hsu's notion of psycho-social homeostasis, originally developed for Chinese character, and then once again conflated with Watsuji Tetsurō's theory of *aidagara* (relationship) which, as I shall presently demonstrate, was itself a neo-Confucian attempt to exploit Heideggerian notions for the construction of a peculiarly Japanese kind of Fascist state ethics.

The end product of these successive accretions of assumption-ridden, highly nationalistic pseudo-theories — embedded as they are throughout with the covert protocols of Japanese cultural uniqueness — appears dressed out in the innocuous jargon of 'a Japanese form of psycho-social homeostasis'. The deeply filiated themes of an insistent national uniqueness thus survive under the happy incognito of the updated jargon of the modern social sciences. We amply see here the theoretical consequences of the failure to reflect and act upon Moloney's conclusion about Kosawa's group, namely that 'Japanese analysts have not been sufficiently analysed or sufficiently trained to practice psychoanalysis themselves.'[27]

But if this continual uncritical modification of uncritical ideas leads to the garbling of thought and its idiom, persistent unravelling of the tangled clews, and constant attention to the sociological realities being consistently mythified by such aggregated fictions may help us turn up surprising, indirect testimony about unresolved tensions in crucial areas of Japanese social life even amid the deranged traditions of its interpretation. Since *amae* exercises a profound appeal within Japan as a theory, it is only natural to probe further to discover what lies behind it. The remarks which follow are tentative fathomings in the direction of such opportunity.

We have earlier touched in passing upon the notion that economic structures of a 'paternalistic' kind deprive the family of the father, which in turn increases the affective intensity of interaction between mother and son, while drastically lowering it between father and son, husband and wife. In this, at least at certain executive levels, Japanese life has preserved a situation frequently encountered in preindustrial societies. Thus it comes as no surprise, when one reads Lannoy on India or Muensterberger on the southern Chinese, to encounter descriptions uncannily like those of Doi on the Japanese. Thus Lannoy notes of Indian life that:

> Prolonged *unilateral dependence* from infancy up to the age of three or more, and the inculcation of *passivity*, docility, obedience and respect, especially when reinforced by excessive (though irregular) *indulgence*, all tend to encourage a son's very deep attachment to his mother. [my italics][28]

This indulgence is linked to aggressive feelings towards the mother, breeding a sense of both omnipotence and *dependence*. Lannoy mentions this in connection with the frightening 'terrible mother' of the *Kāli* myth, but it makes us recall Kosawa's decisive fascination with the Ajātasattu narrative, which betrays the same complex. It is in this context that we should read the recent epidemic of rumours among schoolchildren in Japan about being waylaid by the 'torn-mouth woman' (*kuchisake onna*). These pseudo-theories in Japan seem to hint at an underlying complex of this kind which, as Lannoy notes, tends to develop into a flight from the ambivalent image of the dominating mother towards associations marked by 'depersonalised group solidarity'.[29]

Here we must bear in mind that what is intended in what follows is not a psychoanalysis of the Japanese as a nation; that is an impossibility, and would be an approach bankrupted from the start. What I am trying to focus upon are possible psychological realities underlying the creation, and then ideological appeal, of central images in the *nihonjinron* mainstream by and for the intellectual élite and those who passionately consume their products.

We do well to return to Kuki's discussion of *iki*, which directly influenced Doi's analysis and conceptual orientation.[30] For Kuki, *iki*/chic was a lifestyle modulated or mediated by two formerly opposed values, *shibumi* (elegant restraint) and *amami* (sweetness). *Shibumi* represented a 'negative externality', that is, a cautious reserve against involvement in deep emotional engagements with people, while *amami* was interpreted as denoting a 'positive externality', a pliant desire to identify oneself with others. *Iki* plays ambivalently between these two poles, a technique of seduction whose function is 'to reduce as far as possible the distance (between seducer and woman) without reducing the difference to naught'.[31] Now Kuki argued that in the modality of *amami* (which he rejects), 'A positive route is opened up between the person who presumes (*amaeru mono*) and the person who is presumed upon (*amaerareru mono*).'[32]

We may now appreciate how not only Doi's linguistic technique, but also his notion of *amae* draw off Kuki's work. The difference lies in the way he tilts Kuki's emphasis from the *shibumi* side of *iki* to the aspect of *amami*, in his shifting of the locus of study of Japanese uniqueness from the outlook of the brothel exquisite to that of the patient on the analyst's couch.

Doi informs us that while abroad he felt great difficulty in establishing emotional relationships with his American hosts, and that the reading of Osaragi Jirō's novel *Kikyō* (Homecoming), which recounts the vagaries of a Japanese exile's relationship with his abandoned homeland, chimed in with his own feelings at the time.[33] Now in this novel, it happens that the word *amaeru* is strategically exploited to distinguish the Japanese from the Western lifestyle and outlook. The hero, Moriya Kyōgo, exiled from Japan for a scandal for which he took the blame, renounces his motherland and immerses himself in the 'European' way of life and thought. In fact the Europeanised Moriya is merely the Japanese caricature of the Westerner as reiterated in the *nihonjinron*, namely, one who, in order to preserve his inner autonomy and individuality, egotistically repels emotional bonds, spurning family ties and surviving by a kind of 'contractual' existence with society on the strength of his aggressively cultivated wits.

The narrative relates how Moriya, on returning to Japan after the war, rubs up against the by now alien grain of that world of human sympathy (*ninjō*) he forsook, and momentarily reawakens to that complex web of allegiances, duties and dependence from which he had previously worked to extricate himself. *Amaeru* is used as the verbal signal to underline this, and its negative use is deployed to explain Moriya's 'Westernised' resistance to Japanese life. When asked if he has looked up his wife, he snaps back, 'I can cosy up to nature's scenery, but I don't intend to coax up to people' (keshiki ni wa *amaeru* ga, ningen ni *amaeyō* to omowanu).[34] Indeed, Moriya's dislike of fawning, coaxing and presuming on others[35] is strikingly like Doi's description of his reaction to his patient's flattery (*amae*) in 1953, and thus is traditional rather than Western. Thus Doi's work uses Kuki's technique and *amami* clue in order to give Osaragi's theme a psychoanalytic form, grounding in terms of national characteristics certain difficulties he experienced as a clinical analyst and as a resident abroad in a foreign society.

Now Benedict had already remarked upon the relative difficulty of this generation of Japanese when, on study leave in the United States, they sought to adapt themselves to American life. But with her usual acuity, she puts a different construction on it by treating it as a conflict or tension arising between the formal code governing relationships in Japan, and the informality of American society. That is, 'The specific Japanese problem, as they see it, is that they have been brought up to trust in a security which depends on others' recognition of the nuances of their observances of a code.'[36]

This coincides with the Bernstein–Barnlund material adduced earlier, and we can see that in an informal society, great insecurity is engendered among people reared exactingly by a different code which militates against familiarity. Doi's *amae* theory in this sense rationalises an inability to experience in foreign company that relaxed sense of place which in Japan exists only among intimates, or strangers who vigilantly observe the rules of social interaction. Just as the *kotodama* myth, on which the idea of symbiotic empathy is partially founded, is shown by Miller to have arisen from a self-defensive reaction to the failure of Japanese ambassadors in China to make themselves understood, so *amae* appears to have exercised an intellectual appeal in Japan in order to rationalise similar difficulties in Japan's contemporary intercourse with the outside world.

If Kuki's concept of *iki* and Doi's theory of *amae*, the flirting of the nonchalant seducer and the desire for motherly indulgence, are diametrically opposed in the logic of their emotional structures, they share nonetheless more in common than a mere relationship of conceptual affiliation in the rhetorical tradition of Japanese self-definitions. Conjoined, they strongly suggest those twin pathological types which emerge, under analysis, from the split in object choice. In this light, it may well not be mere accident that it is precisely in regard to the analysis of object relations that Doi's theory displays its most obvious failings and oversights.

In an interesting note, Saul remarked that the split in sexual object choice could be related to the incest barrier, and that clinical work might clarify the crucial role of dependence on the mother in the etiology of this crisis.[37] Freud had already noted that mother-fixation had inhibited the fusion of the erotic and the tender emotions in children, so that object interest and dependence, or in later life, positive sexual pursuits (*cf iki*) and the contrastive passive desire for a dependent relationship (*cf amae*) become dissociated. Women upon whom the drive for maternal dependence is fixed are felt by such people to be lacking in sexual interest (wife treated as a mother), while inversely, those to whom such patients are sexually attracted are treated in a casual, unemotional fashion. Of such a type Saul remarks:

> For him, women were of two classes — those upon whom he could be dependent, whom he looked up to, and idealised, and with whom he was relatively impotent, and those who had a fully dependent attitude toward him, whom he looked down upon, and with whom he fully enjoyed sexual relations.[38]

This cannot but remind us respectively of Kuki's stress upon the uncommitted, purely sexual character of erotic chic (*iki*) and Doi's contrasting emphasis upon the quasi-homosexual character of maternal dependence (*amae*) in coaxing behaviour.[39] The coincidence may therefore not be accidental. We are driven back to our reevaluation of the material on certain social structures which tend to alienate spouses, and drive the mother to seek emotional reparation in her relationship with the son.

At this point in my analysis of the material, I came across a passage in Tsurumi Kazuko's work on 'Japanese Curiosity' which lends striking, if inadvertent, support for this tentatively psychoanalytic reconstruction of the pseudo-psychoanalytic presentation in Japan of such characteristics. Writing about what she calls 'emotions of differing vectors', she remarks that:

> Doi Takeo has analysed lucidly 'coaxing' (*amae*) as the basic emotion of the Japanese, and Kuki Shūzō has discussed 'chic' (*iki*) as an emotion peculiar to the Japanese. I consider the overlapping of these two different emotions to be the basic emotional pattern of contemporary Japanese. According to Doi, coaxing is an emotion felt by a child towards its mother, it is

passive object love, a fusing activity of unity with the mother, of a completely one-sided dependence on another. The *ama* of *amae* is said to be connected with the *ama* of *Amaterasu* and is a primitive, ancient emotion.[40]

On the other hand, chic is an emotion based on sexual love between the male and the female, in which, simultaneously, an intense desire for unlimited access and a concomitant repression of the possibility, or resignation to the impossibility, of becoming completely at one with the other person vie with each other and engender strong feelings of tension. It is an emotion which seeks the beautiful in those parallel lines that, though converging, can never possibly meet, and this is made to be the model of those male–female relationships in the red light districts of feudal society.

In that coaxing is an emotion which considers the dissolution of tension as beautiful, and chic an emotion which regards the aggravation of emotion as beautiful, and further in that coaxing tends to conceal individuality from recognition,[41] while chic is an assertion of strong individuality, they constitute emotions that differ in their vectors.

These two emotions, while differing in their vectors and the historical stages of their first appearance, form a pair, and have been inherited more or less in both men and women in contemporary Japan. Within the family, it seems that it is the emotion of coaxing which chiefly comes into play. Outside of the family, it is predominantly the emotion of chic which operates. The pattern of male behaviour whereby one stylishly spends time flirting with girls (*iki ni asobi*) in bars and clubs, and then seeks the indulgence of one's wife at home (*nyōbō ni amaeru*) is living proof of such a multi-layered structure of the emotions. Further, there is a firm multi-layered structure of emotions corresponding to these in those women who generously permit this sort of behaviour.[42]

Tsurumi's method of diachronic psychology (borrowed from Yanagita Kunio), while positing that one can analyse contemporary behaviour by simply adding up ostensibly historically-located stages of emotion, is clearly defective. What she is doing is simply integrating fanciful speculations about national traits into a composite model, in keeping with the uncritical, eclectic tendency of the *nihonjinron*. But her conjoining of the theories of *iki* and *amae* in this fashion has done us an inadvertent service, in that her synthesis formally expresses what was originally a relation of latent affinity. We have a cultural rationale of that type of split behaviour discussed by Saul in his paper on incest and dependence. Saul concluded that such patients:

> Develop a sexually inhibited, dependent attachment to an idealised woman, and turn to depreciated women for sexual pleasure, the latter being both an escape from the dependence and a means of draining hostilities which cannot be expressed toward the woman who is not only idealised, but on whom the patient is dependent.[43]

The inhibition of sexual expression with the wife occurs because she substitutes for, or reembodies, the mother, while aggressive sexual outlet occurs in fleeting liaisons. This is suggestive for understanding why, according to certain texts, even young married couples, after the birth of the first child, call one another 'mama' and 'papa',[44] and for appreciating the psychological function of that vast world of the 'water trade' (*mizu shōbai*) and *toruko* (bath-house brothels) in contemporary Japan.

Kuki's *iki*, we recall, draws on the culture surrounding the sexual commerce between merchants and harlots in Edo. The strict isolation of the sexes in feudal Japan impeded the growth of social contexts and spaces in which free intercourse between the sexes might flourish. Marriage was strictly linked to considerations of class and property. The dramatic works of the age constantly play on the theme of the doom that awaits lovers who are united by pure elective affinity, and on the idea that *ninjō* (human feelings) are always sacrificed on the altar of *giri* (social obligations). Once marriage was deprived of the possibility of conjugal rapport of an amorous yet freely chosen kind, the bordello world alone, the *maisons closes* of Yoshiwara and Shinbara, fulfilled the need for more informal amorous relationships.

Now Kuki's mother hailed from the Gion quarter of Kyoto, and embodied the culture of that old bordello society. Her affair with Okakura Tenshin shocked Meiji society, and Kuki himself was reared believing that Okakura was his real father. Ambiguous paternity and the influence of a flirtatious, strong-minded mother impressed his youthful mind to such a degree that his later love life constantly betrays traces of unresolved attempts to evade or overcome this oppressive heritage. His first love took the veil as a Catholic nun. He then married his brother's former wife. Finally he remarried a woman hailing from the same Gion quarter as his mother, and his habit of surrounding himself with *geisha* to enjoy their antics as he soberly sipped tea (with, like Baudelaire's dandy, '*l'air froid qui vient de l'inébranlable résolution de ne pas être ému*' — The cool manner which derives from the unflappable resolution not to be stirred)[45] clues us in to the latent autobiography underlying his idealisation of *iki* as a characteristic of the *Yamato* race.[46]

The impossibility of finding a woman to substitute for his mother and the rebuff to his first love when the girl in question renounced secular life for the cloistered existence of Western monasticism, laid the basis for his repudiation of love as 'absolute fusion' and his preference for the world of passing flirtation. His fixation with *geisha*, and his marriage to Nakanishi Kitsue, strongly suggest a quasi-incestuous need for the mother, but one which contains the ever-present, frustrated realisation of the impossibility of such a dependent regression to unity with the mother. Confusing the ideal of Western love with this type of dependence on a motherly type (what Doi understands by *amae*), he elects to define his identity (under the alias of a fictive national type) with the image of the urbane seducer, the cool, detached habitué of a bordello culture of fleeting liaisons.

The transition from such *iki* to *amae* is revealed in Shiga Naoya's autobiographical novel *An'ya Kōro* (Passage through a Dark Night, 1921-3, 1937) which recounts the long, lugubrious quest of its hero Tokitō Kensaku to discover a woman who might substitute for the hero's long-deceased mother. Opening with vivid memories of her, the novel describes Tokitō's neurotic explorations of the cafe society and gay quarters of late Meiji Japan. His first initiative in the direction of marriage with Aiko (tellingly combining two characters meaning 'love' and 'child') proves abortive. She, we note, is the daughter of a woman who was the adoptive daughter of Kensaku's maternal grandparents who reminds him strongly of his own mother, so that in his relationship to Aiko there is an element of incestuous displacement.[47]

Aimlessly drifting about after this failure, he encounters by chance a mother on a tram who attracts his attention because of the way she handles her child. The male infant she cuddles is being watched by another baby, the daughter of another woman passenger, and when he notices and returns her gaze, the young child begins to clutch and clamour in the little girl's direction. His mother coyly notes to the young girl that her little boy appears to want to talk with her, but then, impulsively she covers her child's face with kisses and he, tickled with pleasure, writhes in delight. Kensaku is overcome by a strange 'mushy sentiment' (*amattarui yō na ki*)[48] in observing how, while smothering her child's throat with kisses she inadvertently exposes her own neck to view, and averts his gaze in embarassment while thinking that, 'This woman was clearly far cleverer in the art of coaxing (*amattarete iru*) than her baby, who was as yet ignorant of the ways of such coaxing (*amattarekata no shiranu akago*).'[49] The passage plays insistently on a word cognate with *amaeru*.[50] Where Doi says that the child initiates coaxing around six months, Shiga has the mother do the coaxing while making the one year old child still unaware of such playful fawning.

The psychological movement of this brief scene is complex and fascinating. It is as if the young mother, seeing her young son attracted by the female child, unconsciously feels envious, seeing her as symbolic of an eventual threat to her hitherto unchallenged hegemony over her own male child. Confident in her power to coax his attention back to herself, she smothers him in kisses, thus arresting his emergent interest in the outside world. It is the mother who initiates the coaxing in order to maintain her child in a state of absolute dependence.

But the soft sexuality of the scene, which disturbs Kensaku, hints that her own child somehow appears to be an emotional substitute for her husband. Kensaku takes her behaviour to be uncharacteristic of a mother, and more suggestive of the kind of conduct that, in his own fantasy, he expects between a woman and her husband.

> Kensaku, when he thought of how the coaxing relationship (*amattarui kankei*) of a young father and mother here re-emerged, unconsciously, with the young child as the object of such feelings, was overcome by a strange feeling of embarassment and, at the same time, by a sense of moderate discomfort. ... Trembling, he began to envisage having just such a person come to him one day as his own wife, and the idea made him extraordinarily happy. Indeed for a moment he felt so happy that there was nothing else in the world he thought he could desire.[51]

Thus we see that Kensaku, frustrated by the early death of an otherwise unresponsive and indeed occasionally harsh mother, in later years idealises her, while at the same time seeking to recuperate the real absence of maternal affection in a relationship with other women. Thus here, when he observes the mother and her child, he naturally thinks that this coaxing intimacy between them is what wives and husbands do, not mother and child. This confusion constitutes the ambivalence which hinders his search for 'love'. His excursions to the brothels leave him unsatisfied (and here he differs from Kuki) because his need is for a wife as *ersatz* mother (the vector of *amae*).

This ambiguity means that his estrangement can never be overcome in terms of human rapports. The resolution, and that a temporary one, of such isolation emerges only in his sudden sleepy glimpse of a sense of mystical fusion with nature as he lies prone on the breast-like prominence of a mountainside.[52] And thus, as so often in Japanese culture, it is the landscape, rich, lonely and unpeopled, which must serve for the discharge of those deepest feelings which the formal exigencies of a minutely regulated social intercourse and the structure of family life inhibit from their fullest human expression.[53]

The *nihonjinron*, as attempts to rework *samurai* traditions in such a way as to render them valid for Japan through her entry into the modern, and now postmodern, world, constantly pit themselves against bourgeois culture (identified as 'the West') as they aggressively extend their ideological hegemony over the world of Japanese interpretation. Thus many of the recent myths legitimise the Tokugawan heritage, and to understand them fully we must return to that feudal soil from which they sprang.

Tokugawan order was based on the old rule of divide and conquer on the compartmentalisation of powers (*cf* the *fudai-tozama* system), meticulous social surveillance and the use of any institution that might safeguard central authority, i.e. taxation and expropriation to divert the accumulation of potentially disruptive capital resources by merchants or fiefs. In Maruyama's analysis, we read that this policy, with its enforced exclusion of some 90% of the population from political and social life, forced them over the centuries, 'To "depend" (*yorashimu*) passively on the given order as no more than the objects of political control'.[54] The key word here *yorashimu* derives from a philosophical axiom which was formulated from a misinterpretation of Confucian texts, according to which, 'The people should be made to depend upon (the Way) but not be informed about it.'[55]

Doi's theory of dependence, in historical context, thus reflects the force of this political tradition, which demanded a radical self-accommodation by the people to a highly reticulated system of social controls over the individual's life. This was revived by the ideologues of the thirties, for whom, '(w)hat we normally refer to as "private life" is, in the final analysis, the way of the subject'.[56]

Likewise Maruyama's analysis throws light on the social roots of *iki*. Relegated to the role of being 'parasitical' outcasts by virtue of their involvement with commerce and money, the merchant townsmen were impeded from converting their capital accumulation into social power. When not appropriated by sumptuary laws or borrowed by indebted *samurai*, it was diverted into a kind of conspicuous consumption in the red light districts, which lay beyond the pale of the normal social order. Wealth that might have been used to create a quasi or proto-bourgeois power base, spheres of public representation of private interest against the total power of the centre, was dissipated innocuously in the ephemeral delights of the gay quarters.[57] Parallel to this profligate dispersion of merchant wealth was the draining of *daimyō* capital imposed by the *sankin kōtai* institution. This entailed enormously expensive overheads for the biennial commuting of the clan chiefs and their retinues from their rural fiefs to the capital, and thus exhausted wealth that otherwise might have been salted away for armaments and the forging of alliances aimed at the eventual overthrow of Tokugawan despotism.

The third leg of such absolutism lay in securing the system by reinforcing the alienation of social groups, clans, classes and sexes through the structure of mutually exclusive hierarchies whose nature naturally subverted horizontal alignments between common interest groups. Stability was thus ensured by the blocking of social solidarity, which in turn, in the modernising period, had to be created by massive ideological integration (hence the *nihonjinron*). Indeed the word *kō*, wrongly understood to refer to the notion of 'public', could mean little more than an individual samurai's allegiance or loyalty to his master, and 'public' service could be defined as nothing more than the relationship of obligation to one's lord, as secured by a feudal stipend.[58]

The arrival of Western imperial powers at precisely the juncture when the machinery of this total absolutism was being increasingly undermined by internal forces of change ironically saved the system from collapse. The 'revolution from above' could draw on Western technology and bureaucratic structures in order to 'modernise' a world which, on its own terms, was doomed to collapse. The *kō/shi* problem, the myth of silence and *yamato kotoba* (appealing as it does against authoritarian modernisation as expressed in the linguistic dress of bureaucratic jargon in Sino–Japanese), the expropriation of the father from the family by the feudally structured corporation, the persistence of *miai* or arranged marriage, and the double-bind socialisation which ensues, all reflect the dead weight of a barren past which constantly aims at usurping the budding fertility of a culture rooted in the autonomous individual. It is this same heritage, through its invasive penetration of the inner person, which dooms so many to misinterpret the alien, and to appreciate the promising diversity of the inner and the outer world. Doi's massive failure, despite his ambition, is eloquently paradigmatic; for his attempt to 'endogenise' psychoanalysis, the highest expression of bourgeois consciousness and individualism, ineluctably collapses back into an infantile celebration of that narcissistic dependence which this feudal world imposed.

Yet Doi's version, we must recognise, remains the most liberated form of what passes for psychoanalysis in Japan precisely because it bears an implicit nuance of criticism. The authoritarian character of Japanese psychotherapy emerges more pronouncedly with Morita and Naikan therapy, which are explicit in their advocacy of increasing self-repression as an indispensable first step in the cure of neurosis.

Morita therapy is named after Dr Morita Shōma (1874-1938), a neurasthenic who, following the age-old prescription of 'physician, heal thyself', tried to develop a distinctively Japanese therapy which might aid him in living with his neurosis. For Morita, the Japanese were prone to a peculiar kind of emotional disorder characterised by self-absorption, hypochondria and neurasthenia, for which he coined the term *shinkeishitsu* (nervosity). He elaborated a theory of its psychogenesis, and developed an equally 'unique' therapy for its cure.[59]

For Morita, normal people have a *sei no yokubō* or strong desire to live fully, but in neurasthenic patients this natural need is thwarted by what he called 'the psychic interaction of attention and sensation' (*seishin kōgo sayō*), a process triggered off by the most trivial of occurrences. When one's attention is, by chance, distracted by some disagreeable sensation, the tension provoked by this momentary discomfort endows the symptoms with increasing significance. The more one is aware of the discomfort, the greater the apparent distress, and an obsessional mechanism of circular interaction between apparent symptoms and symptom-anxiety is engendered, in which each act of attention merely annexes and reinforces one's preoccupation with these apparently menacing symptoms. Such people become liable to a state of captivity (*toraware*), that is they become captives of anxious thought as they exaggerate the severity of their original symptoms, until the point is arrived at where intellectual obsession with them leads to a complete withdrawal by the patient from an active life.[60]

Morita suggested that this *angst* had its sources in the fear of death, and it is significant that he himself traced his own neurasthenic *timor mortis* (fear of death) to the impact of seeing a Buddhist scroll depicting the agonies awaiting those in hell, when he was a mere child. He affirmed that the state of nervosity experienced by a *shinkeishitsu* patient is common to all people, differing only in the intensity with which it strikes the real neurotic.

According to Morita, thinking too much was the root of such neurotic alienation from both one's self, and outward social life. Thought cut one off from the palpable experience of vivid reality, for intellectual labour made one think in terms of 'how things should be' instead of 'how things are'. Only by conditioning the patient to a 'thoughtless' existence, to taking things 'as they are' could a cure be procured. This involved teaching the patient to coordinate his mind with the external flow of reality (*aru ga mama*), (Lebra's 'nature tak(ing) its course', or Reynolds' 'the acceptance of phenomenological reality').[61] 'Reality' thus takes precedence over the mind's interpretation of that reality (*jijitsu hon'i, jijitsu yuishin*). This flight from intellectual abstraction to concrete phenomenalism simply reflects feature 26,26' and F,F' in tables 6 and 7 of chapter 4, in the paradigm of contrasts, but in effect what is involved here is a sanitising of social 'reality' and a concomitant diagnosis of the cognitive and reflective intellect of the individual as pathogenic.

The therapy consists in enforced rest and indolence, to reduce the working span of 'bad intellect', and then a gradual readaptation to physical activity directed towards the resumption of the routines of one's previous workaday existence. When one proves capable of working and living in terms of the old roles of workplace and the family, irrespective of one's symptoms, then one is considered cured. The high recovery rate, however, is predictable from the practice of screening out patients not susceptible to Morita treatment. But if *shinkeishitsu* is similar to classical nervosity, then we should not be surprised, since nervosity also is not disabling and does not impede the conduct of one's daily activities significantly. Failure to cure is attributed not to problems with the technique, but rather to 'hereditary factors' that render the patient unresponsive to this kind of treatment.[62]

Books on Morita therapy are textbooks in self-contradiction. Patients must see things 'as they are', but treatment is marked by constant authoritarian inverventions in which the patient is exhorted with innumerable 'do's and don'ts', which tell him how he 'ought to be' or 'ought to feel'.[63] It is also a highly anti-intellectual therapy, since the patient is forbidden to inquire about his treatment, and enlightenment about the nature of these anxieties is avoided because 'rationalistic' (i.e. 'Western') comments might only strengthen the patient's captivity in his neurosis.[64]

Rebellious patients are isolated, while those who mimic the stages of cure are praised and held up before the others as proof of the method's value.[65] Here, clearly, shame sanctions are exploited in order to repress the outward expression of the neurosis. Those whose ideas conflict with the analyses of the doctors are told to 'integrate their thinking with that of other people' (*cf* Tanizaki and Suzuki on *junnō*, self-synchronisation). Dreams are ignored, and verbal slips, so crucial to Freudian analysis, are 'corrected'. To rephrase this in Morita's terms, the abnormal, socially 'unreal' language of the patient's troubled self is 'reformed' so that his speech pattern will 'harmonise' itself with the formalised *aru ga mama* of conventional usage, that is, towards the non-disclosure of the self.

Doctors exercise their control of the patient by predicting his symptoms, and by pigeon-holing him before he has succeeded in expressing the nature of his anxiety-neurosis. In fact, they are prone to supply the patient with the 'proper' words as he stumbles to disclose his feelings. Given all this, it is extremely difficult to understand how Reynolds and others can publicise this as an 'alternative' therapy which somehow exposes the latent 'cultural' assumptions of Western psychotherapy, since it so manifestly betrays the defective assumptions of nineteenth century psychiatry which modern mental health theories have, for almost a century, so incessantly attempted to dissect and transcend. Indeed, under the alias of 'cure', Morita therapy simply reinforces or reinstates those social controls of induced self-regulation typical of Japanese secondary socialisation in patients whose neuroses are, in the first place, admitted to be, 'The extreme product of a form of socialisation that works too effectively on some persons.'[66]

Morita therapy is merely a relatively unmodified offshoot of earlier Western psychiatry, surviving in an ostensibly 'unique' Oriental guise. It shares strong analogies with both Victor Frankl's logotherapy and the 'psychotherapy' dealt out to Soviet dissidents.[67] It neatly exposes the hidden falsity of the *nihonjinron* view of Japanese social relationships, since there is no hint here of 'empathy' with the patient, but simply punishment for his neurotic sense of being out of key with the rest of society. A theory which considers thinking too much as pathogenic, and which exhorts patients to accept wholeheartedly social 'reality as it is', reveals that Morita's programme in essence is concerned only with the suppression of feelings which tend to place the person 'out of kilter' with the regulating codes of social relationship in Japan.[68]

The paradox remains that Western researchers reared on antipsychiatry and determined to find an alternative therapy to the 'alienating', 'authoritarian' discipline of Western psychiatric care, should embrace and extol a system of psychiatric control hostile to rationality, indifferent to explanation, repressive of individuality and conducive to the maximalisation of the doctor's authority, as resocialising agent, over the patient. Reynolds concludes that Morita's ideas may provide us with a new stimulus for the construction of a metatheory of psychotherapy,[69] and we are here reminded of Doi's equally ambitious project with his 'hide and seek' concept.

Doi, who believes he has the keys, in *amae*, for founding a universal psychotherapy uniting 'East and West', has had to cope with the rival claims of his forerunner. He acclaims Morita's insight into the fact that captive obsession (*toraware*) was integral to nervosity (*shinkeishitsu*), yet argues that the theory of the reciprocal interaction of attention and sensation is inadequate, and must be understood in the light of his theory of *amae*. Thus for Doi, *toraware* (being captured by thought) is merely the result of an obstruction of the desire to have one's dependency needs indulged.

Predictably then, Doi explains nervosity as arising from an inability to have others indulge one's coaxing in a relationship of passive dependence:

> As we have mentioned, Morita's originality consists in his having raised into focus the psychology of obsession, and his theory of nervosity (*shinkeishitsu*) could be said to be based upon a surpassingly Japanese conception. However, human psychology does not vary that much from place to place after all. Given that it may appear to differ, nonetheless it will invariably be found to have a common foundation. In particular the nervosity which Morita studied can also be observed in the West, so that it would be quite strange to make out that Western patients do not have the psychology of obsession which Morita pointed to. It is simply that in the past, no Western scholar noticed it, and that is probably due to the existence among Westerners in general of a psychological tendency which makes it difficult for them to become aware of this type of psychology.[70]

To return from point-scoring fantasy to the facts, we might begin by noting that Morita's analysis is in no way an advance upon Hamlet's soliloquy in which, pondering on suicide as a possible means of escaping his existential indecision, he remarks that killing himself would be attractive but for the fact:

> ... That the dread of something after death,
> The undiscovered country, from whose bourn
> No traveller returns, puzzles the will,
> And makes us rather bear those ills we have,
> Than fly to others that we know not of?
> Thus conscience does make cowards of us all,
> And thus the native hue of resolution
> Is sicklied o'er with the pale cast of thought
> And enterprises of great pitch and moment,
> With this regard their currents turn awry,
> And lose the name of action.[71]

If *toraware* (thought captivity) arises from the fear of death, and, in making the active man a prisoner of an anxious intellect, incapacitates his power to function in the real world, then Hamlet, whose will to act is 'puzzled', for whom reflection (conscience) impedes the prompt execution of tasks, and makes him withdraw from life, and for whom the natural resolve (native hue of resolution), like Morita's *sei no yokubō*, is paralysed by melancholy (thought), is clearly a *shinkeishitsu* candidate.

Morita's 'unique' theory of *shinkeishitsu* is already found in Coleridge's famous interpretation of the play, in which Hamlet's indecisiveness was seen to relate to the way in which, for him, 'the external world, and all its incidents and objects, were comparatively dim'.[72] For Coleridge, action is the end of existence and thought useful in so far as it parallels but does not usurp reality (*cf aru ga mama*); that is:

> In healthy processes of the mind, a balance was maintained between the impressions of outward objects and the inward operations of the intellect; if there be an overbalance in the contemplative faculty, man becomes the creature of meditation, and loses the power of action.[73]

Coleridge's views here owe much to philosophical currents in German romanticism, as does Kierkegaard's analysis of the melancholy of the autopathic individual, who keeps existence at bay by 'the most subtle of deceptions, by thinking'.[74] Far from being unique, Morita theory and therapy merely revitalise in a Japanese idiom a moribund tradition of psychiatric cure in the West. We see it as early as Swift in his satire on Laputa, where a strict regimen of practical labour is advocated to cure Yahoos of neurasthenic spleen and anthropophobia (*cf shinkeishitsu* and *taijin-kyōfushō*).

Morita's work reshapes ideas he gained from his supervisor Kure Shūzō, who popularised the clinical psychiatrist E. Kraepelin's descriptive nosology and advocated the Pinelian system of humane treatment for the mentally ill. His theory recapitulates the eighteenth century view of melancholy, which considered that such patients were 'captured' by a somnolent dream of a visionary world, from which they could be recalled only by the imposition of a routine of physical labour in the 'real world'. Here, the dreamy thought world of the neurasthenic was effaced by a strict quotidian regimen of physical activity which revealed 'the exactness of a social order, imposed from the outside'.[75]

The nostalgia for such a simple solution perhaps motivates those foreigners who see in Morita an ostensibly 'alternative' psychotherapy. But contemporaneously, we should note, Morita's own disciples are rewriting his whole approach along more modern, Western-influenced lines, in order to cater to their patients' insistence on less authority, more explanation and greater verbalisation.[76] It is thus difficult to maintain the fiction of uniqueness when the method itself derived from Western therapies, and the newer Moritists are engaged in not only melding the method with foreign psychotherapy, but proving unable to agree among themselves on precisely what constitutes the essential character of Morita's original method.[77]

Naikan therapy, finally, openly exposes as a positive value what is only latent in this preceding therapy. Here neurosis is seen as 'ingratitude', and mental illness a cause for shame. 'Cure' consists in stimulating a sense of 'infinite guilt' among patients towards innocent and 'significant others'.[78] Presumably, being neurotic makes one insignificant.

This 'therapeutical' technique was developed by Yoshimoto Inobu (b. 1916) for the reform of people in correctional institutions, and draws on Buddhist ideas (esp. the *Jōdoshin*, or Pure Land Sect) for its theory, though the ideas are increasingly conflated with notions drawn from Protestant existential theology. Its recent extension to the population at large suggests that the victims of suburban neuroses are guilty of the same anti-social behaviour as the criminal miscreants for which this technique was originally formulated.

For Naikan therapists, man is fundamentally selfish and guilt-ridden, but, at the same time, favoured by the 'immeasurable benevolence of others'. The patient is made to realise his 'authentic guilt' by being manipulated into a controlled emotional breakdown or regression in which he must dredge up and meditate on any image of having once been cared for. A single instance of kindness is, we might argue, hardly evidence for 'immeasurable benevolence'. He is induced thus to acknowledge that his neurosis is an act of egotistic self-indulgence which insults the 'infinite love' shown to him by others. Naikan is essentially an instrument for reintegrating the criminal/neurotic back into society by repressing grievance. If neurosis has social constituents, this would entail making the patient submit himself, in guilty apology, to the very people who, in fact or fantasy, may have played some provocative role in his original estrangement. It is the most extreme form, therefore, of that repressive resocialisation which Moloney considered to be characteristic of Japanese psychoanalysis whereby:

> The Japanese psychoanalyst faced with the problem of curing the mentally ill person, must first of all diagnose him as 'ill' because he does not adhere to the rigidly prescribed culture patterns I have outlined. The cure upon which the analyst embarks constitutes the opposite of a cure by Western standards. Instead of endeavouring, as do occidental psychoanalysts, to free the individual from his inner thongs, the Japanese analysts actually tighten those thongs.[79]

Psychotherapy, which started out as a technique for releasing the individual from internalised constraints, has become an instrument of coercion and punishment for those who break down under the weight of a disindividualising socialisation. Neurosis is seen as a perilous defection from the ideal of anonymous identity with the 'group'. Yet it is precisely in the neurotic, with his private and estranging suffering, that the totalising verdicts on identity in the *nihonjinron*, are strikingly contested, and it is perhaps only in the opening out of such disequilibriated voices that the search for an authentic identity, untrammeled by authority and unintimidated by the silencing ethic of self-synchronisation, may begin and develop.

Notes

1. R. Shaplen, *A Turning Wheel* (Andre Deutsch, 1979) pp.340-1.
2. Doi, *'Amae' no kōzō*, ibid. p.9; *'Amae' zakkō*, ibid. pp.8-9.
3. F. Gibney, *Japan: The Fragile Superpower* (W.W. Norton, New York, 1975) pp.119-33, p.120.
4. C. Carr-Gregg, *Japanese Prisoners of War in Revolt* (Queensland University Press, St. Lucia, 1978) pp.144ff.
5. G. Clark, *Nihonjin — yuniikusa no gensen*, ibid. pp.80-3.
6. D. Mitchell, *AMAERU: The Expression of Reciprocal Dependency Needs in Japanese Politics and Law*, (Westview Replica ed., Boulder, Colorado, 1976). Were Doi's analysis correct, there could never be any reciprocity in Japanese life.
7. As reported by Tony Thomas, 'Academic has CSR hopping mad' in *The Age* (Melbourne) 21 July 1978, p.17.
8. T.S. Lebra, 'The Role of Supernatural "Other": Spirit Possession in a Japanese Healing Cult', in William P. Lebra (ed.) *Culture-Bound Syndromes, Ethnopsychiatry and Alternate Therapies*, (University Press of Hawaii, Honolulu, 1976) pp.88-100. See also Lebra, *Japanese Patterns*, ibid. pp.232-47.
9. Wen Shing Tseng, 'Folk Psychotherapy in Taiwan' in Lebra, *Culture-Bound Syndromes*, ibid. pp.164-78, p.176.

10. As quoted in J. Temple, *Asian Insight*, (University of Queensland Press, St Lucia, 1977) p.13. Brzezinski inverts the order making the need for dependence produce the hierarchy. Thus the Japanese social fabric 'Appears to be responsive to the Japanese desire for a clearly demarcated social hierarchy'. Z. Brzezinski, *The Fragile Blossom: Crisis and Change in Japan*, (Harper and Row, New York, 1972) p.3.

11. Doi, *'Amae' zakkō*, ibid. pp.41-2. Doi in *'Amae' to shakai kagaku*, ibid. p.7. Kawashima remarks on 'The great attraction of Doi's ambitious project of trying to develop and clarify a new analytical instrument that is not the product of European science.' (*'Amae' to shakai kagaku*) p.iii.

12. Doi Takeo, 'Psychotherapy as 'Hide and Seek' ', in Lebra (ed.) *Culture-Bound Syndromes*, ibid. pp.273-77.

13. M. Argyll and M. Cook, *Gaze and Mutual Gaze*, (Cambridge University Press, England, 1976) p.15.

14. See J. Lacan, *Ecrits I* (Editions du Seuil, Paris, 1966) pp.111-208. English version in J. Lacan, *The Language and the Self*, trans. and annot. Anthony Wilden (Delta Books, New York, 1975) pp.85ff pp.163-4. See also, A. Lemaire, *Jacques Lacan*, 3rd ed. (Pierre Mardaga, Bruxelles, 1977) pp.99ff. See S. Freud, *Beyond the Pleasure Principle*, in *The Standard Edition*, vol. 18 (Hogarth Press, London, 1953-74) pp.4-18.

15. S. Freud, *Beyond the Pleasure Principle*, ibid. pp.14-15. Lemaire, *Jacques Lacan*, ibid. p.100. Bowlby, *Separation*, ibid. pp.426-8.

16. Okonogi, *Moratoriamu ningen*, ibid. p.196, see also p.232. Doi, *'Amae' zakkō*, ibid. p.180 records that his readers were uncertain as to whether he approved or disapproved of coaxing.

17. See the colloque between Doi and Okonogi in *Moratoriamu ningen*, ibid. pp.326-38, p.337-8. The reference is to *'Amae' no kōzō*, ibid. p.93. Doi explains that by *'amae o kokufuku suru'* he means, 'To make conscious the seeking for indulgence/coaxing (*amae*) of the unconscious', a parody of Freud's famous dictum, *Wo Es war, soll Ich werden'* (Where It (the *id*) was, I (the ego) shall become). *cf* S. Freud, *New Introductory Lectures*, ibid. p.112, with the translator's note to J. Habermas, *Knowledge and Human Interests*, trans. Jeremy J. Shapiro (Heinemann, London, 1972) pp.235-6, and note 31 ad.loc.

18. An analysis of the types of methodological mistakes Doi is prone to may be found in Y. Sugimoto and R. Mouer, 'Doi Takeo-setsu e no hōhōronteki gimon', in *Gendai no me*, 20:9 (Sept 1979) pp.200-213, and the same authors' volume, *Nihonjin wa'nihonteki'ka*, ibid. passim, esp. pp.164ff.

19. Okonogi, *Gendai seishin bunseki*, ibid. pp.150-1.

20. E. Erikson, *Childhood and Society*, rev. ed. (Triad/Paladin, London, 1977) pp.222ff.

21. Doi, *'Amae' zakkō*, ibid. p.173.

22. Kimura Bin, *Hito to hito to no aida*, pp.147-66, p.147.

23. Kimura, *Hito to hito*, ibid. pp.161ff.

24. Hamaguchi Eshun, *'Nihonrashisa' no saihakken*, ibid. pp.135ff, esp. pp.137, 139.

25. Hamaguchi, *'Nihonrashisa'*, ibid. pp.141-2.

26. Hamaguchi, *'Nihonrashisa'*, ibid. p.147.

27. Moloney, *The Japanese Mind*, ibid. p.135.

28. R. Lannoy, *The Speaking Tree* (Oxford University Press paper. 1975) p.106.

29. Lannoy, *The Speaking Tree*, ibid. p.110. For omnipotence and dependence, compare Doi's case of the student with the Emperor complex.

30. Doi, *'Amae' no kōzō*, ibid. p.89.

31. Kuki, *'Iki' no kōzō*, ibid. p.21 (on *bitai*). *cf* R. Nakamura, R. de Ceccaty,

Mille ans de littérature japonaise, (aux editions de la différence, Paris, 1982) pp.271-77, p.274. *cf* For d'Aurevilly's dandy, 'Aimer ... c'est toujours *dépendre*, c'est être esclave de son désir', *Du Dandysme*, ibid. p.686.

32. Kuki, *'Iki'no kōzō*, pp.50-1, p.51.
33. Doi, *'Amae'no kōzō*, ibid. p.9.
34. Osaragi Jirō, *Kikyō* (Ōbunsha Bunko, Tokyo, 1974) p.141.
35. Osaragi, *Kikyō*, p.142, 143, 324.
36. Benedict, *The Chrysanthemum and the Sword*, ibid. pp.225-7.
37. L.J. Saul, 'Two Observations on the Split in Object Choice', in *Psychoanalytic Quarterly*, 20 (1950) pp.93-5.
38. Saul, 'Two Observations', ibid. p.93.
39. Doi, *'Amae'no kōzō*, ibid. pp.134ff, esp. p.141.
40. See above, ch. 8, note 22. For a hypothetical etymology of *ama* (unrelated in any case to *amae*) see Murayama Shichirō, *Kokugogaku no genkai*, (Kōbundō, Tokyo, 1975) pp.187-191.
41. Reading *kosei-maibotsuteki* for the printed *kosei-botsuriteki*, a reading confirmed by Hamaguchi's gloss on *shozoku-shūdan e no maibotsu* as *tappuri amaeru koto no taiken*, '*Nihonrashisa*', ibid. p.136.
42. Tsurumi Kazuko, *Kōkishin to nihonjin*, ibid. pp.125-6.
43. Saul, 'Two Observations', p.94.
44. Suzuki Takao, *Kotoba to bunka*, ibid. p.189. Contrast Miura, *Nihongo no bunpō*, ibid. pp.54-62.
45. Baudelaire, Le Peintre de la vie moderne, ibid. 92.
46. *cf* Yasuda and Tada, ' *"Iki" no kōzō' o yomu*, ibid. pp.13ff, pp.59-60. Minamoto Ryōen, *Giri to ninjō*, ibid. pp.167-8 contrasts the violent end of those who chose love over *giri* to the cautious restraint of the Edo *tsūjin* whose flirtations avoid the risk of excessive passion.
47. Shiga Naoya, *An' ya kōro*, (Kadokawa Bunko ed., Tokyo, 1967) p.49ff.
48. Shiga, *An'ya kōro*, ibid. p.65.
49. Shiga, *An'ya kōro*, ibid. p.66.
50. On *amattareru* = *amaeru*, see Doi, *'Amae'no kōzō*, ibid. pp.90-1.
51. Shiga, *An'ya kōro*, ibid. p.66. On the weakness of the husband and wife bond, Doi remarks that the conjugal relationship in Japan is 'intimate but not personal'!, 'Psychiatry and Culture in Japan', ibid. p.135. See also Doi, '*Amae' zakkō*, ibid. p.55; F.S. Hulse, 'Convention and Reality in Japanese Culture', in Silberman, (ed.) *Japanese Character and Culture*, ibid. pp.298-307, p.306; Lebra, *Japanese Patterns*, ibid. p.62.
52. *An'ya kōro*, ibid. pp.452-3. His 'marvellous sense of rapture' involves a feeling of *his mind merging with his flesh* within nature. The word *tōsui* (intoxication) in the form *jiko-tōsui*, signifies narcissism. For an excellent study of this see now W.F. Sibley *The Shiga Hero*, (University of Chicago Press, Chicago and London, 1979) passim, esp. pp.95-6, citing the same passage in Norman Brown as that referred to above ch. 4, n. 5.
53. Nietzsche, *Menschliches, Allzumenschliches*, 508: 'We delight in being out in nature because it entertains no ideas about us'. *cf* Doi, *'Amae' zakkō*, ibid. pp.91-101; Lebra, *Japanese Patterns*, ibid. p.3.
54. Maruyama Masao, *Studies*, ibid. p.330.
55. Maruyama Masao, *Studies*, p.330, n. 4.
56. *The Way of the Subject*, cited Maruyama, M. *Thought and Behaviour*, ibid. p.7.
57. Maruyama, *Studies*, ibid. pp.329-30; Sansom, *The Western World*, ibid. p.219; B. Moore Jr *Social Origins*, ibid. pp.239-40.
58. Maruyama, *Studies*, ibid. p.332.
59. Miura Momoshige, Usa Shin'ichi, 'A Psychotherapy of Neurosis: Morita

Therapy' in T.S. Lebra, W.P. Lebra (eds.) *Japanese Culture and Behaviour*, ibid. pp.407-30. Lebra, *Japanese Patterns*, ibid. pp.215-31, D.K. Reynolds, *Morita Psychotherapy*, ibid. passim.

60. Reynolds, *Morita Psychotherapy*, ibid. pp.5-9; Miura & Usa, 'A Psychotherapy', ibid. pp.409-11; Lebra, *Japanese Patterns*, ibid. pp.217-18.

61. Reynolds, *Morita Psychotherapy*, ibid. p.109; Lebra, *Japanese Patterns*, ibid. p.223.

62. Miura & Usa, 'A Psychotherapy', ibid. pp.416-22; Lebra, *Japanese Patterns*, pp.227-9; Reynolds, *Morita Psychotherapy*, ibid. pp.13ff, pp.27-40.

63. Reynolds, *Morita Psychotherapy*, pp.216-17. Virtually every statement in Reynolds' book about Morita therapy can be contradicted by other statements in the same book.

64. Miura & Usa, 'A Psychotherapy', ibid. p.420, x. In fact the reason for this lack of explanation may be found in Reynolds' statement that, 'many Morita therapists seemed to have difficulty distinguishing explanation and description, reality and analogy, scientific proof and philosophical explanation'. (Reynolds, ibid. p.216).

65. Reynolds, *Morita Psychotherapy*, ibid. pp.72-3.

66. Reynolds, *Morita Psychotherapy*, ibid. p.101.

67. cf Reynolds, *Morita Psychotherapy*, ibid. pp.163ff. On the parallel with brainwashing, Reynolds, ibid. pp.180-194.

68. Indeed Reynolds notes the reluctance of Moritists to explore 'the family discord, the suppressed aggression, and the repressed sexuality that, I believe, motivate many of the neurotic disorders in Japan' (ibid. p.138).

69. Reynolds, *Morita Psychotherapy*, ibid. p.220.

70. Doi, *'Amae'no kōzō*, ibid. p.120.

71. *Hamlet*, Act 3, Scene I, lines 78-88.

72. See E. Schneider (ed.) *Samuel Taylor Coleridge: Selected Poetry and Prose*, 2nd ed. enlarged (Reinhart Press, New York, 1971) p.461.

73. As reported in the *Bristol Gazette*, cited Schneider, ibid. p.467.

74. S. Kierkegaard, *Concluding Unscientific Postscript*, trans. David F. Swenson, Walter Lowrie (Princeton University Press, Princeton, paper. ed. 1968) p.226.

75. M. Foucault, *Histoire de la Folie*, (1018, Paris, 1961) pp.183-5, p.185.

76. Reynolds, *Morita Psychotherapy*, ibid. p.126, 135.

77. Reynolds, *Morita Psychotherapy*, ibid. pp.139-42, 149-50.

78. Reynolds, *Morita Psychotherapy*, ibid. pp.175-180; Lebra, *Japanese Patterns*, ibid. pp.201-214, esp. p.205; Murase Takao, 'Naikan Therapy', in Lebra and Lebra, *Japanese Culture and Behaviour*, ibid. pp.431-442.

79. Moloney, *The Japanese Mind*, ibid. p.213. On paranoid or persecuted people's belief that the parents who in fact abuse them love them, see M. Schatzman, *Soul Murder* (Penguin, 1976) p.49. Note that Kensaku, immediately after recounting a violent memory of being beaten by his mother, remarks that she was the only person who loved him. Shiga, *An'ya Kōro*, ibid. p.8.

10 THE SHAME OF A SHAME CULTURE

'If we honour others,
We must dishonour ourselves.'
Goethe, *West-östlicher Divan*, Rendsch Nameh

It should be roughly clear at this point that much of what passes for a 'Japanese kind of logic' in the *nihonjinron* arises from a severe, defensively combative endeavour to overcome a diffuse sense of inferiority to the West, a West which, in the first place, we must understand as a symbolic entity, as the image of a hostile diversity, the Oedipal, the social, the presence of the father within the self. The restless habit of measuring oneself against some monolithic 'other', engaging as it does powerful internal forces of shame, honour, and sensitivity to status, leads to a mode of consciousness in which, as Rousseau remarked, 'once the heart has taken on this habit of making comparisons, it becomes impossible not to feel aversion for anything that surpasses us, lowers us, restricts us, anything that simply by being there prevents us from being everything.'[1]

Shame over a self-perceived backwardness was a major spur for 'catching up and overtaking' (*oitsuke, oikose!*) the West which formed the external model for modernisation. This shame towards one's traditional past produced a literature of reverse identity, which placed all things foreign on a pedestal and demeaned anything smacking of the Orient. For any Westerner to praise 'things Japanese' in this early period was tantamount to a subtle put-down. When a sense of parity with the West was achieved, then shame is displaced as motivating agent by the pride of honour, Westernisation by a resurgent nostalgia for the authentically indigenous patrimony of culture.

To put this another way, when the ego-ideal was defined in terms of 'Westernisation', all discussion of Japan's 'cultural uniqueness' tended to engender feelings of shame and inferiority. But when the Japanese economy began to mount a challenge to the hegemony of the West, the sense of shame switched to focusing upon the lost, original tradition. The subsequent retrieval of esteem thus enjoins a need to discredit the outside world, and the alien or new values (emerging from industrialisation) which, though emerging within the modernising society, are seen as external corruptions or subversions of the 'unique' traditional *Weltanschauung*.

An insight into the emotive logic underlying this complex may be gained by studying the way the *nihonjinron* have responded to Ruth Benedict's comparison between Western 'guilt culture' and Japanese 'shame culture', which has become one of the major points of contrast (15,15' in table 4, chapter 4) in the *nihonjinron*. Her book *The Chrysanthemum and the Sword*, published shortly after Japan's defeat, was widely cited to prove the 'distorted' character of Japanese cultural institutions, and its negative implications were so seriously felt that the grey eminences of Japanese learning devoted themselves to a collective review and counter-attack on her methodology.[2] This intense reception and response has had a large impact upon the *nihonjinron*, and here I wish to summarise briefly four critiques of her work on Japan as a 'shame culture' which are both representative and influential.

Sakuta Keiichi took exception to Benedict's apparently simplistic view of shame as mere fear of external sanctions, and argued that one must distinguish '"public" shame' (*kōchi*) from 'private' shame (*shichi*).[3] Here the *kō/shi* distinction (14,14' in table 4) is amuletically conjoined to the notion of shame to suggest that Benedict is unaware of the 'interiority' of the Japanese sense of shame. That is, her distinction between shame as governed by external sanctions and guilt as determined by internal sanctions is refined by the *kō/shi* antithesis in order to create definitions diametrically opposed to those of Benedict, namely, '"private" shame' as an inner sanction, and '"public" guilt' as an external sanction arising from criminal action and its punishment in the courts.[4] Guilt, as the inner result of parental punishment, also may be said to arise from external sanctions and thus, for Sakuta, Benedict's neat distinction is false and, indeed, a product of 'the way of thinking centered on Christianity which tacitly assumes the superiority of guilt cultures over shame cultures.'[5]

Elsewhere, Sakuta links this shame (Japan)-guilt (West) contrast to Nakane's distinction between the 'warp' (verticality) and the 'weft' (horizontality) (*cf* 11,11', table 4) in order to argue that, 'In the West, guilt is conceived of in terms of the warp thread (*tate-ito*) of man vis-à-vis God, whereas in Japan it is conceived of in terms of the weft-thread (*yoko-ito*) of man vis-à-vis man.'[6] The application of the *tate-yoko* contrast thus enables Sakuta, metaphorically, to invert the usual contrast between an egalitarian West and an hierarchical Japan to the latter's advantage (in a technique by now familiar from our reading of Watanabe, Suzuki and Doi), by interpreting, spatially, Western guilt as vertical, and Japanese shame as horizontal. We are working within the theatre of concepts as talismanic tokens of cultural status.

For Doi Takeo, Benedict's work is vitiated by value-judgements, 'Namely when she says that guilt cultures set a value upon internal norms for action, whereas shame cultures value external norms for action, *it is clear that in her subjective judgement the former is superior and the latter inferior.*' (my italics)[7] Further, Doi argues that where Benedict treats shame and guilt as diametrically opposed, the two are in fact closely related, for, 'The person who has committed a "*sin*" is very often *ashamed* of what he has done.'[8] We are somewhat disconcerted here because Doi is conflating, not guilt, but rather sin, with shame. Bester's translation does not avert us to the difficulty here, namely that the Japanese word for guilt, *tsumi*, bears connotations quite distinct from the Western words it serves to translate. *Tsumi o okasu* can mean to commit a sin or crime, but there is an important difference between the commission of a crime, as defined by the community, and the inner compunctions of guilt (which as psychological punishment does not necessarily entail real crimes, but merely superego anxiety for some thought).[9]

To show that 'guilt' (qua *tsumi*) and 'shame' (qua *haji*) are closely linked, Doi cites the expression *tsumi o hajiru*, which Bester translates as 'a sense of guilt accompanied by a sense of shame'.[10] Again this is misleading, for the expression literally means 'to feel ashamed about one's *tsumi*'. Were *tsumi* a precise equivalent of what is understood by the Western concept of guilt, then the phrase would translate 'to be ashamed of one's guilt', a strange expression which would imply rather a sense of discomforted embarrassment about guilt feelings, and not a contrite and shamed repentence for the commission of a moral or legal 'crime'. We begin to perceive that, underlying these arguments, there is a verbal equivocation.

Doi argues that Japanese guilt is distinct from Western guilt in that it is associated with a sense of betraying one's group. Thus 'guilt feelings' are a function of human relationships, and most keenly felt when one's *tsumi* endangers *giri* bonds. On such occasions, rupture is avoided by saying *sumanai*, taken by Doi to mean 'my obligation to you has not ended'. Thus:

> In this way, the Japanese sense of guilt exhibits a very distinct structure, beginning in betrayal and concluding in apology, and it is for this very reason that it is the *archetype of guilt*, and it must be said that the reason why Benedict did not observe this was primarily because of her cultural prejudice.[11]

Effectively, Doi is saying that Benedict's ethnocentrism impedes her from recognising the existential superiority of Japanese guilt, and it is no use apologising for the oversight because, 'Westerners are, in general, not easily given to expressions of apology'.[12] Doi then tries to show that Japanese 'shame' is also superior to Western guilt because:

> A sense of guilt frequently contains the assumption that one might well have gotten away with something without having to feel guilty. This is probably the reason why Westerners are much fonder of guilt feelings. It is the sense of shame which is much more basic in that one feels one's very existence itself is incomplete and inadequate.[13]

And again:

> Guilt rather than shame suits the nature of Western man since he can thereby display the latent power of the self.[14]

Doi's conclusion is that:

> Far from being internal, the feeling of guilt is simply a superficial awareness of having infringed external sanctions.[15]

In brief, then, Doi in his usual manner of intellectual table-turning chides Benedict for her assumption of superiority, then turns her arguments on their head by trying to demonstrate that both Japanese shame and guilt are superior, more archetypical, than their Western equivalents. Like Sakuta, he has reversed the definitions proposed by Benedict, by making guilt 'external' and shame 'internal'.

The sinologist Mori Mikisaburō approaches the crux from the

perspective of Confucian ethics. He paraphrases *Analects* 2:3 in the following way:

> If one tries to unite a people forcibly, by means of punitive sanctions and political authority, the people will only think of evading the meshes of the law without feeling shame for their evil deeds. If one leads the people by morality and propriety however, they themselves will come to be ashamed of their evil deeds, and will naturally behave in the correct manner.[16]

That is, shame becomes an inner moral sanction when learned by imitating exemplary others, whereas 'guilt' is a superficial thing arising in the context of external sanctions like those of punishment. The Chinese text here does not speak of 'guilt' but 'punishment' (*hsing*), however, but Mori takes this as implying guilt since 'the object of punishment is nothing other than *guilt*'.[17] Even if we were to concede this, such 'guilt' is not what Benedict is referring to in her original discussion. These scholars are consistently reading her concept of psychological guilt in terms of judicial guilt.

Mori modifies this previous formulation somewhat by arguing that two forms of both guilt and shame exist. If guilt is the object of social penalties then it is an external sanction; and if an internalisation of divine punishment, then it is an inner sanction. Likewise, shame as a consciousness of debts to the world, and as social face, may be considered to be external, but if it is fixed within consciousness by learning, then it is an inner sanction.[18] In this latter regard, he cites the word *shen-tu* (*shindoku*), moral circumspection in private life, as linguistic evidence that shame in the Orient is in part an inner code. Thus he concludes that, 'In the final analysis, it is unsuitable to distinguish shame and guilt, as Benedict does, as respectively "external" and "internal"'.[19]

He rounds off his discussion by arguing that if modernisation corresponds to a renunciation of religion, then Japan and China, which were deficient in religious beliefs, stand in the vanguard of world progress with their secular shame culture, and well in advance of those Western countries where the guilt culture of Christianity still holds reactionary sway.[20] Again shame is taken here to be, *pace* Benedict, a proof of Japanese superiority, and guilt a sign of Western backwardness.

Aida Yūji attributes the popularity of Benedict's work to the fact that it was published when it was fashionable to badmouth things Japanese.[21] Benedict's distinction implies, in his reading, that the Japanese are 'typical opportunists', in that a shame-value allows people to keep their consciences clean if no one knows about their evil-doing.[22] For Aida:

> The idea that 'shame' and 'guilt' are essentially different is nothing more than a product of that arrogance of the Europeans who consider themselves to be deeper and more advanced (than other peoples).[23]

In fact, he tells us, Western guilt is nothing more than a cringing fear of hell fire, and far from being an internal norm, it is produced by the ever present sense of being under the scrutiny of other, censorious Christians. Thus, 'By guilt consciousness is to be understood nothing more than the consciousness of being observed by such people.'[24] Aida tries to illustrate this by citing a number of anecdotes to corroborate his view that guilt is an external sanction. Catholic priests always live in company because the presence of others is the only thing that will ensure their celibacy. Having thus shown that 'Western guilt' is merely a degraded form of that definition of shame which Benedict attributed to Japan, he then offers a sop to those who still hanker after feeling guilty in a sophisticatedly modern way. Public opinion is a prime source of shame sanctions in Japan and so:

> If this sense of 'society' (*seken*) of the Japanese can be broadened to some extent, it may thereby be possible to establish, not a shame culture, but rather a guilt culture — a 'guilt culture' which is less hypocritical, more natural and human than that of Europe.[25]

Aida's treatment draws out in an explicit manner what is said in a low-key way by the other writers, and we should expect this since he is a declared enemy of the very civilisation whose culture he is an influential (mis)interpreter of. He displays little knowledge of Benedict, employs mudslinging to point-score against the 'West', and confuses everything by the strange assertion that guilt is a version of shame, and may be nurtured authentically only by remaining faithful to the indigenous strength of shame sanctions. At this point, we are justified in noting that the tradition of criticism has become completely unhinged from Benedict's original formulation.

Benedict's analysis was tacitly indebted to Margaret Mead's use of the shame-guilt distinction and the Weberian contrast between Protestantism's notion of interior dignity and Confucianism's emphasis on external dignity. For Benedict, in a shame culture the major sanctions for conduct derive from external, socially-based criteria, whereas in guilt cultures generally, ethical attitudes are regulated by the inculcation of an absolute, internal authority within the individual. Guilt may be absolved by confession (that is by making public what is private) and atonement, whereas shame arises precisely when others become aware of an individual's violation of prescribed norms, *or when the individual fears such exposure to social scrutiny.*[26]

The Japanese writers all seize on Benedict's initial formulation of shame as 'an external sanction' in order to controvert her by showing it has an interior dimension within the individual (*cf* Sakuta's 'private shame', Mori's *shindoku*). But this critical challenge overlooks the fact that Benedict had already made precisely this very distinction, in writing that, 'A man is shamed either by being openly ridiculed or rejected, or by fantasying to himself that he has been made ridiculous.'[27]

All four writers confuse her definition of guilt with this notion in early Christianity. But Benedict's usage is not religious or legal but Freudian. For Freud, guilt arises from the child's fantasy of having violated taboos, as a reaction formation to the child's aggressive and sexual feelings against his parents. It is not therefore inculcated from outside, but rather occasioned by the sense of a 'crime' which in fact never took place outside of the impulsive desires of the imagination, when wish and enactment are still confused.[28]

Further, Benedict's distinction is used heuristically, not mechanically. She explicitly remarks not only that the Japanese, 'Are terribly conscious about what other people will think of their behaviour, and *they are also overcome by guilt when other people know nothing of their misstep,*' (my italics)[29] but also that in her own United States, the guilt-heritage of Puritanism was on the wane, while shame was playing an increasingly forceful role in judgements of conduct.

The Japanese responses here stem from a loose or indifferent reading of her text, and show an extraordinarily touchy concern for possible status implications in this foreigner's judgement. This leads them to read into her book ethnocentric values which they then, having ostensibly exposed them as invalidating, ironically invert and turn to Japanese account. To rephrase Goethe, in dishonouring Benedict's 'guilt culture' they honour their own 'shame culture' with the very terms of superiority and cultural value judgements which they have previously projected into her discussion in order to invalidate it.

The results are of an enormous conceptual confusion. This mechanical inversion of foreign definitions is a widespread technique within the *nihonjinron*, and another example is provided by Okonogi when he remarks that:

> One cannot schematise so simply the psychotherapy of shame as other-directed, and the psychology of guilt as autonomous and inward. For in shame there is both a psychology of dependent shame (*izonteki na haji*), and one of autonomous shame (*jiritsu na haji*) and in guilt consciousness there are other-directed elements (*tasha-shikōteki na mono*) and autonomous, autogenic (*jihatsuteki*) elements.[30]

Here *izonteki* is a technical, Sino–Japanese gloss for *amae*, and thus Doi's theory is being amuletically connected with Riesman's distinction to bring out and contort a distinction already explicit in Benedict. The result of these textual manipulations is that Benedict's original contrast has been polemically incorporated into the *nihonjinron* in a conceptually unrecognisable form, and thus deprived of its initial heuristic value, as we can again see in Kimura's judgement that:

> The Japanese consciousness of guilt is completely a consciousness of shame and the Japanese consciousness of shame is completely one of guilt ... The guilt of the Japanese, as a breach of *giri*, is a guilt, and is a shame, which transcends the distinction between shame and guilt.[31]

Conflating the two terms in this way makes nonsense of the original distinction in the first place. None of the writers seems aware that *tsumi* does not correspond to the meaning of guilt as understood by Benedict. It is this linguistic snare which accounts for the strange way in which they assail Benedict's thesis. The word *tsumi* appears to be an external sanction to them because in Japanese it often implies the idea of *blame* (*cf tsumi o kaburu*, to take the blame, rap).[32] The Chinese character used for *tsumi* (*tsui/ zai*) appears to have originally meant to be caught for a crime. If, in addition, *tsumi* were related etymologically to *tsubi* (vagina), then instead of the Freudian correlation between shame and the genital organs,[33] we would have in the Japanese instance *tsumi* as 'guilt' being related to the *pudenda*. This might help explain why the four Japanese scholars here all tend to interpret 'guilt' in terms of shame feelings. The essence of the confusion seems to lie in the fact that shame and guilt have two distinct historical senses, and the Japanese are reading the later psychological meaning of the Western words in terms of the pre-modern purport.

Instructive is Fenwick Jones's use of Benedict's categories in the context of German cultural development. He warns us against interpreting 'guilt culture' among the early converts in terms of a sense of remorseful self-reproach independent of social sanctions (i.e. the modern sense). Guilt was first understood as liability to punishment, that is, exactly the sense that Mori discerns in the early Confucian texts.[34] Likewise with shame, in ancient Germany, 'it is fear of being shamed, not ashamed, as it is in our post-Kantian world.'[35] The Japanese hostility to Benedict's thesis may arise therefore from an inadvertent reading of her post-Kantian concept of guilt in terms of its pre-Kantian value in Japanese, and concomitantly, of failing to appreciate adequately the distinction between being shamed, and being ashamed.

Where Benedict's ideas have been fruitfully deployed, extended and developed in a broad field of cultural studies in the West,[36] in Japan, to gather from these four discussions, they appear to have fallen on barren ground. Partially this may be explained by reference to the linguistic preconceptions tacitly underlying their misinterpretation of her work. But it is also the consequence of a failure to immerse oneself in empirical, broad cross-cultural comparisons, to draw on the wider scope of world learning. These four writers are transfixed by an emotive concern with redeeming an honour apparently scathed by the value implications read into her work. Mori is an exception but even his work wholly ignores, to its detriment, important empirical studies on Chinese shame, such as Eberhard's in which it was found that guilt rather than the canonical shame of Confucian ideological texts, was an important element in popular culture.[37] The result of this isolation is that the tradition of Oedipal shadow-boxing in scholarship continues, so that amuletic manipulations of contrastive categories of a very simplistic kind prevails over objective research.

There is no point in creating a category like that of 'private' shame as a purely internal moral sanction, merely by meditating on what people say Benedict apparently said. One must scrutinise carefully her text, appreciate its intellectual context, be wary of facile associative ideas in the *nihonjinron* and, above all, go back through Japanese historical literature to test both her and any other scholar's hypothesis against traditional usage. Sakuta's pseudo-category of 'private' shame, for example, is not merely based upon a misunderstanding of Benedict, but simply ignores the fact that the notion of 'private' shame not only pre-existed his formulation, but also contradicts his definition of this as an inner moral sanction. Tsuda cites a text which runs, 'Even if one's daughter becomes a prostitute, so long as no one knows about it and it remains a matter of 'private shame' (*naishō no haji*) then the family name (or honour) is not injured'.[38]

The insistent challenge to Benedict's *bona fides* perhaps stems from the fact that she was trying to expound Japan's difference precisely at the time when, after the war, that country set about remodelling itself along Western lines. Since status was equated with identity with the West, this implied 'status damage'.[39] Rather than being an attempt to preempt facile moral judgements in terms of Western values about Japanese wartime behaviour (Benedict's real intention), her thesis was read as a vainglorious snub to a defeated country by one of the impudent victors. Whatever the value of her thesis, the curious *gekokujō* logic of those who have assailed it suggests that she has touched a painful nerve. For these scholars, at least, there appears to be something shameful about being characterised as denizens of a shame culture as Benedict defined it.

The instance only serves to underline how a good deal of the reception and response to foreign culture in Japan comes up hard against parochial resistances in which shame, honour, the senses of status and inferiority (or superiority compromised) play a major part. We are angling in deep waters indeed, and what I have remarked on barely touches the surface of these psychological dimensions of the *nihonjinron* reading of both Japan and the West. Suffice it to remark here the intriguing pertinence of Freud's views on shame, and on the sense of inferiority as rooted in the erotic feelings, and his laconic view of the latter as a narcissistic scar.[40] The outsider who questions uniqueness engages, unawares, dynamic forces of psychological identity all but invisible in the superficial forms of these debates.

Notes

1. Cited in J.H. Huitzinga, *The Making of a Saint* (Hamish Hamilton, London, 1976) p.69.
2. The results are summarised in J.W. Bennett and M. Nagai, 'The Japanese Critique of the Methodology of Benedict's "The Chrysanthemum and the Sword"', in *American Anthropologist*, 55 (1953) pp.404-11.
3. Sakuta Keiichi, *Haji no bunka saikō* (Chikuma Shobō, Tokyo, 1967) pp.9-26. His distinction between 'public' and 'private' shame is predictably acclaimed as a 'unique concept' by Koschmann, *Authority and the Individual in Japan*, ibid. p.305.
4. Sakuta, *Haji no bunka saikō*, ibid. passim, esp. pp.23-4.
5. Sakuta, *Haji no bunka saikō*, ibid. p.24.
6. Sakuta, 'Shi to no wakai' in *Haji no bunka saikō*, ibid. pp.155-83, pp.182-3.
7. Doi, *'Amae' no kōzō*, ibid. p.48. *cf* Doi, *'Amae' zakkō*, ibid. p.146.
8. As translated by Bester, *The Anatomy of Dependence*, ibid. p.48; *cf* Doi, *'Amae' no kōzō*, ibid. p.49; *'Amae' zakkō*, ibid. p.147.
9. *cf* 'It's harder to confess the sin that no one believes in/Than the crimes that everyone can appreciate,' T.S. Eliot, *The Elder Statesman*, Act 3.
10. Doi, *'Amae' no kōzō*, ibid. p.55; Bester, *The Anatomy of Dependence*, ibid. p.53.
11. Doi, *'Amae' no kōzō*, ibid. p.51.
12. Doi, *'Amae' no kōzō*, ibid. p.52.
13. Doi, *'Amae' no kōzō*, ibid. p.58. The phrasing and content is such that one cannot but presume that here Doi is tacitly inverting a judgement he found in Erik Erikson's *Childhood and Society*, ibid. p.227: 'Too much shaming does not lead to genuine propriety but to a secret determination to try and get away with things, unseen.' (*cf* Doi, ibid. p.57).
14. Doi, *'Amae' no kōzō*, ibid. p.57, again mocking Erikson, ibid. p.229.
15. Doi, 'Amae' zakkō, ibid. p.146.
16. Mori Mikisaburō, *'Na' to 'haji' no bunka*, (Kōdansha Gendai Shinsho, 1971) pp.137-8.
17. Mori, *'Na' to 'haji' no bunka*, ibid. p.153.
18. Mori, *'Na' to 'haji' no bunka*, ibid. p.154. Mori's distinction implies a notion of 'public' guilt and 'private' guilt, paralleling Sakuta's on shame.
19. Mori, *'Na' to 'haji' no bunka*, ibid. pp.155-6.
20. Mori, *'Na' to 'haji' no bunka*, ibid. p.185.
21. Aida Yūji, *Nihonjin no ishiki kōzō*, ibid. pp.135ff.
22. Aida, *Nihonjin no ishiki kōzō*, ibid. p.135-6.
23. Aida, *Nihonjin no ishiki kōzō*, ibid. p.140.
24. Aida, *Nihonjin no ishiki kōzō*, ibid. p.142.
25. Aida, *Nihonjin no ishiki kōzō*, ibid. pp.144-5.
26. R. Benedict, *The Chrysanthemum and the Sword*, ibid. pp.222ff.
27. Benedict, *The Chrysanthemum and the Sword*, ibid p.223.
28. *cf* Erikson, *Childhood and Society*, ibid. p.79.
29. Benedict, *The Chrysanthemum and the Sword*, ibid. pp.2-3.
30. Okonogi Keigo, *Moratoriamu ningen no jidai*, ibid. p.260.

31. Kimura Bin, *Hito to hito to no aida*, ibid. pp.73-9, pp.76-7. See also Hamaguchi Eshun, *'Nihonrashisa' no saihakken*, ibid. pp.84-96.
32. cf Osaragi Jirō, *Kikyō*, p.29.
33. Compare German *Scham, Schamteile*; Latin *pudor, pudenda*; Greek *aidōs, aidoīa*. Freud held shame's original purpose to be 'the concealment of genital deficiency.' cf S. Freud, *New Introductory Lectures*, ibid. p.166.
34. G.F. Jones, *Honour in German Literature* (Northern Carolina University Press, 1961) pp.38-9.
35. Jones, *Honour in German Literature*, ibid. pp.31-2 (on *Scham*).
36. cf W. Eberhard, *Guilt and Sin in Traditional China*, (University of California Press, Berkeley and Los Angeles, 1967); J.G. Peristiany (ed.) *Honour and Shame — The Values of Mediterranean Society* (University of Chicago Press, Chicago, 1966). Benedict's formulation has been widely used in Greek studies to refine Gilbert Murray's original analysis of *aidōs-nemesis* (which may well have influenced both Mead and Benedict). See E.R. Dodds, *The Greeks and the Irrational*, (University of California Press, Berkeley and Los Angeles, 1951) pp.28-63; and J.N. Redfield, *Nature and Culture in the Iliad* (University of Chicago Press, Chicago and London, 1975) pp.113-19. Redfield's definitions of *aidōs* (shame) as 'a vulnerability to the expressed ideal norm of society; the ideal norm is directly experienced within the self, (cf Mori on *shindoku*) as a man internalises the anticipated judgements of others on himself,' (Redfield, ibid. p.116) is suggestive for the Japanese context.
37. Eberhard, *Guilt and Sin*, ibid. p.13.
38. Tsuda Sōkichi, *Waga kokumin shisō*, ibid. 6:128.
39. Conversely, 'boundary damage' is created when, upon the firming of a sense of economic and cultural parity with the West, foreigners suggest that what is being promoted as uniquely Japanese may be paralleled in other countries.
40. S. Freud, *On Psychopathology*, Angela Richards (ed.) (Pelican Freud Library, 10, 1979) pp.180-1; *New Introductory Lectures*, ibid. pp.97-8.

11 MONKEY BUSINESS

'Monkeys put to death any members of their community who show a desire to live apart. And what the apes do, men do too, in their own manner.'
Hitler, *Table Talk*, 14 May 1942.

In this penultimate chapter, I should like briefly to survey the impact of the *nihonjinron* on various fields of scientific research. As off-the-cuff speculative endeavours at national self-definition which programmatically eschew 'Western' rationalism, we should not expect the *nihonjinron* to venture into the severe fields of empirical science. In their obsessive concern for conceptualising the unique, these writers inadvertently deprive themselves of the ability to make valid generalisations. And yet, it is perhaps the inherent fragility and necessary inadequacy of all models hitherto proposed in the *nihonjinron* which strengthen the temptation to ground these theses of unique identity in the firmer idiom of an empirical science.

Sakagami's attempt to distinguish comportmental differences between 'Japanese' and 'Western' honey bees which are seen to correspond precisely to cultural differences between the Japanese and Westerners is an outstanding example.[1] It appears that Western bees will colonise with alacrity the discarded hives of Japanese bees, but Japanese bees refuse to inhabit Western hives, breaking them up instead in order to construct a new one. Secondly, Japanese honey bees appear to be tolerant hosts of Western bees released into their colony, whereas Western bees to the contrary attack Japanese bees that enter their hive and annihilate them. Thirdly, they defend their respective hives in tellingly different ways. Whereas the Western bee cools the hive by poking its head out menacingly while fanning, its Japanese counterpart exposes its rear to the outside world while beating its wings, thus exposing itself to danger.[2]

Aida Yūji for one has seized upon this work without pausing to ask himself what is meant precisely by calling bees 'Western' or 'Japanese' (*apis mellifera vs apis cerana*?) in order to explain, among other things, the difference in battle tactics between British and Japanese forces in the battle of Imphal. His reading is analysed in table 15.

This apparently uncanny coincidence between the respective bee behaviour and cultural style of Japan and the West is explained in ecological terms. European environments are characterised by poor soil, and have few flowers, which thus makes for the selection of aggressive, competitively efficient bees in the struggle for limited nectar (*cf* 2,3 in table 1) whereas the bounteous nature of Japan provided native bees with a surfeit of flowers so that there honey bees never had to fight among themselves for scarce resources (2,'3' in table 1). Thus an argument from api-culture has been inducted in order to suggest a kind of biological basis for cultural differences between the Japanese and Westerners, in which science seems to confirm empirically the peaceful coexistence of the former, and the malign imperialism of the latter.

An ostensibly more impressive attempt to ground the *nihonjinron* ideology on a scientific basis was provided by Tsunoda Tadanobu's recent bestseller on the 'Japanese Brain'.[3] Tsunoda tries to show that, while morphologically identical (an important concession), Japanese and Western brains differ in the hemispherical localisation of certain neurological functions. That is, by a strange key-tapping method, he asserts that he has obtained laboratory results which indicate that, while consonants and vowels are handled together in the left hemisphere of Japanese brains, in occidental brains consonants are processed in the left hemisphere, and vowels in the right hemisphere. The essential point underlying this thesis is that the left brain of the Japanese *unifies* the perception of natural acoustic phenomena (linguistic, musical and natural sounds), whereas these are treated separately,

Table 15: Bee Behaviour

'West'	'Japan'
Dwell in foreign nests (continental, nomadic;* 1,6.)	Dwell in their own nests (insular, settled habitat; 1',6'.)
Insensitivity to dirt of others (= impurity)	Sensitivity to the dirt of others (purity, *cf* Araki, above ch.5, pp.57f)
Intolerant (23)	Tolerant (23')
Divisive (principle D)	Harmony (principle D')
Bellicose (20)	Peaceful (20')

*See tables 3-7

or alienated from each other, in Western brains.[4]

Tsunoda's project here is to provide empirical verification for what is the central unifying thesis of the *nihonjinron* ideology, namely, as he would put it, the identity of *logos* and *pathos*.[5] In an extremely involved and eccentric argument, Tsunoda attempts to sustain this view by holding that Japanese is a 'vowel language' in contrast to Western languages, which he regards as 'consonantal'. Underlying this antic distinction we may discern, in a modified form, the old thesis contrasting *yamato kotoba* to *kango/gairaigo* which, as we have earlier seen, is itself a wholly invalid, non-linguistic assumption. And therefore, it is not surprising that his linguistic material has been shown to be highly dubious.[6]

Judgement on Tsunoda's work must await independent verification by competent scientists (preliminary work has, it would appear, if predictably, failed to confirm his findings).[7] What is certain is that Tsunoda's book exploits his experimental results to corroborate a large number of ideological fictions concerning Japanese uniqueness as surveyed in this book, and that his broader cultural interpretations of the implications of his research are wild, if not fantastic. He has argued, for example, that the declining success of Japanese athletes in global competitions in the postwar period is due to the damage to neurological reflexes caused by the study of foreign languages, which, being consonantal, confuse their uniquely vowel-wired brains.[8]

Tsunoda's theory belongs to that stream of *nihonjinron* in the seventies which calls for a return to a pure, authentically Japanese pattern of thought, in which the ostensible fundamental unity of Japanese man with nature is the keystone. Tsunoda cites with approval the work of Japanese primatologists as proof of the originality and productive rewards of adopting a 'purely Japanese' approach in scientific research, and specifically the following passage from a work by Umesao Tadao:

> The reason why individual discrimination (*kotai shikibetsu*) progressed smoothly is because the Japanese have something like a sense of personal affection for individual monkeys. It seems that many Western scholars cannot help but entertain grave doubts about the possibility that Japanese scientists may discriminate between monkeys individually merely by looking at their faces. It is true that Carpenter would tattoo monkeys he had captured for the purpose of distinguishing them indi-

vidually. But it was Japanese scientists, without doubt, who advanced one step further into the inner core of the monkey mentality. Without losing their objectivity, their papers have inserted a scalpel into the very depths of the monkey mind. Many of these works are marked by penetrating insights. It is my belief that a depth psychology or psychoanalysis of monkeys may be developed by the work of these Japanese scientists.[9]

Tsunoda comments that:

By identifying themselves with an object (in the external world) in this way, these scholars have made definite scientific discoveries of a kind which differ from the 'scientific' concepts that form the marrow of the Western framework.[10]

In both these passages we discern an explicit intention to re-found science on a kind of Japanese epistemology which apparently involves a process of the observer/experimenter's conscious self-identification with the object under analysis. Not only these primatologists, but also Tsunoda, with his identity of *pathos* and *logos*, and indeed Doi, with his collusive identification with his patients' *amae*, appear to believe that the Japanese are culturally invested with a unique mode of cognition of subject–object identity, wherein the alienation of the observer from the world external to him thought typical of the 'Western mentality' (*cf* 26,D in tables 6 and 7) is somehow miraculously transcended.

We are closing upon the philosophical kernel of the ideology of Japaneseness here and we do well to follow up Tsunoda's hint by examining the field of Japanese primatology, which is frequently held up in the *nihonjinron* as the one field of nationalistic thought which has reaped rich, internationally recognised, results. This school was founded by Imanishi Kinji (b. 1902), a scholar who, through his teaching and thinking at Kyoto University, in the pre-war period a theoretical hot bed of nationalism, has exercised a significant influence on the postwar *nihonjinron*. Though originally concerned with elaborating the ideas of philosophers and thinkers like Nishida Kitarō and Watsuji Tetsurō (his erstwhile colleagues) in the field of biological sciences, his ideas have had an impact on a younger generation of scholars like Umesao Tadao and Aida Yūji concerned with much broader issues of culture.[11]

Deprived of the resources of a research station in Mongolia at the end of the war, Imanishi returned to Japan, to a country too poor to finance his ambitious programmes. He often sounds as if at this period his ethnological work were a continuance of war by other means, since he is said to have concluded that, as he could not beat 'the yanks' (*amechan*) on their own terms, he would outdo them by reversing their procedures. That is, he would do fieldwork instead of laboratory research (hence his lifelong suspicion of genetics), use men instead of scientific equipment, and concentrate on longterm studies rather than speedy results. In this way, he hoped 'to take the wind out of their sails' by demonstrating that 'though we've been beaten in the war, we won't be done in by their scholarship'.[12]

Directing his students towards a variety of studies, from 'the social dynamics of pet rabbits' (Kawai Masao) to 'the social interference theory of tadpoles' (Umesao Tadao),[13] Imanishi eventually settled his attention on research into the troops of *Macaca fuscata* monkeys which roam the Japanese wilds. Here, his school developed three techniques which are often cited as the unique outcome of a Japanese way of interacting with nature and animals. Firstly, emphasis is placed on the putative capacity of Japanese to 'individuate monkeys by sight' (*kotai shikibetsu*). Secondly, there is the practice of having observers intermingle with the monkeys at specially constructed feeding stations; and thirdly, stress is laid on interpreting primate behaviour in terms of 'social' and 'cultural' values.[14]

The idea that in this there is something 'uniquely Japanese' stems from a curious amnesia, for it is clear that Imanishi borrowed the idea of both feeding monkeys and recognising them by sight from the pioneering work of C.R. Carpenter. Umesao says that Carpenter had to tattoo monkeys in order to individuate them, but advantageously fails to mention that Carpenter soon disposed of this marking system because, 'Many could be recognised on sight because of individual differences in appearance.'[15] Carpenter records having moved among the monkey troops (breaking with the rule of neutrality) and feeding them sweet potatoes in order to record the underlying dynamics of the social systems.[16] Thirdly, the idea that cultural transmission among monkeys was a Japanese discovery overlooks the fact that this same view was implicit in Alfred Carpenter's observation that Burmese macaques used stones as breaking tools to open up oysters (1887), and in Eugene Marais' contention that chacma baboons had discovered the intoxicating properties of a local shrub leaf and regularly used them in euphoric feasts.[17]

This quibbling is important because both Imanishi's school, and the various *nihonjinron* that draw inspiration from it, repeatedly link these procedures to a peculiar Japanese *Weltanschauung*, and stress how different this is from that underlining the arid objectivism of Western science. Thus we are told that Western ethnologists and anthropologists either do not mix with native peoples or do not get on with them, and treat animals as objects, whereas (again, according to Umesao Tadao):

> The development of primatology in Japan is due to the intimacy which subsists here between man and monkey. For Europeans, of course, there is an unbridgeable gap between man and the animal kingdom, ...[18]

In a similar vein Kamishima Jirō tells us that:

> Umesao Tadao has presented an interesting typology regarding relationships between man and monkey. According to this, the theory of evolution arose in the West precisely because man and money are *disconnected*. In Japan, man and monkey form a continuous link (*cf* D',E' in table 7), the monkey differing from man only by a hair's breadth. Therefore, our thought pattern was so inherently evolutionist as not to require a formal theoretical elaboration. Because of this, it came to be thought that, with man and monkey serially linked, there could be a psychological current exchanged between them.[19]

As Doi with Freud, so here Umesao with Darwin. Namely, *homo nipponicus* did not develop psychoanalysis nor a theory of evolution theoretically because the Japanese *Weltanschauung* already embodied this outlook which only centuries of intellectual endeavour in the recent West have managed to understand.

Imanishi's work had as its aim an ambitious challenging of Darwinian thought, which it attempted to overthrow by establishing an alternative, authentically oriental, model of evolution. A reading of Imanishi's theory in its entirety would extend this chapter beyond reasonable limits, and here I will concentrate only on those aspects which highlight both his nationalism and his relationship to the *nihonjinron*. As I have already hinted, his formulations owe a great debt to certain social and theoretical ideas which were anti-individualist, linked in part to the rise of fascism in Japan, and explicitly aimed at 'overcoming the modern'. A deeper analysis would quickly show how his theory melds Watsuji's notion of *aidagara*, Nishida's subject–object epistemology and Tanabe Hajime's 'logic of the species' in a biological idiom.

For example, his development of the notion of *kotai shikibetsu*, though initially derived from Carpenter, bears a heavy load of philosophical theorising. He holds that though evolution is a process of increasing specialisation, repeated differentiation has never ruptured the underlying, original biological affinity linking all biological orders. Affinity (*ruien*) here is defined as 'a principle which orders relationships that can be seen as both dissimilar and analogous at the same time'.[20] Man, being part of this natural order, can thus make 'correct or necessary anthropomorphisms'[21] from himself to other species by attributing to them social, cultural and spiritual forms which, in the West, are usually considered unique to the human species. He backs this by an epistemological theory which runs as follows:

> Going back to a state prior to discrimination, in which discrimination as a product had not yet appeared, if we try to think about the standpoint of our immediately observing things, then this (perception) is not a mere mechanical thing, without meaning, like the reflection of things in a mirror. Rather, I consider that our perception of things is one in which we perceive these things in the relationships, existing from the beginning, with which the things which constitute this world are furnished. In other words, we always perceive simultaneously also those points of similarity between things.
>
> That is, if this simple cognition that I mean here is one that grasps things in their relatedness, as it were, by immediate, intuitive perception (*chokkanteki ni*) without so much as going through the process of actually comparing one thing with another and rendering a judgement, then I would say that our understanding of the mutual resemblances and differences between things has a sort of *a priori* (or transcendental) character fundamentally inherent in our cognitive mode itself. That is to say, this (cognition) has a profound basis in the way that the things which constitute this world were originally differentiated and developed from the one primal material, namely

that even we ourselves have neither burst forth into the world in our present form, nor come here from another world, and in that sense, we are not entities heterogeneous to the world itself. Rather, precisely because we ourselves have experienced within our own bodies this process of differentiation and growth of this world, this (*a priori*) character in our cognition) came to be, at one time or another, endowed in us.

Thus it is not only that the various things which constitute this world are not heterogeneous to us, but that we also formed and developed alongside the formation and development of these things. Considered in this way, the fact that we are able, without contrivances, to perceive the relationships pre-existing between these things is rather due to an hereditary disposition with which we have been endowed, or to put it more simply, it is only one of our inherent instincts (*honnō*).[22]

Here, as the language itself suggests, Nishida's theory of 'pure experience' (*junsui keiken*), as modified by his later notion of 'active intuition' (*kōiteki chokkan*), underlies the idea of 'simple cognition', and appears melded to a biological version of Watsuji's theory of *aidagara* in which a transindividual bond between man and man is replaced by a cognitive bond unifying man and other species in the natural kingdom.

Secondly, Imanishi has attempted to overthrow Darwinian theory by an attack on the twin poles that support it, namely, random, spontaneous mutations in individuals which then spread by breeding through the species, and the theory of natural selection. Underlying this critique is, curiously enough for someone who advocates as a unique field observation technique the discrimination of individuality in monkeys, a strong bias against individualism. Indeed, Imanishi's attempt to replace the individual with the species as the unit of evolutionary change coincides with the *nihonjinron* contrast between an individualist West and a groupist Japan (10,10' in table 4).

For Imanishi, when environmental change presents a species with a challenge, then the species, by drawing on its pre-existing repertoire of possible mutations, throws out the appropriate genetic trump card[23] enabling it to adapt precisely to these new conditions, and thus the management of evolution is controlled by the species itself. All the individuals within the species, or most of them, must change simultaneously and in the same way. His argument, in attributing to the species a power of endless self-transformation, assumes a teleological dimension. Mutations only arise when there is a need for them and do not occur when they are not required.[24]

His development of the theory of a 'species society' (*shushakai*) as the fundamental unit of evolutionary change draws on Lamarck but betrays a certain conceptual affiliation to the 'logic of the species' (*shu no ronri*) of Tanabe Hajime's ultranationalistic philosophy.[26] 'Species' here is the mediating ground of the nation, midway between the genus of mankind and the individual, which coerces or negates the individual, or as Tanabe quaintly put it, may 'force the individual's spontaneous obedience'[26] but is, in turn, negated by the totality, thus being the 'expedient means' (*hōben*) through which the individual apparently realises himself in 'Absolute Nothingness'.

Some of this has clearly rubbed off on Imanishi's thinking, particularly in the notion of the species (effectively the race community) as negation of the individual. Imanishi's *sumiwake genri* (which derives from F.E. Clements' theory of plant succession and climax, and Shelford's adaptation of the same to animal societies),[27] ideated to replace Darwin's struggle for survival with the concept that each species assumes a 'spatial niche' in order to live unantagonistically with other animal communities in an organic harmony marked by 'prosperity and order',[28] comes curiously close to giving biological form to the idea of a 'Greater Co-prosperity Sphere' in the natural world parallel to that which the fascist government was extending into Asia during the war. It also plays off, in the contrast with Darwin, features 18,18' and 20,20' in tables 4 and 5.

Imanishi's greatest impact has been in the field of Japanese primatology. The strange things about some of the published reports (in a field where much empirical work has been of great value) is that they tend to corroborate too nicely the ideological presuppositions underlying Imanishi's work. Thus the noted case of Imo, the macaque which discovered how to wash and flavour potatoes on the island of Kōshima, and was thereafter imitated by the troop, is spoken about as if there were something of mystical proportions in the method of cultural propagation. We are told that the discovery, spreading rapidly throughout a colony of macaques, seems to have been diffused simultaneously to other macaque troops on other islands and the mainland, and this is somehow linked with the birth of a new youngster to the original troop.[29] This seems to confirm two of Imanishi's theories.

It is firstly used to sustain the view that monkeys have both subjectivity and a transmissible culture, constantly changed by new discoveries, and secondly to support his thesis that evolutionary adaptations occur spontaneously throughout the species. But it might be noted that Imanishi's ideas on spontaneous mutation throughout the species, however much they may be motivated by nationalist ideology, do bear rough comparison to Sheldrake's heterodox hypothesis of 'morphogenetic fields', according to which, once a new form occurs it will provoke the emergence of similar forms by resonance through both space and time.[30]

The oddest thing however about this school is that their descriptions of the psycho-social characteristics of the Japanese macaques dovetail or overlap with the *nihonjinron* analyses of those social relationships and values deemed unique to the Japanese. Monkey society, we are told, is male-dominated, while rearing is entrusted to submissive females. The group (*mure*) orders relations in terms of an hierarchical (*cf tate*) pecking order. Individualism is excluded, and the lone monkey learns through early disciplinary training (*shitsuke*) to submit to the consensual 'laws of the troop' (*mure no okite*). Stress is laid on the 'skinship' of the mother–child bond, while the rules of social precedence (*jun'i*) may be ignored only by the very young, who are allowed to presume on relations of dependence, or to coax (*amaeru*). Monkeys learn by mimicry (*sarumane*: *cf* the old hare about Japanese technology), and baby monkeys overindulged by their mothers develop symptoms of social withdrawal similar to those of Morita's *shinkeishitsu* patients.[31]

In one recent campaign to 'learn from the chimpanzee' (because they are 'more human than Man') it appears that the Japanese public, in viewing these films on primates, felt that they highlight in their behaviour something 'precious lost in human society', namely trust between the group and its boss, and that compassion (*ninjō*) community leaders in the monkey world feel for their underlings. Such is Joe, the head of a chimp troop at Tokyo's Tama Zoo, who wears himself out in worry to maintain order, protect the weak and safeguard the welfare of the group. He even humbles himself before his subordinates in order not to intimidate them, something which the modern Japanese executive has apparently lost sight of. The Tokyo Metropolitan government was reported to be planning to use such films to teach its directors 'management without control', and the Sports Association to train Japan's Olympic coaches.[32]

In this new sense of identity with monkeys a curious historical reversal has taken place. For one of the Western stereotypes given high profile in the *nihonjinron* and a frequent source of bitter rancour is that which compared the Japanese spitefully to monkeys. Richet, we are told, even thought of them as at a stage intermediate between monkey and (white) man'.[33] This old slur, kept very much alive in the Japanese imagination by the *nihonjinron*, has by virtue of Imanishi's primatology been stood on its head. The old disparaging stigmatisation of foreigners becomes an internalised compliment, presumably because, 'the *mutual* understanding between Japanese monkeys and the Japanese people is deep'.[34] If Jane Goodall is concerned with elucidating how 'the chimpanzee has a primitive awareness of Self',[35] the *nihonjinron* masters playing on this theme do the opposite. While one humanises the ape, the other makes a monkey out of himself.[36]

Notes

1. Sakagami Shōichi, *Mitsubachi no tadotta michi*, (Shisakusha, Tokyo, 1970). I rely on the summary in Aida, *Nihonjin no ishiki kōzō*, ibid. pp.30ff. It is referred to as an important work in 'Comparative Animal Sociology' in Umesao Tadao, Kira Tatsuo hen, *Seitaigaku nyūmon*, (Kōdansha Gakujutsu Bunko, Tokyo, 1976) pp.85-7.
2. Aida, *Nihonjin no ishiki kōzō*, ibid. pp.30-9.
3. Tsunoda Tadanobu, *Nihonjin no nō — Nō no hataraki to tōzai no bunka*, (Taishūkan Shoten, Tokyo, 1978). His work is summarised and reviewed briefly by Makita Kiyoshi, in *Journal of Japanese Studies*, 5:2 (1979) pp.440-49; R.A. Miller, *Japan's Modern Myth*, ibid. ch. 4, pp.64-83; Shibatani Atsuhiro, *Science '80'*, 1:8 (1980) pp.24-6. Shibatani is a former student of Imanishi Kinji, in apparent exile from that school (See Imanishi Kinji, *Watakushi no reichōruigaku*, (Kōdansha Gakujutsu Bunko, Tokyo, 1976) p.262).
4. In his book on Japanese music entitled 'The Ears of Japan', Ogura formulates the principle that, 'A race forms its own unique world of sounds by selecting those sounds which are proper and suitable (*fusawashii*) to its ears'. Ogura Rō, *Nihon no mimi*, (Iwanami Shinsho, Tokyo, 1977) p.5.
5. Makita, ibid. pp.442-4.
6. Tsunoda, *Nihonjin no nō*, ibid. p.131, *cf* the review editor's note to Makita's comments, ibid. pp.449-50, referring to the data in Tsunoda, ibid. pp.291ff. The view that Japanese are poor speakers of foreign languages because of a difference in language processing is clearly wrong. It is well known that these difficulties ensue from the way language training in Japan is designed to impede fluency.
7. See the paper by Cooper and O'Malley cited in Makita, ibid. p.447.

8. *cf* his remarks on the Japanese brain and creativity in Kimura Shōsaburō, Kamishima Jirō et al. *Shin nihonjinron*, (Kōdansha Tokyo, 1980) pp.229-281, esp. pp.238, 259-60, 278. *cf* Tsunoda, *Nihonjin no nō*, ibid. pp.369-76.

9. Tsunoda, *Nihonjin no nō*, ibid. p.363. He is citing from Umesao, Tadao, *Nihon Tanken* (Chūō Kōronsha, Tokyo, 1960). A résumé of Umesao's views may be found in John Frisch, 'Japan's Contribution to Modern Anthropology' in Joseph Roggendorf (ed.), *Studies in Japanese Culture* (Sophia University Press, Tokyo, 1963) pp.225-44, pp.238ff.

10. Tsunoda, *Nihonjin no nō*, ibid. p.363.

11. Imanishi headed the North-West Research Centre in Changchiak'ou (Kalgan) in Inner Mongolia during the war, and the nature of the work done there, and its relationship to the war, is an unwritten chapter in the *nihonjinron*. He directed there such scholars as Umesao Tadao and Ishida Eiichirō in studies on nomadic life, and this has had a considerable impact upon the postwar images of Western pastoralism as a contrast to Japanese agriculturalism (1,1'; 6,6' in tables 1 and 3) through Imanishi's influence at the Research Centre for the Humanities at Kyoto University.

12. *cf* Ueyama Shumpei, *Nihon no shisō. Dochaku to ōka no keifu*, (Simul Shuppankai, Tokyo, 1971) pp.198-9. The quote is Ueyama's way of summing up Imanishi's attitude.

13. *cf* postscript to Miyaji Densaburō, *Saru no hanashi*, (Iwanami Shinsho, Tokyo, 1966) p.185.

14. *cf* Frisch, 'Japan's Contribution', ibid. esp. pp.234-41. It is even claimed that monkeys have an (ethical) value system, for which see Yamada Keiji hen, *Gakumon no chizu*, (Asahi Shinbunsha, Tokyo, 1979) pp.23ff. Umesao, *Nihon Tanken*, ibid. p.234 says that the aim is to develop a 'cultural primatology' in direct opposition to the 'cultural anthropology' of the West.

15. C.R. Carpenter, 'Sexual Behavior of Free-Ranging Rhesus Monkeys' in *Journal of Comparative Psychology*, 33 (1942) pp.113-62, pp.115-6. The practice of giving separate names to individual monkeys is also employed by Jane Van Lawick-Goodall, *cf* her *In the Shadow of Man* (Fontana paper. London, 1976) p.44.

16. Setting up feeding stations for primates runs the risk of altering the behaviour of these animals, thus rendering objective observations difficult if not impossible. See Frisch, 'Japan's Contribution', ibid. pp.237-8, and Lawick-Goodall, ibid. pp.143ff.

17. A. Desmond, *The Ape's Reflection* (Blond and Briggs, London, 1979) p.143. E. Marais, *The Soul of the Ape* (Penguin, 1973) pp.90ff. He also used a method of individual discrimination (ibid. p.140).

18. Ishida Eiichirō, in Umesao Tadao, Tada Michitarō hen. *Nihon bunka no kōzō*, ibid. pp.69-70.

19. Kamishima Jirō, *Nihonjin no hassō* (Kōdansha Gendai Shinsho, 1975) p.52.

20. Ueyama, *Nihon no shisō*, ibid. p.209 citing Imanishi's hastily drafted book (before he was dispatched by the army to Mongolia) *Seibutsu no sekai.*

21. Imanishi Kinji, *Ningen izen no shakai*, (Iwanami Shinsho reprint, Tokyo, 1956) pp.9, 19.

22. As cited in Ueyama, *Nihon no shisō*, ibid. pp.209-10. It is this theory of discrimination which underlies his idea of *kotai shikibetsu*.

23. Imanishi Kinji, *Shinka to wa nani ka* (Kōdansha Gakujutsu Bunko, 1976) p.27.

24. Imanishi, *Shinka to wa nani ka*, ibid. pp.24-5, 30, 33-4, p.131.

25. Imanishi, *Shinka to wa nani ka*, ibid. p.31, pp.128ff. For Tanabe see G. Piovesana, *Recent Japanese Philosophical Thought*, ibid. pp.145-58. A translation

of chapter 1 of his 'Dialectic of the Logic of the Species' by David Dilworth and Taira Satō may be found in *Monumenta Nipponica* XXIV:3-4 (1969) pp.273-88.

26. Tanabe, 'Dialectic of the Logic of the Species' ibid. p.274.

27. Imanishi, *Shutaisei no shinkaron* (Chūkō Shinsho, Tokyo, 1980) pp.101ff; Ueyama, *Nihon no shisō*, ibid. pp.201ff; Umesao, Kira, *Seitaigaku nyūmon*, ibid. pp.49-54, pp.57-60.

28. Imanishi, *Ningen izen no shakai*, ibid. pp.23-35; esp. pp.33-4. Ueyama, *Nihon no shisō*, ibid. pp.201-3. His idea of peaceful coexistence in opposition to Darwin's theory of competition may owe something to Kropotkin's *Mutual Aid.* It is to be noted that Kropotkin's translator, Ōsugi Sakae, also translated two French books of entomology (an early interest of Imanishi's) widely read in Japan. See T.A. Stanley, *Ōsugi Sakae: Anarchist in Taishō Japan* (Harvard University Press, Cambridge, 1982) p.49, pp.148-9.

29. See the mysterious report of this in L. Watson, *Lifetide* (Coronet paper. London, 1980) pp.173-4. See also Miyaji, *Saru no hanashi*, ibid. pp.146ff.

30. R. Sheldrake, *A New Science of Life* (Blond and Briggs, London, 1981).

31. Mizuno Hajime, 'Saru to hito to wa doko ga dō chigau ka', in *Chūō Kōron* 4 (1979) pp.247-55, esp. pp.247f. Doi, '*Amae' zakkō*, ibid. p.122, contests the view that monkeys can 'coax'.

32. *Mainichi Daily News*, 4 November 1978, p.12.

33. Hirakawa Sukehiro, *Wakon yōsai no keifu* (Kawade Bungei Sensho, Tokyo, 1976) p.176. See also Aida Yūji, *Nihonjin no ikikata* (Kōdansha Gakujutsu Bunko, 1976) pp.19ff. See the extraordinary exchange between Ueyama and Itani in Yamada Keiji hen, *Gakumon no chizu*, ibid. pp.170ff, where the chimpanzee, being nearer Europe, tends to adopt a rational approach to problems unlike the Oriental macaques and orang utangs which show a Zen-like meditative approach.

34. Kawabe Sumiko, *Saru no Akachan*, (Chūkō Shinsho, Tokyo, 1964) p.10. Kenmochi Takehiko, '*Ma' no nihon bunka*, ibid. p.71, actually speaks of Japanese and monkeys conducting 'dialogues'.

35. Goodall, *In the Shadow of Man*, ibid. p.243.

36. *cf* The wordplay between Japanese *hitonami/monkī-nami* in Aida Yūji, *Sekai no naka no nihonjin* (Kawade Shobō Shinsha, Tokyo, 1974) p.141. It is this range of ideas which lies behind Watanabe's remark cited above, ch. 5. But it is not the Japanese male who should be worried about this proximity. On the basis of leucocytes samples Kasuya Isaku concludes that 'the personality nucleus of a Japanese monkey is not that of a human infant, but that of a human adult; or, more specifically, that of a human young woman highly conscientious and sternly devoid of sociability in character'! See his *Leucocyte and Personality: An Introduction to Micro-constitutional psychology* (Doshinsha Press, Tokyo, 1974) pp.121-2.

12 ON IDENTITY AS DIFFERENCE

'In jeder geistigen Haltung ist das Politische latent'
(Politics is latent in every spiritual attitude)
Thomas Mann, cited in T. Reed, Thomas Mann: *The Uses of Tradition*, 1974 p.306.

'It seems almost as if Japan differs from the rest of the major traditions of the world, all of which would accept the Socratic dictum that "the unexamined life is unfit to live". Japan might even counter by saying that it is the examined life that is unfit to live, because it is not life.'
Charles Moore, in *The Japanese Mind*, p.289.

The Twilight of Meiji

Although many scholars regard the almost obsessional preoccupation with the analysis of ethnic identity in Japan to be, itself, distinctive to Japanese intellectual culture,[1] national identity as a theme of inquiry in Europe dates back to the eighteenth century, to an age when an older vein of ethnocentrism was transformed by secular and bourgeois trends into a fully-fledged political programme of national revival. It played, as propaganda, a significant role in the overthrow of the *ancien régime*, and spread contagiously through the continent in the wake of Napoleon's armies, finding a particularly congenial home in Germany. There, thinkers like Hegel, Fichte, Schlegel and Jahn, in expounding the idea of the organic state, its *völkisch* community and *Volkstümlichkeit*,[2] established an intellectual momentum for nationalism which was to exercise a profound influence on later political and social culture.

If originally European nationalism owed much to certain currents of bourgeois liberalism (though in Germany bourgeois illiberalism as a reaction against the Enlightenment was also of decisive importance), after the defeats of 1848 this liberal character in nationalism tended to wither before the rising force of conservative nationalism. By 1870 we witness the emergence of imperialist nationalisms in which internal consolidation and external annexation begin to constitute the twin poles of the national ideal. When in 1867 Japan opened its doors to the West (as a model for modernisation), it encountered among these imperial powers a variety of conservative nationalism in which:

> The ruling class and the monarch were glorified as the embodiment of the nation, its hierarchy and traditions expressing the essence of the nation's historic culture and social unity. At the same time, these nationalisms possessed an aggressive modernising drive with strong militarist overtones.[3]

In this sense, the dramatisation of the Meiji Restoration as a radical attempt to modernise an Oriental absolutism along Western lines is misleading. Thought in late Tokugawan times is marked by the fact that the stronger the momentum of decay in the rigid caste system and the economic foundations of its aristocratic, anti-mercantilist élite, the more pronounced were the ideological emphases on totalitarian radical reform. As we see in the remarkable anticipations of modern absolutisms in such thinkers as Satō Nobuhiro, Ninomiya Sontoku and Honda Toshiaki, indigenous notions of an organic, totally mobilised nation–state had already been brought to fruition, but the administrative means, industrial base and economic techniques required for its realisation were wholly lacking.

The opening up to the West provided the only means whereby the twin elements of such visionary totalitarianism could be achieved, namely internal consolidation under restored Imperial authority and foreign annexation by force of modern arms. The conservative revolution from above thus in effect sought to revitalise this moribund world order within by tactical recourse to foreign civilisation which held the instruments, not for the transcendence of feudalism, but for its survival and 'modernisation'. The timing was decisive, since the nationalism they saw exemplified in the West was, at this precise juncture, both imperial and conservative. Crucial to the success of this herodian restructuring of Japan was the thwarting of that alliance between radical intelligentsia and entrepreneurial class which, as nationalist antagonists to the absolute state, proved decisive for the emergence of bourgeois culture and society in the West.

It is for this reason that we find the ideological charters for Japanese nationalism deeply imbued with either a mystical or aristocratic coloration and why, instead of justifying their self interest in terms of social amelioration, the emerging entrepreneurs of Japan tended to defend their capitalist endeavours in terms of 'the national interest'.[4] In this sense, Japanese fascism, unlike its German counterpart which was established only through the destruction of bourgeois social institutions, could build naturally on traditional foundations.[5]

While 'modernisation' was thus in many respects a selective reinforcement of traditional institutions under the deceptive alias of 'Westernisation', to the intellectuals of the time the rapid changes were frequently read as indications of a radical change in polity. After a generation of hectic reform justified by appeal to the Western example if, more often than not, propelled by traditional Confucian and samurai codes of 'rising in the world',[6] enthusiasm for the foreign began to give way to nostalgia for the past, as the costs of industrialisation, perceptions of the disconcerting contrast between the new bourgeois ideals and Western *Realpolitik*, colonial carpet-bagging and difficulties in revising the humiliating treaties, began to be weighed up in the balance against the renewed urgency of preserving the national essence (*kokutai hozon*), that intangible complex of the uniquely Japanese which campaigners like Shiga Shigetaka, Miyake Setsurei and Kuga Katsunan began to write on from the mid 1880s.[7]

If infirm and tentative at the outset, this doubt over what passed for 'Westernisation' and vague nostalgia for autochthonous culture was transformed overnight into a sense of positive repudiation and national pride with the Japanese victory over China in 1895, a victory which, though profoundly indebted to Western armaments and logistical know how, was seen as endorsing the fledging sense of a return to indigenous spirit.

In this transitional phase between a superficial programme of Westernisation and later reactionary regression to endogenous tradition, a key role was played by men poised precariously between the two poles. Westerners like Lafcadio Hearn and Ernest Fenellosa, employed to teach Western science and culture, were quickly enamoured of that very culture which they had been hired to surmount. The very instructors of modernity thus paradoxically lent their name and prestige to a revival of interest in antiquities which was later to assume symbolic weight in the revolt against modernity. Hearn with his 'queer thrill' for the 'outward strangeness' of old Japan, hitched his own mediocre waggon to the accelerating train of uniqueness and in exploring the unplumbed oddity of Japan found prodigal scope for the vicarious conquest of his finde-siècle malaise and deracinated hostility to the West he had repudiated.[8] In doing so he inadvertently abetted the very forces of cynical nationalism in Japan whose brazen power-mongering he was otherwise so dedicated to unmasking in the Western context.

In Hearn there is an unresolved contradiction between his love for Japanese values, and his acute awareness of the force of centuries of martial authoritarianism conditioning them.[9] He is seduced by a social modality which seemed to preserve intact the edenic world of the Greek *polis* and the simplicity of a child's fairyland. On the other hand, the rising generation of men like Nitobe Inazō, many of them converts to Christianity, while indelibly drenched in the dyes of traditional socialisation, tempered their innate fidelity to this residual *samurai* heritage with a recognition that, ineluctably, Western style institutions were indispensable for progress. Where the Westerner assuages his disillusionment with his native world and its tensions with the anodyne of this Oriental, preindustrial society, the Japanese, equally disturbed by the problems of backwardness in their local culture, sought redress in the developing promise of Western institutions.

These two figures stand out in the restoration of national pride after the initial phase of adulation for all things foreign (with its concomitant contempt for local culture) had exhausted itself. But they display an ambivalence which prefigures the contradictions characteristic of all later *nihonjinron* written by their less illustrious epigones. For both Hearn and Nitobe, the 'uniqueness' of Japan consists in the way it appears to preserve all of the institutional structures and values which they associate, respectively, with archaic Greece and medieval Christianity. Paradoxically therefore, they set out to illustrate the distinctiveness of Japan by paralleling many aspects of its culture with the superannuated traditions of Europe.

Uniqueness here is not properly a *sui generis* phenomenon, without parallel in the documented testimonies of civilisation. Rather it is a distinctiveness *vis-à-vis* the contemporary West, how the singularity of Japan is seen to lie in the way it preserves either the inchoate forms of human experience (Hearn) or the full-force of feudalism (Nitobe) into the modern era. But in simple terms, all this really means is that Japanese 'uniqueness' consists in being historically retarded with respect to the industrial development of the West. In their terms, every non-Western moderniser must be 'unique'.

Uniqueness thus became a code word applied to exotic phenomena whose attractiveness lay precisely in the way they gave lively contemporary witness to a world and life style transcended by the march of time and progress in the West. Nitobe for example contradicts himself in speaking of the parallels between *bushidō* and the chivalric codes of the medieval West by asserting at one point that, 'Few historical comparisons can be more judiciously made than between the Chivalry of Europe and the *Bushidō* of Japan,'[10] only to justify elsewhere his retention of the native term bushidō in an English text on the grounds that, 'A teaching so circumscribed and unique, engendering a cast of mind and character so peculiar, so local, must wear the badge of its singularity on its face.'[11]

Their two most influential books were published around the time of the Russo–Japanese war (1904-5), and victory here, this time against a Western power, was decisive in confirming a full scale ideological drive against exogenous models of development. The years from 1906 to 1912 constitute perhaps the critical turning-point in modern Japanese intellectual history, and despite recent inroads into this sociocultural complex, Bowring's judgement that the late Meiji period is 'as yet a relatively uncharted field'[12] remains valid.

With the failure of obtaining war reparations after the huge economic and physical costs of the war with Russia, the year 1906, marked as it is by the publication of the first philosophical formulation of national socialism, Kita Ikki's *Outline of a Proposal for the Reconstruction of Japan* (a bible of later right wing revolutionaries), and the coining of the word *genmetsu* for the idea of 'disillusionment',[13] witnesses the emergence of a brilliant, if short lived movement towards alternative political activism and literary naturalism. In the midst of urban *anomie*, virulent pollution as symbolised by the Ashio Copper Mine, peasant protest and sabotage, riotous demonstrations, the breaking of rural ties and the fragmentation of the family, increasingly visible economic corruption and political crisis, we observe a vibrant upsurge in a new type of fiction embracing such figures as Shimazaki Tōzon (*Hakai*, 1906), Tayama Katei (*Futon*, 1907), Natsume Sōseki, Shiga Naoya, Nagai Kafū, Tanizaki Jun'ichirō and Mori Ōgai in his second period. At the same time we observe the emergence of radical activists like Ōsugi Sakae and Kōtoku Shūsui who aim at nothing less than a total subversion of the imperial state.

Flourishing under the auspices of the 'liberal' Saionji cabinet, this social and literary burgeoning of a modern culture deeply disturbed conservative quarters. To confront the peril posed by 'dangerous thoughts',[14] the old conservative guard led by Yamagata Aritomo had first to provoke the downfall of Saionji, and this done, place the hardliner Katsura Tarō back in position. As a prophylaxis against 'thought', compulsory education was extended, state textbooks on ethics redrafted, Shintō and the emperor cult entered into curricula, and rural youth groups were subject to mass ideological mobilisation.[15] There is a visible upsurge in books on national ideology, from a mere one volume in 1908 to 10 works in 1910.[16] Press laws were passed, censorship controls radically tightened, novelists brought to trial for obscenity (while popular, traditional pornography, as a fantasy outlet, was untouched), revolutionaries imprisoned, and in the case of the Kōtoku Shūsui 'plot' against the Emperor, executed *en masse.*[17]

Yet it is precisely at this juncture, when the battle against modernity was at its peak, that the government found a spontaneous ally among intellectuals working in theoretical areas of research. The next generation of thinkers enters on centre stage in the years around 1910, which were a watershed for what might be called, by adapting a phrase from Thomas Mann, 'the intellectualisation of Japanese conservatism'.[18] This aid emerging from non-official quarters, which provided a high calibre culture of reaction missing from the demagogic works on ethics issued by government officials,[19] is grounded in the writings of academics and thinkers who, for the most part, pertain to that generation born in the first years of the Meiji Restoration between 1870-75. In summarising the common thread underpinning their independently constructed theories I must for reasons of space abbreviate an analysis which requires a far closer reading of the texts involved.

Nishida Kitarō (1870-1945) undertook with the publication of his work *A Study of Good* (1910) to sketch out the philosophical ground of an autochthonous school of thought. His key notion of 'pure experience', though phrased through a vast number of concepts and terms lifted eclectically from both Western and Oriental thought,[20] attempts to reconstitute and validate the notion of no mind and *satori* in Buddhist philosophy. As he writes programmatically at the outset:

> Experience means to know reality exactly as it is (*jijitsu sono*

mama). It is to know by entirely abandoning the artifices of the self and by following reality. Since usually those who discuss experience actually conjoin thought of some kind to the idea, 'pure' means precisely the condition of experience in itself, without the admixture of any thinking or discrimination. For example, it means, at the instant of seeing colour or hearing sound, the experience prior not only to thinking that it is the function of an external thing or that it is my feeling, but even before the judgement of what this colour or sound is, has been added. Therefore pure experience (*junsui keiken*) is identical with immediate experience (*chokusetsu keiken*).[21]

Whether we discern here an attempt to grasp the notion of *samadhi* (transformation of the mind into the object it contemplates in profound meditation) via Western philosophical categories, or remark only an admixture of Wang Yang-Ming and Buddhist mysticism under the gloss of occidental jargon,[22] it is clear that the idea of 'pure experience' provided Nishida with a happily up-to-date vehicle for reaffirming a pre-modern, pre-Kantian, epistemology, whose essence he sums up as involving 'the unity of subject and object' (*shukaku gōitsu*) and 'the state of undifferentiation of subject and object' (*shukaku-mibun no jōtai*),[23] a mode of cognition increasingly seen as unique to Oriental man.

Morita Shōma (1874-1938) developed his concept of *shinkeishitsu* as a condition uniquely Japanese roughly in the same period, around 1909.[24] As we have seen, this entailed the view that 'nervosity' resulted from the mind's captivation by thought, a condition of intellectual obsession which alienated man from life. For Morita, thinking was the root of neurosis, in that it estranged man from a vivid engagement with reality as it is (*aru ga mama*), and only a 'mindless' routine of work, as therapy, could restore a patient to his original experience of identity with phenomenological reality. Thought here is thus seen as a pathogenic wedge which ruptures the smooth interface between subjective feeling and the objective world. The similarities of this position with Nishida's epistemology are striking. Where one speaks of the 'artifices of the self' the other talks of 'the workings of bad intellect', and both concur in viewing the discriminating function of logical consciousness as deauthenticating man's immediate harmony with the world.[25]

In 1911, Muraoka Tsunetsugu (1884-1946) published his monumental study of *Motoori Norinaga*, which revived interest in the autochthonous school of classical philology. His book is a long interpretation of the leading thinker of the nativist school of intellectual thought in the Tokugawa period, and its significance lies in the way he tries to show how this indigenous philologist independently developed and anticipated principles of criticism that were to emerge in Western scholarship only decades later. Specifically, Muraoka thought he could discern in Motoori's approach an independent discovery of the principle underlying Böckh's *Philologie*, which aimed at 'the recognition of that which was once cognised' (*Das Erkennen des Erkannten*).[26] That is, philology aspired to re-enact or make re-appear (*saigen*) the consciousness of the people of antiquity, what is represented (*shazō*) in this consciousness, not only in terms of intellectual content but also in regard to their feelings, intact in its pristine form (*cf sono mama*).[27]

Muraoka held that Motoori's purpose of 'throwing light upon/ clarifying the pristine antiquity of the Empire',[28] though not as clear as Böckh's philosophical formulation, is tantamount to the same thing. The native school of philology, thus revalorised, provides an objective critical means through which the dead past of Japan, as centred in the culture of the Imperial line, may be not only resuscitated but reexperienced by contemporary man in its original form.

Fourthly, the father of Japanese folklore studies, Yanagita Kunio (1875-1962) published his pioneering study of peasant oral traditions, *Tōno Monogatari* (Tales of Tōno) in 1910. If Nishida and Morita attempt to transcend the estranging dimensions of 'Westernising' culture by affirming the unity of subject and object, then Yanagita, though formally hostile to *samurai* culture, takes a tack which parallels the course of Muraoka's study, by endeavouring here on in to reconstruct from peasant culture the ideal of the 'common Japanese man' (*jōmin*).[29] In the 'natural consciousness of the primeval Japanese' discerned in this prototypical *jōmin*, Yanagita discovered an authentically endogenous base for modernisation to contrast to that alienating mode exploited by those 'foreign culture bearers', the Meiji samurai élite. In Tsurumi Kazuko's words:

He refuses to equate modernisation with Westernisation. To

him modernisation is a process 'like peeling off again and again the outer crusts to bring into existence the truly worthy core of our culture'. That process has been going on noticeably among people long before Japan's contact with the West.[30]

A curious theory this, indeed, in which progress is interpreted as reversion to type back through time. *Tōno Monogatari* was addressed to Japanese students abroad, to remind those about to return to government service that the essence of being Japanese consisted in fidelity to this fictional prehistorical archetype of peasant consciousness. It is only by a return to a preforeign, archaic outlook, as an existential locus of authentic identity, that one can rediscover the true Japanese self. There is thus a negation of history in Yanagita, and a pronounced tendency to interpret the whole structure of oppression and exploitation in Japanese historical culture as a false imposition of alien values deriving from China and the West onto that endogenous, purely Japanese culture born by peasant tradition.[31]

A similar nostalgic return to the uncomplicated world of an earlier age may be found in the works of Mitamura Engyō (1870-1952). Where Yanagita seeks pure identity through contemporary reaffirmations of solidarity with primeval peasant consciousness, Mitamura, in a series of works evoking the traditional lifestyle of the Edo townsman, recreated a lost or fast-disappearing world of customary urbanity as a nostalgic contrast to the harassed and hectic milieu of the new, rapidly industrialised Tokyo.[32] It was also around this time that Suzuki Daisetsu (1870-1965), who had a significant influence on Nishida's thought, undertook to introduce to the West his Zen Buddhistic interpretations of Japanese culture, placing at the heart of Japan's pre-Western outlook the culture of monastic discipline.

Again, it is at this juncture of late Meiji that Kawakami Hajime (1879-1946) began to turn his interest away from economics to cultural problems.[33] In an essay penned in 1911, he contrasts how in Japan the individual's value consists only in his being an instrument of national growth, in direct antithesis to the Western order. In particular, he describes an opposition between Western individualism (*kojinshugi*) which is founded on *jinkaku* (the frame of individual personality), and the Japanese family-state (*kokkashugi*) which is founded on what he calls *kokkaku* (the frame of the nation). In this difference between occidental *person-*

ality and Japanese *nation*-ality he discovered the uniqueness of his country, where there was an absolute identity of the individual's 'private' (*shi/watakushi*) interest with the national 'public' (*kō/ōyake* = imperial) interest.[34] In affirming the indivisibility of the individual, the nation and the Emperor, Kawakami enunciates here another version of the Nishidan fictive unity of subject and object, but while cautiously ascribing this outlook to popular religion, he hints of his awareness that the cult of nationality owes much to government propaganda. The whole essay resonates with a barely subdued concern for the implications of the government's crackdown and prosecution of socialists, and the plotters against the Emperor.

For Kawakami, Japan is living through an 'age of contradiction' (*mujun no jidai*), which is most painfully felt by the intelligentsia (and, apparently, the bureaucrats) because this emerging cult of the imperial nation-state is a recrudescence of primitive religion wholly out of keeping with modern science. The modernising class of scholars and bureaucrats are commanded to import and master the new knowledge from the West which destroys the older knowledge of the traditional world view, but are told at the same time to guard against agitating or unsettling traditional beliefs of the kind which now underpin the Meiji state. They are ordered, paradoxically, to advance while remaining at a standstill (*susume susumu na*),[35] for there is no way round the fact that the knowledge they master is destructive of the traditions which, revived, are being used to legitimise the nation-state. This radical contradiction was to provoke Kawakami to embark on a long, arduous reflection which lead him eventually to revolutionary Marxism.

Less constrained by the coercive presence of government authorities, the doyen of Western studies on Japan, Basil Hall Chamberlain, in a lecture delivered in London in 1912, raised a cry of alarm at the mass falsification of the past being enacted by the Meiji bureaucracy. For him, we were witnessing a massive cultural fraud, involving the creation of a new religion by the Meiji élite, in which the imperial cult, Shintō and Bushidō prefigured. Shintō, a primitive, discredited cult, was being dusted off and revived; reverence for the Emperor was being proselytised as if it were a traditional piety when in fact he had always been treated in a cavalier fashion, and the code of the *samurai* was being hailed as an ancient value system integral to Japanese culture when no modern researcher had so much as heard of the word *bushidō* until

On Identity as Difference 211

the turn of the century.[36]

We observe therefore that in the final years of Meiji, not only did the élite find it necessary to formulate and propagate an ideology of illusion to counter that disillusioning vision of modern life which marked the emergence to maturity of Japanese naturalistic fiction,[37] but also that a significant wing of the intelligentsia, in relatively unconstrained autonomy, defected from the modern by a theoretical regression to archaic or feudal consciousness, and thus inadvertently supplied a sophisticated armoury of ideological ammunition to the very state from which they themselves often felt estranged.

The brilliant efflorescence of introspective studies of private subjectivity was truncated, and in the battle between realistic, honest autobiographical fiction and the surreal fabrications of disindividualised national identity, the *force majeure* of the imperial state prevailed. The freedom of the novel was vanquished by the coercive fiction of the *nihonjinron*, and a close comparison of these two genres amply confirms that this ideological eclipse of introspection constituted a repressive flight from that intense sexual awakening which challenged the *samurai* ethic that would 'keep love and sex out of the family and in the brothel where it belongs'[38] (*cf* Kuki). This evasion, by relocating the individual's identity in the anonymous, desexualised group, resuscitated narcissism in the compensatory idiom of national uniqueness,[39] and leased a regressive life to that concomitant aggression against the external world (identified as the intrusively alien 'West' of the modernising process) and the real self it inhibits and frustrates, which it was the task of modernity to strive to transcend.[40]

In these various formulations, official and unofficial, of authentic identity as disindividualised synchronisation with the mythic world of archaic tradition, the implication is both constant and necessary that all forms of social and personal crisis, the sense of deracination and estrangement, are attributable to the irruption of an alien mode of cognition and social organisation. The genesis of alienation though rooted in the structure of both Japanese socialisation and modernisation itself, was hoisted on the extraneous world of the industrialised West.

Now in the modern Western tradition, alienation means the 'externalisation' (Entäusserung) of the subject from itself through the objectifying process of man's activity as social agent in the world.[41] Or, in Freudian terms, alienation occurs when the child transcends his pure subjectivity by emerging from his narcissistic absorption through the development of object relations, in which he becomes aware of the difference between self and other, self and the objective world. But in the *nihonjinron* conceptualisation, as we have just seen, the essence of Japanese culture and the uniqueness of the 'Japanese mentality' is seen to lie in the non-alienation of the subject from itself, in the fusion of self and other. The process of alienation therefore is used only to refer to the irruptive dynamic of imported Western civilisation, which, in 'externalising' the 'natural' state of subject–object identity within Japan, destroys the ostensible harmony existing between the Japanese and their world, and compels them to enter and dwell in that 'inauthentic' world of critical reflection which posits a dialectical opposition between the self and the other.

Thus the ensuing dialectical contrast in the *nihonjinron* between 'Westernness' and 'Japaneseness' conceals under the guise of conflict between radically different cultural patterns what is in fact an inevitable internal antagonism, of both socialisation and historical modernisation, between self and society. Just as the quest for uniqueness betrays an urge towards narcissism, so the image of the 'West' here functions as an external metaphor for all aspects of the Japanese social structure during modernisation which constrain the child to submit to a society hostile to his individual interest. Developed in the crucial years 1909-11 as fantasies for transcending the alienating realities of Meiji industrialisation, these theories identified with a pure, dialectically unconditioned, past. In this sense they embody an inner structure of infantility as the locus of national identity. The expression of solidarity with a pre-Socratic and pre-Oedipal culture, in which subject–object unity is still affirmed, can only be sustained when the emotions and the intellect disavow through fictions that mature consciousness which is brought about painfully by modernity itself. It is in this sense that we should read the late Meiji government's attempt to repress the naturalistic 'I novel', and replace it with an ideological genre that discusses 'us Japanese'.

The third generation of Meiji thinkers born around the years 1870-1875, after modernisation had begun, achieves the aim only dimly envisioned by the earlier group centred round the *Seikyōkai*, and the intermediate nationalists represented by Hearn, Nitobe, Okakura Tenshin and others. That is, they succeed in erecting an elaborate structure of theory for the development of autochthonous thought in philosophy, psychiatry, philology, folklore, religion and state theory, and are subsequently lauded as 'unique', 'indigenous' thinkers. This threefold phase of Meiji nationalism, culminating in the illusive declaration of complete cultural autonomy, not only determines but anticipates the general redevelopment of the *nihonjinron* in the postwar period (table 16).

The paradox of this achievement consists in the ineluctable fact that the determination of an apparent conceptual autonomy in the analysis of Japanese culture and society was secured at the expense of an infantomorphic intellectualisation of this same world, and it is precisely this image which their epigones in the *nihonjinron* of the 70s, such as Doi, Watanabe, Suzuki, Hamaguchi and others, covertly reinstate or unconsciously sustain in their 'new' formulations.

Table 16: Progress Towards Cultural Autonomy

Era	Dominant Mode	Inferior Mode	Affect
1867-87 (1945-60)	'West' Western cultural ascendency as ideal model	'Japan' Japan a feudal backwater of outmoded traditions	Shame
	Japanese uniqueness consists in primitive values and institutions not to be found in the 'rational' West		
1887-1905 (1960-1970)	Transitional Phase Attempts made to compare and relativise the two categories. Growing doubts about the 'ideal' character of the 'West' conjoined with tentative reappraisals of certain values in old Japan		Mixed Feelings
	Japanese uniqueness seen to bear comparison with former values and institutions in the West. They may be anachronistic, but embody certain values which are not to be sacrificed but rather transformed		
1906-1911 (pattern till 1945) (1970-?)	'Japan' Reascendency of native traditions as absolutely unique	'West' Ideas and institutions are wholly alien to the essential style of Japanese culture and to be avoided	Honour
	Japanese uniqueness conceived properly as something *sui generis*, and as an exemplary model for the outside world		

Self Eclipsed

As I have occasionally hinted throughout this book, the reticulated elaboration of Japanese concepts of uniqueness in the modern period is immensely indebted to the theoretical world of German nationalism. The discovery in mid-Meiji of a strong affinity between Japan's situation and that of Germany's late modernisation led to an increasing dependence on the German example, to legitimise the authoritarian heritage of the Tokugawan state while ostensibly remaining faithful to modernisation on Western lines. In this retarded, yet rapidly industrialising, highly centralised economy, where the bourgeois revolution had been effectively suppressed and the mandarinate closely integrated into the state system, uncanny similarities were to be found to bear light upon Japanese problems. The German nationalist reaction to modernity, with its celebration of community, the soil, aristocratic culture and Teutonic singularity, with its archaic depth, and its hostile repudiation of the 'decadent, bourgeois, cosmopolitan and democratic West', provided in its various forms all that politicians and conservative intellectuals required in order to sustain the authority of tradition.

The Japanisation of German nationalism has sent deep roots into the academic soil of Japan, and survives there intact, if frequently unrecognised, because of the peculiar jargon of authenticity employed to translate these concepts of foreign provenance. It may thus be paradoxically remarked that under the incognito of a 'unique Japanese way of thinking' there often stirs the hidden form of an occidental ethnocentrism all but forgotten in the postwar West. It is this fact which produces that constant sense of vague *déjà vu* to the foreigner who studies the *nihonjinron*. If the real problem posed to the world since the Meiji Restoration is that of 'how Western civilisation will be Nipponicized',[42] as Hasegawa thought, then we are tempted to remind him that his enthusiastic vision is second-hand, and all too familiar to those who have read Nietzsche's mockery of the German belief that their unique development would work 'to Germanise the whole of Europe'.[43] If it is a puzzle for Tada as to why the Japanese are preoccupied with their uniqueness as Japanese, for others it is nothing more than a late twentieth century variant of those Germans for whom, as Nietzsche wearily commented, 'the question "what is German?" never dies out'.[44]

The *nihonjinron* therefore, in their central ideological structure, often give us at second-hand, in oriental guise, the essence of ethnocentric self-definitions already fully explored within the earlier nationalist, and often fascist wing, of European intellectual history. Often what is residually original is a result of the incompetence of the transmitter, unless these reformulations are consciously designed to obscure the foreign origins of the ideas in the first place.

If it is a somewhat disturbing proposition to assert that in order to understand the ideas in the *nihonjinron* we have to deepen our familiarity with the trajectory of German nationalism from 1808 to 1945, it is nonetheless supported by significant indications in the Japanese literature itself. It is even more disturbing to note that much of the conceptualisation of Japanese nationalism owes a deep debt to the influence exercised over Japanese scholars by both popular and sophisticated currents of German ultra-nationalism from late Weimar times through to Hitler's exercise of power. In particular we might note the impact of Heidegger's ideas on such men as Kuki Shūzō and Watsuji Tetsurō. Indeed we might argue that the ideological tradition of 1909-11 which identifies the kernel of Japaneseness in the unity of subject and object (itself heavily indebted to German sources) was mediated to the postwar generation through the extensive reformulations of scholars who immersed themselves in German thought during the twenties and thirties.

It was in 1933, for example, that Kosawa Heisaku began to meld Freudian psychoanalysis with Japanese nationalism and Nishida and Morita's ideas by defining neurosis as a consequence of 'Westernisation', in which the primary fusion of son and mother in Japanese character was repressed. This led to what he called, in terms echoing both Nishida and Buddhist thought, the 'spiritual darkness' (*mumyō*) of individualised consciousness, namely the emergence of object relations. As therapy, Kosawa advocated a return to the pre-Oedipal state which precedes 'the alienation from the oneness of subject and object',[45] in which Nishida's subject–object identity is clearly being redeployed in terms of the ideal of mother–son fusion. Where in 1933-4 German national socialism banned Freud's works and his movement, Kosawa mutilates his concepts to render them adaptable to the pietistic code of patriarchal nationalism in Japanese fascism, employing a different technique to achieve what was, in effect, the same end.

Of the scholars who had a hand in drafting the *Kokutai no hongi* (Hisamatsu Sen'ichi, Watsuji Tetsurō, Yamada Yoshio (a literary collaborator of Tanizaki's, and Inoue Takamaro), Watsuji was perhaps the one most versed in contemporary German intellectual currents, and it is probably to his reading of Thomas Mann that we may ascribe the phrasing 'true words most often become true deeds', used to trick out the Confucian dictum, 'A gentleman in naming things must use proper words. What he says (*yen/gen*) must be put into effect (*hsing/kō*)'.[46] What is involved here, apparently, is the use of the *Hsün-tzu* discussion on the 'rectification of names' as a means by which the ruler, as if by magic, unifies the passive people with the Way,[47] in order to interpret Japanese poems as constituting a native tradition of silent compliance and unthinking execution of verbal orders issued by the Emperor or his representatives. In this document of 1937, we see the notion of subject–object identity conflated with Oriental concepts (*kotodama, cheng ming*) of the identity of word and reality, with a dash of the Christian *logos* as creative word,[48] in order to exile reflection from the subject's consciousness and replace it with unswerving loyalty.

Thirdly, we have seen that Watsuji had already in 1922 explained the aesthetics of *mono no aware* as a subjective state in which the particular was united to the universal, another variant of Nishida's formulation. Watsuji's study abroad in the late twenties enabled him to sophisticate this early celebration of Japanese culture's ostensible pre-Kantian cognition with devastating effect. Deeply influenced, as was his colleague Kuki, by Heidegger's philosophy and analytic method, and specifically by his hermeneutic technique of 'etymologising realism', Watsuji applied *mutatis mutandis* his German mentor's method of juggling concepts out of the rabbit hat of Greek and German 'etymologies' to the analysis of the ethical vocabulary of Chinese and Japanese. In his *The Significance of Ethics as The Study of 'Man'* (*Ningen*), written just after his return in the early thirties, he argues on the basis of his analysis of the Confucian vocabulary that in the Orient the concept of man is always relational, social and supraindividual in contrast to the individual resonance of Western words like *anthrōpos, homo, man* and *Mensch*.[49]

Ethics, for example, in Sino–Japanese *rinri*, is broken down into its constituent elements of *rin* and *ri*, and then read through the native Japanese *kun* glosses to signify the 'reason' (*kotowari = ri*) of 'companionate association' (*nakama* = *rin*).[50] Likewise the Sino–Japanese word for man, *ningen*, is construed to refer to a 'relationship between' (*aida* = *gen*) 'men' (*hito* = *nin*), and *ningen* is thus men when in society and society (*yo no naka*) itself. While self and other (*jita*) are absolutely other to each other, yet individuals are '*men*' only in so far as they constitute a communal existence. Thus 'the locus of ethical problems lies not in the consciousness of the isolated individual but in the relationship between men (*hito to hito to no aidagara*)',[51] and in the notion of a transindividual self (*chōkojinteki naru jiko*).

Now the conversion of Heidegger's ideas into a Japanese ethical tradition by Watsuji involves, predictably enough, the radical extinction of those residual elements in Heidegger in which the uniqueness of the individual is preserved, and in this his translation perfectly parallels Kosawa's reworking of Freud. Namely, while the theory of *aidagara* (man as relationship) builds on the Heideggerian analysis of *Verhältnis*, relation as 'holding oneself toward' (*sich verhalten*), and 'being-in-the-world' (*In-der-Welt-Sein*), for Heidegger's emphasis on man's relationship to tools in this process, Watsuji substitutes as a deeper priority, *Mitsein* as a condition of mutual relatedness in which the world (*Welt* = *yo no naka*) is understood wholly as the social world.[52] And even in this move, he draws on a Western authority, namely Heidegger's student Karl Löwith, in which apparently an anthropology of 'betweenness' between self and other is developed on the basis of an analysis of the human, non-natural, meaning of the word *Welt* (world).[53]

The point is that where Heidegger distinguished between an authentic and inauthentic mode of 'being with others', and characterised inauthenticity in man by the degree to which his individual existence is depersonalised by the intrusive dominance of the 'public', in which chat (*Gerede*) displaces speech (*Rede*) in consciousness, Watsuji moves to a position which denies autonomy to private, individual consciousness itself, going to the extreme of asserting that, 'The greater the degree of the compactness of community of existence (*sonzai no kyōdō*) the denser is the 'private' (*shi/watakushi*) of a man.'[54] And again that, 'Conscience is the crying out (*yobigoe*) of the original totality'.[55]

The Heideggerian individual's reclamation of authentic being through his transcendence of history as errancy is here supplanted by Watsuji's subsumption of a historically emergent sense of individuality among the Japanese[56] back into the archaic structure of disindividualising relationship (*aidagara*) characteristic of the ethics of the Way. Little wonder that even sympathetic readings concede that in this form Watsuji's *aidagara* theory amounts to little more than a 'totalitarian state-ethics'.[57]

Watsuji concludes his essay by referring to 'climate' (*fūdo*) as a conditioning structure, different from place to place, in which human national existence achieves its concrete expression. Man as an abstract universal does not exist, and universal human existence may only be realised through the particular form of the nation.[58] The full elaboration of this doctrine occurs in his work *Fūdo* (1935), where it is explained not as a purely natural phenomenon but as a structure within human existence.[59] In a strange analysis inspired by Heidegger's study of *ex-sistere*, Watsuji tries to show that it is never 'I' that feels such climatic effects as cold, but 'We', and man as a we discovers himself in this self-apprehension within climate.[60]

Illustrating the effects of Japan's monsoonal climate on national character through such things as house design, he argued that architectural necessity makes for a house which excludes private space, and this in turn negates the possibility of individuality within the family. Thus the conjugal relationship which emerges in such climatically-determined structures is one of an 'unbarriered fusion' (*hedate-naki ketsugō*), which he reformulates neatly as an existential condition of the 'unduality of self and other' (*jita fuji*).[61] We have finally arrived at the redeployment of the Nishidan thesis of the unity of subject and object in the sphere of uniquely Japanese human relationships, and yet here, and in the related *aidagara* theory, we cannot but remark the cunning recreation as a distinctive Japanese ethical structure of what was, contemporaneously in Europe, known as a fascist doctrine according to which, "Immanent in the concept of the individual is the concept of society".[62] The irony is unrecognised.

Nightmare of Solitary Community

Despite the explicit contextualisation of the concepts of identity elaborated in 1909-11 within the ideological framework of Japanese fascism during the late 20s and 30s, the postwar *nihonjinron* draw openly and consistently on them as if the conceptualisation of culture were wholly divorced from politics, something which the modern history of Japan thoroughly discredits. But in popularising and trivialising these prewar sources, in a sense, the *nihonjinron* expose to view their essence, divested of the *recherché* jargon of the original formulations. And we do not need to reflect far in order to discover that underlying the varied discursive ideas of Japaneseness outlined in the preceding pages there exists a unified theme which defines the essence of Japanese uniqueness in terms of what, in Western discourse, passes for the condition of infantility.

In the sphere of linguistics, we have noted the key role played by the fictive category of *yamato kotoba* in sleuthing for autochthonous identity. Constituting the 'voices of the blood', they antedate history in reflecting the pure form of tribal sentiment and ethnic homogeneity. The literature defines *yamato kotoba* as words which are immediate and concrete, a repertoire of lyrical sentiment which, in Watanabe's telling phrase, are as 'soft as a mother's skin', in contrast to foreign words in Japanese which are abstract, used when 'the mind works intellectually and at a distance from objects'[63] and thus verbal agents of alienation from the primal Japanese experience of unity with his (social) world. *Yamato kotoba* are thus assumed to express the user's unmediated identity with the world or the other. As Kishimoto Hideo puts it:

> It is not necessary in Japanese to specify the subject by explicitly stating whether 'I' am feeling lonesome, or the scenery is lonesome ... Analytically, the sentiment is the result of the collaboration of the subject and the object. ... One of the characteristics of the Japanese language is to be able to project man's experience in its immediate and unanalysed form.[64]

In the *kotodama* formulation, these 'maternal' *yamato kotoba* harbour a 'unity of word and reality' (*meijitsu ittai*) which induces in the Japanese a 'concurrence of word and deed' (*genkō itchi*), or in Wang Yang-Ming's formulation, so central to revolutionary fanaticism in Japan,[65] 'the unity of thought and action' (*chikō gōitsu*). As the literature itself occasionally suggests, this is the way the primitive or the child fantasies about the power of words over reality.

In the field of human relations, Suzuki Takeo analysed the code of reticent empathy as one in which interlocutors aspire to the ideal of 'the unity of self and other' (*jita gōitsu*), a linguistic variation on Watsuji's *jita fuji*. This is explicitly linked to the putatively 'weak ego structure' of the Japanese, and Doi clarifies by relating this to the existence of coaxing (*amae*), the emotion felt by the child at his mother's breast before the onset of object relations, which for him marks all mature life among the Japanese and is an attempt to heal the rupture between subject and object by recuperating the identity of self and other and the harmony of subject and object.[66] Doi alone of these writers recognises the infantility of this, and argues that it must be transcended by the discovery of the subject and of the independent existence of the other.[67]

Again we have seen that Imanishi's approach to primatology rephrases the notion of the identity of the subject (as naturalist/observer) and the object (the sphere of living things, monkeys) in order to challenge Darwinian evolution. His rooting of 'simple cognition' (*soboku na ninshiki*) in the instincts as a transcendental apperceptive mode which unites in a harmony of relatedness all living things merely knits together Nishida's proposition of *shukaku gōitsu* and Watsuji's concept of *aidagara* in the theatre of animal behaviour. Tsunoda's theory also, we might add, aims from an analysis of the way *yamato kotoba* are audially registered to give empirical corroboration to the thesis that Japanese experience unites *pathos* and *logos*, another variation of the formula.

Watsuji's theory is one which persists under a large number of guises. Kimura Bin, in a perplexing conflation of Nishida, Dōgen, climate theory, and Watsuji's *aidagara* insists that the subject–object harmony of the Japanese is rooted in the 'acclimatisation' of the individual self in a unique 'kinship of blood identity', which transcends the Western notion of ego by a psychological concept whose basic unit is 'We' (*wareware*). The *Blut und Boden* imagery apart, someone should remind him that '"We" is not a term of psychoanalysis'.[68]

Hamaguchi is even more eclectic, but here again the *aidagara* theory underpins the whole shaky edifice of his hypotheses. He contrasts the individualism underlying the 'Western theory of personality' to the 'social relationism' of Japanese groupism. Following Watsuji, he differentiates the Western notion of mankind as a sum of individuals from the 'Oriental' notion of man as a collectivity. His originality consists in a jejune trick of semantic juggling which presumes to make an advance on Watsuji's formulation of *ningen* as *hito no aida*. Understood as 'between men', *ningen* is contrasted to *kojin* (one man = individual). Now, *ningen* was originally pronounced *jinkan*. By reversing the two constituent Sino-Japanese characters from their original order, one obtains *gennin*, ancient pronunciation *kanjin*. All this elaborate operation permits is to enable Hamaguchi to promulgate, as *his* own, novel contribution, an ostensibly new conceptualisation of Oriental personality as social relationship, in which *kanjinshugi* (betweenmenism) is radically contrasted to Western *kojinshugi* (individualism).[69]

Finally Kamishima Jirō explains the motive behind all of this amuletic recooking of concepts (and we might note that in effect *kanjinshugi vs kojinshugi* marks no advance, after 60 odd years of hectic nationalism, on Kawakami's contrast between *kokkaku* and *jinkaku*, which undoubtedly influenced Watsuji himself). For Kamishima, it is necessary to transcend the objective sociology of the West by doing away with its premise of the individual as an entity isolated from society.[70] Moulding Doi's dependency coaxing to Kimura's racial 'infra-personalism' within the matrix of Hsu's psychosocial homeostasis, and then mounting this on the framework of Watsuji's Confucianist reworking of Heidegger (a totalitarian state-ethics) which itself rests on the Meiji foundations of Nishida's epistemology and Kawakami's *kokkaku*, Hamaguchi and Kamishima, with the slightest touch of linguistic sleight-of-hand, can now promote to the world a new vision of sociological thought. The programme is already under way, with Kumon Shumpei's recent publication of a paper on Japanese 'contextualism' in an American journal,[71] and thus *kanjinshugi*, innocently translated as 'contextualism', though ultimately derived directly from a fascist formulation in the West, stands ready to sweep the world as an 'alternative' to the alienating mode of individualistic analysis hitherto current in the Occident.

Watsuji's original analysis of relational existence as one in which identity is 'I as a we and we as an I'[72] was itself a remarkably deft larceny in that it expropriated by the subtlest kind of bold plagiarism Hegel's definition of the absolute Spirit, which constitutes the unity of self-consciousnesses, wherein '*Ich, das Wir, und Wir, das Ich ist*'.[73] The anarchist Bakunin played off this in remarking 'I do not want to be an I, I want to be a We',[74] as did Yevgeny Zamyatin in his novel *We* (1924) in such extravagant formulations as 'all and I are the one We,' and 'nobody is one, but one of'.[75] Zamyatin's prophetic parody of the Soviet state profoundly influenced in turn Orwell's own novel on totalitarianism *1984*.

Nishida once defined history as a 'process of transforming the content of racial life into the Platonic ideas'.[76] In restrospect, the intellectual trajectory of Japanese nationalism achieves this project by a covert induction into native thought of ideas in that very Western tradition against which they outwardly assert their uniqueness. The 'discovery of Japanliness' is obtained through unacknowledged appropriations of concepts which, in the postwar critical tradition of their original homeland, are considered as fascist or totalitarian. Deployed within Japanese discourse, these notions are reworked in a way that constitutes identity in terms of pre-Oedipal, infantile consciousness. The idiom of unique authenticity is established through the conceptual revalorisation of regression, as if the aim were to invert Freud by proposing that 'where I was, the *id* shall be'. As Nietzsche would remind us, 'pleasure in the herd is older than pleasure in the I (*cf* ego)' and thus 'the sly, loveless Ego ... seeks its profit in the profit of the many'.[77]

The irony is that not only do the mandarins define as *sui generis* to Japan a modality which in Western terms is understood as either totalitarian or infantile, but that many foreigners extol in this image 'Japan as Number One'. What impedes one from perceiving this instructive homology between our barely transcended past and the image of contemporary Japan is the juggled idiom of Japanese discourse, the outer strangeness of its arcadian dialect of uniqueness; or else, our own secret sympathy.

The vision of such a 'Japan' is sustained, both within and abroad, by those who in Revel's words, 'Aspire to a hierarchical society in which — as Michel Foucault's nightmare or the all too real India described by Dumont — the individual neither exists nor thinks for himself but only in relation to the group.'[78] In constructing a mythology of culture which denies the existential distinction between 'I' and 'Thou', and in supplanting that original and ineluctable estrangement between self and other with a cosy affirmation of the identity of subject and object as an ethnic ontology, the mandarinate legitimates a world in which neither the individual nor the group may obtain a pregnantly dialectical relationship of enhancing exchange. In this ideological exclusion from Japanese culture of a principle of mutuality and equilibrium between the individual and his society, neither the potentialities of the self nor those of the community can ever achieve, or aspire to, a more complete realisation.

Most disturbing of all is the fact that this fictive confounding of self and other rebuffs and disclaims the possibility of love itself. In its stead, we find the impoverished *ersatz* of a disguised narcissism submerged beneath the disembodied image of a disindividualised collectivity, in which the idiom of identity is both tribal and anonymous.[78] In such a world of contrived discourse, one is permitted no ripe articulation and reciprocal expression of instructive difference, but only a fallow and banal silence, a dumb solidarity of the unknown self with an unknown world.

Notes

1. *cf* Doi, *'Amae' zakkō*, ibid. pp.5-6; Minami, *Nihonjinron no keifu*, ibid. p.3.
2. 'The unique character of one nation as against other nations', and thus a perfect equivalent of *kokutai*. See F. Stern, *The Politics of Cultural Despair*, (University of California Pr, Berkeley and Los Angeles, 1961) p.120.
3. A.D.E. Smith, *Nationalism in the Twentieth Century* (Australian National University Press, Canberra, 1979) pp.6-9, at p.9.
4. On the non-bourgeois character of mystical, aristocratic nationalisms see Smith, *Nationalism*, pp.6-7. On the self-promotion of businessmen as disinterested nationalists see B. Marshall, *Capitalism and Nationalism*, ibid. passim. B. Moore, Jr, *Social Origins*, remarks that 'Japanese capitalism never became the carrier of democratic ideas to the extent that commercial and manufacturing interests did in nineteenth century Europe' (p.298).
5. Moore, *Social Origins*, ibid. pp.299ff, esp. pp.304, 313, on the essential continuity between traditional institutions and Japanese fascism.
6. E.H. Kinmonth, *The Self-Made Man in Meiji Japanese Thought*, (University of California Press, Berkeley and Los Angeles, 1981), esp. pp.54-8.
7. K.B. Pyle, *The New Generation of Meiji Japan* (Stanford University Press, Stanford, 1969) ch. 3, esp. pp.53, 67, 136, 164ff. Shiveley, 'The Japanisation of the Middle Meiji' in Donald Shiveley (ed.) *Tradition and Modernisation*, ibid. pp.77-119, p.78 remarks on the use at this time of German ideas to counteract English and French concepts, in order to perpetuate traditional institutions, noting that 'This is a kind of "native" reaction in the sense that the objective is conservative–traditional even though the means is Western.'
8. *cf* Hearn's early letter cited in D.W. Enright, *The World of Dew* (Secker and Warburg, London, 1955) p.159.
9. *cf* Hearn, *Japan: An Attempt at Interpretation*, ibid. pp.457-8.
10. Nitobe Inazō, *Bushido: The Soul of Japan*, (Shōkwabō, Tokyo, 1901) 5th. ed. p.122.
11. Nitobe, *Bushido*, ibid. p.3. On Nitobe see Kinmonth, *The Self-Made Man*, ibid. pp.255-6, and Rodan, *Schooldays in Imperial Japan*, ibid. pp.200-10.
12. R.J. Bowring, *Mori Ōgai and the Modernisation of Japanese Culture* (Cambridge University Press, Cambridge, 1979) p.125.
13. J. Rubin, *Injurious to Public Morals* (University of Washington Press, Seattle, 1984) p.60.
14. Rubin, *Injurious to Public Morals*, ibid. p.58 traces the origin of the term *kiken shisō* to Ōmachi Keigatsu, writing in 1904.

15. Rodan, *Schooldays in Imperial Japan*, ibid. p.195; Rubin, *Injurious to Public Morals*, ibid. pp.108ff. It is of note that officials like Hiranuma Kiichirō and Koyama Matsukichi who played key roles in both censorship and bringing radicals to trial in the period 1907-11, reemerged as the architects of thought control in the thirties. See Rubin, *Injurious to Public Morals*, ibid. pp.82-3, Mitchell, *Thought Control*, pp.36ff, 143-4.

16. *cf* The figures from Reed's study of the *kokutai* cited in Marius B. Jansen, 'Changing Japanese Attitudes toward Modernisation' in M.B. Jansen (ed.) *Changing Japanese Attitudes Toward Modernization* (Princeton University Press, Princeton, New Jersey, 1965) pp.43-89, p.82.

17. The crisis of the Meiji success ethic, the increasing difficulties in finding jobs for graduates, is no doubt linked with not only the political radicalism and new introspection of naturalist writers, but also with the desperate repression by the government. See the excellent analysis by Kinmonth, *The Self-Made Man*, ibid. chs. 6, 7, esp. pp.206-10, pp.222-4, pp.242ff.

18. *cf* '*Die Vergeistigung des deutschen Konservatismus*', cited T.J. Reed, *Thomas Mann, The Uses of Tradition* (Oxford, Clarendon Press, 1974) p.282.

19. *cf* The critique of Watsuji Tetsurō's ethics made by Tosaka Jun in the thirties in his *Nihon ideorogii ron*, in *Tosaka Jun Zenshū*, 2 (Keisō Shobō, Tokyo, 1966) pp.223-38, p.309.

20. Nishida borrowed the term 'pure experience' (*junsui keiken*) from William James (through Suzuki Daisetsu). See David Dilworth, 'The Initial Formations of 'pure experience' in Nishida Kitarō and William James, in *Monumenta Nipponica* 24:2 (1969) pp.93-111, who shows that in Nishida's reworking the concept restores a (Zen-rooted) transcendental idealism which James sought to criticise. Nishida's conceptualisation owes something to Mach, Schopenhauer (*cf reine Anschauung, reine Erfahrung*) Schelling and Fichte (*cf Identität*). See Shimomura, *Nishida Kitarō*, ibid. pp.48, 108, 206, 237ff., and Ueyama, *Nihon no shisō*, ibid. pp.114ff, 161.

21. As translated by Dilworth, 'The Initial Formations', ibid. p.95. There is also something here, besides Zen influences, of Chu Hsi's doctrine of man's true nature being identical to external nature (*t'ien jen ho i*) and Wang Yang-Ming's concept of the unity of thought and action (*chih hsing ho i*) and the text here betrays traces of a passage influenced by these Chinese thinkers in Bashō, for which see Bashō, *The Narrow Road to the Deep North*, trans. Nobuyuki Yuasa, (Penguin, 1982) p.33. An instructive parallel may be found in Heidegger's doctrine of *Vor-Augen-Sein* where '*Sein* is something made present to the eye. As such, it is unthought (*Ungedacht*), and has not been made articulate in language.' G. Steiner, *Heidegger*, ibid. p.78.

22. *cf* Shimomura, *Nishida Kitarō*, ibid. p.102; Ueyama, *Nihon no shisō*, p.138, p.159.

23. Nishida Kitarō, *Zen no kenkyū*, (Iwanami Bunko reprint, 1979) p.16. *cf* The glosses *butsuga sōbō* and *chii yūgō*, ibid. p.54.

24. Kondō Kyōichi, 'The Origins of Morita Therapy' in *Culture-Bound Syndromes*, ibid. pp.250-8, pp.251-2.

25. Reynolds, *Morita Psychotherapy*, ibid. pp.9, 55 (truth as 'the harmonisation of subjective experience and objective reality'), and p.154 citing Levy to the effect that 'when the self was not self conscious, it was healthy'.

26. Muraoka Tsunetsugu, *Motoori Norinaga* (Iwanami Shoten reprint, 1958) pp.341-380, esp. pp.343-4, p.355, 365, 372, 379. *cf* Maruyama, *Studies in the Intellectual-history*, ibid. pp.xx, 143.

27. Muraoka, *Motoori Norinaga*, ibid. p.343.

28. Muraoka, *Motoori Norinaga*, ibid. pp.341, 361.

29. According to Miyata Noboru, *Nihon no minzokugaku* (Kōdansha Gakujutsu Bunko, Tokyo, 1978) pp.52ff. esp. p.58, *jōmin* was coined in late Meiji

times as a 'value neutral' word for common people, equivalent to *Volk*(!), abandoned for *heimin* in the Taishō period, and then reused from 1935. Compare Miyata's discussion to Toyoda, *Nihonjin no kotodama shisō*, ibid. p.228.

30. Tsurumi Kazuko, 'Yanagida Kunio's Work as a Model of Endogenous Development' in *Japan Quarterly*, 22:3 (1975) pp.223-38, pp.223-4. As to the view of the Yanagita school that Japanese culture is structured in layers preserving intact the culture of each epoch and class (see Tsurumi above, and her *Nihonjin to kōkishin*, ibid. pp.124ff) it is not only wholly false but, were it true, hardly unique. For an Indian parallel see Lannoy, *The Speaking Tree*, ibid. pp.xvi-xvii.

31. While distinguishing *jōmin* from *samurai* culture, the *jō* supposedly refers to quotidian aspects of lifestyle shared by all Japanese from the Imperial house downwards. Secondly, there was considerable osmosis (not to speak of the effects of constant repression) from *samurai* culture to peasant culture. The idea, therefore, of a transhistorical culture based on peasant consciousness is riddled with contradictions. *cf* Miyata, *Nihon no minzokugaku*, ibid. pp.52-3, 62-3, 66-69.

32. I follow the account in Henry D. Smith II, 'Tokyo as an Idea', ibid. p.67.

33. G.L. Bernstein, *Japanese Marxist: A Portrait of Kawakami Hajime 1879-1946*, (Harvard University Press, Cambridge, 1976) dates his interest in Tokugawan economists to 1907 (p.62) and his turning to an exclusive concentration of cultural contrasts to 1911-15 (p.72).

34. 'Nihon dokutoku no kokkashugi' in *Kawakami Hajime Chosakushū*, 8 (Chikuma Shobō, Tokyo, 1964) pp.185-210, esp. pp.190-1.

35. Kawakami, 'Nihon dokutoku no kokkashugi', ibid. p.203. Compare Mori Ōgai's *Ka no yo ni* (1912) which, on German precedent, suggests that the crisis between the intellectuals and the state may be resolved by allowing sceptical research among thinkers (to control anarchism and dissidence), conjoined to the maintenance of popular faith in the myths of Japanese culture (Mori Ōgai, *Abe Ichizoku, Maihime* (Shinchō Bunko, Tokyo, 1968) pp.92ff) and the summary and discussion in Bowring, *Mori Ōgai*, ibid. pp.189ff.

36. B.H. Chamberlain, *Japanese Things* (Charles Tuttle reprint, Vermont and Tokyo, 1974) pp.531-44, esp. pp.533-6. The word *bushidō*, though rare, does however occur in premodern texts, see Saitō Shōji, '*Yamatodamashii*' *no bunkashi* (Kōdansha Gendai Shinsho, Tokyo, 1974) pp.96ff.

37. Rubin, *Injurious to Public Morals*, ibid. p.110.

38. Cited Kinmonth, *The Self-Made Man*, ibid. p.147.

39. That the mother was the driving force behind these men (Nishida, Mori, Ōsugi, Kawakami, Kōtoku, Kitamura Tōkoku, Yanagita etc,) in their ambitious bids for social or academic success in the patriarchal world of imperial Japan is something that requires deeper study.

40. This failure may be neatly traced by examining the trajectory in Mori Ōgai's novels from sexual awakening (*Vita Sexualis*, 1909) through the desire to master and repress the erotic impulse (*Seinen, Gan*), a probable flirtation with the notion of homosexuality in *Kaijin* (1912) to, finally, a regressive lapse back into the historical novel focused on sacrifice and death. See Bowring's survey, *Mori Ōgai*, ibid. pp.137ff.

41. On *Entäusserung*, see the exposition in G. Lukács, *The Younger Hegel: Studies in the Relations between Dialectics and Economics*, trans. R. Livingstone (MIT Press, Cambridge, Massachusetts paper. 1976) pp.537ff.

42. Hasegawa Nyozekan, *The Japanese Character*, trans. John Bester (Kodansha International, Tokyo, 1966) p.35.

43. '*Ganz Europa zu verdeutschen*', Nietzsche, *Jenseits von Gut und Böse*, 244.

44. Tada Michitarō, in *Nihon bunka no hyōjō*, ibid. p.8. Nietzsche, *Jenseits von Gut und Böse*, 244.

45. *Shukaku ichinyo kara no sogai sunawachi mumyō*, cited in Okonogi, *Gendai seishin bunseki*, ibid. p.145. The identification of neurosis with

226   On Identity as Difference

Westernisation is shared by Doi, Morita, and Okonogi and signifies that neurosis is identified with the emergence of object relations, that is that the ego (Westernisation) is pathological, and narcissism normal.

46. Lun Yü. 13.3. Tosaka in his review of Watsuji's Ethnics, *'Nihon ideorogii ron*, ibid. p.304 had already commented on how Watsuji's 'unique' philosophical methods of analysis were in fact merely distillations of a motley mixture of foreign impurities commingled with Japanese sources.

47. J.J.L. Duyvendak, 'Hsün-Tzŭ on the Rectification of Names', ibid. p.240, (Chinese text p.242). One wonders whether the *Man' yōshū* line 'A land where *kotoage* (word-raising) is not done' in this context is cited with the subsequent line in the Hsün-Tzŭ in mind: 'What need was there of force of arguments?' (Duyvendak, ibid. p.240).

48. As again Miller, 'The "Spirit" of the Japanese Language', ibid. p.260, n. 16 acutely observes.

49. Watsuji Tetsurō, *Ningen no gaku toshite no rinrigaku no igi*, revised and incorporated in his *Rinrigaku* (1937) and available in the postwar, discreetly toned-down version in *Watsuji Tetsurō Zenshū*, 10 (Iwanami Shoten, Tokyo, 1962) pp.11-31. It is available in English in 'The Significance of Ethics as the Study of Man' trans. David A. Dilworth, *Monumenta Nipponica*, 24:4 (1971) pp.395-413.

50. Watsuji, Ningen no gaku, ibid. pp.12-15: Dilworth, 'Significance of Ethics', ibid. pp.396-9. The phrasing 'companionate association' is Dilworth's.

51. Watsuji, 'Ningen no gaku', ibid. pp.17-18, Dilworth, 'Significance of Ethics', ibid. p.401. The citation comes from Watsuji, 'Ningen no gaku', p.12 and is also cited in Lebra, *Japanese Patterns*, ibid. p.12 as if it were, not an ideological construct, but an 'emic' point of view. Despite the sophisticated formulation, Watsuji's analysis of *ningen* merely recovers the old peasant interpretation of the character for man, *nin/hito*, as two people supporting each other. See J.F. Embree, *Suye Mura* (University of Chicago, Illinois) reprint paper. (1972) p.321.

52. Watsuji, 'Ningen no gaku' ibid. p.19; Dilworth, 'Significance of Ethics', ibid. p.402. See also Tosaka, *Nihon ideorogii ron*, ibid. pp.305ff. On Heidegger's analysis, see Steiner, *Heidegger*, ibid. pp.82ff, 87ff; J. Macquarrie, *An Existentialist Theology*, (Penguin, Harmondsworth, 1973) pp.38ff, 85ff.

53. *cf* His *Das Individuum in der Rolle des Mitmenschen*, 1928, cited in Watsuji, 'Ningen no gaku', ibid. pp.19ff.

54. Watsuji, 'Ningen no gaku', ibid. p.29. A close reading of this passage suggests that the influential study of Aruga Kizaemon on the *tate* structure of *kō/shi* ('public', 'private') mentioned above ch. 5, n. 26, derives in turn from Watsuji's formulation.

55. Watsuji, 'Ningen no gaku' ibid. p.27.

56. *cf* Watsuji, 'Ningen no gaku', ibid. p.17 says that the Japanese have 'converted' (with a nuance of *diverting* from the proper sense) the word *ningen* into meaning man as an individual.

57. Piovesana, *Recent Japanese Philosophical Thought*, ibid. p.143.

58. Watsuji, 'Ningen no gaku', ibid. pp.30-1.

59. Watsuji Tetsurō, *Fūdo*, in *Watsuji Tetsurō Zenshū*, ibid. vol. 8, p.7. On *fūdo* see Piovesana, *Recent Japanese Thought*, ibid. p.138.

60. Watsuji, *Fūdo*, ibid. pp.7-14.

61. Watsuji, *Fūdo*, ibid. pp.140, 142. The expression *jita fuji* here represents a reactionary attempt to refute Mori Arinori's concept of *jita heiritsu* (the equal standing of self and other), a key motif in mid-Meiji education. Yet it misrepresents the past, since Confucian tradition held that 'there should be a distinction between husband and wife' (*fūfu betsu ari*). On these points see I.P. Hall, *Mori Arinori* (Harvard University Press, Cambridge, Mass., 1973) p.91, n. 45, pp.441-7.

On Identity as Difference 227

62. Gentile, *Genesi e structura della società*, ibid. p.33. See also Zeev Sternhell, 'Fascist Ideology' in Walter Laqueur (ed.) *Fascism: A Reader's Guide* (Pelican, Harmondsworth, 1979) pp.325-406, pp.364f. Gentile's concept, inspired by the Hegelian idea of the ethical state, was elaborated in his *Fondamenti della filosofia del diritto* (1916) esp. IV, 7 where the intimacy of legal authority lies in 'l'essere la società non già *inter homines* bensì *in interiore homine*' (Human sociality is not constituted by a relationship between individuals but rather exists within each individual man). cf S. Zeppi, *Il Pensiero Politico dell'Idealismo italiano e il Nazionalfascismo* (La Nuova Italia Editrice, Florence, 1973) pp.152-3, p.162. In Watsuji, *inter homines (aidagara)* is located *in interiore homine*. Marx in his sixth gloss on Feuerbach, in writing that 'the human essence ... is the ensemble of social relations' (see the exposition in L. Sève, *Man in Marxist Theory*, trans. John McGreal (Harvester Press, Sussex, 1978) pp.69ff) had a profound effect, through syndicalist thought, on the conceptualisation of man in fascism. See A.J. Gregor, *Italian Fascism and Developmental Dictatorship* (Princeton University Press, Princeton New Jersey, 1979) pp.34ff.

63. Watanabe Shōichi, *Nihongo no kokoro*, ibid. p.25.

64. Kishimoto Hideo on *sabishii*, 'Some Japanese Cultural Traits and Religions', in Moore (ed.) *The Japanese Mind*, ibid. pp.110-121, p.110.

65. cf Mishima Yukio, *Kōdōgaku no nyūmon* (Bunshun Bunko, Tokyo 1974) pp.189ff.

66. See Doi, *Seishin bunseki to seishin byōri* (Igaku Shoin, 1965) p.4. See also Doi, *'Amae' zakkō*, ibid. p.173; Hamaguchi, *'Nihonrashisa' no saihakken*, ibid. p.136.

67. Doi, *'Amae' no kōzō*, ibid. pp.93-4.

68. Erikson cited by Marcus Cunliffe in the *Times Literary Supplement*, 23 October 1981, p.1241. cf Lasch, *Culture of Narcissism*, ibid. p.33. Compare Kimura, *Hito to hito to no aida*, ibid. pp.1-12, on '*wareware nihonjin*'.

69. Hamaguchi, *'Nihonrashima' no saihakken*, ibid. pp.50ff.

70. Kamishima, *Nihonjin no hassō*, ibid. pp.73-83 where Watsuji's *aidagara* theory is confronted with Buber's 'I' and 'Thou'.

71. Kumon Shumpei, 'Some Principles Governing the Thought and Behaviour of Japanists (Contextualists)', in *Journal of Japanese Studies*, 8:1 (winter 1982) pp.5-28, esp. pp.17ff. For Kumon the 'Japanese psyche' is almost 'pathological' but he refuses to dissent from nationalism' (p.6).

72. Watsuji, *Fūdo*, ibid. p.10 where we read '*Wareware de aru tokoro no ware, ware de aru tokoro no wareware de aru*'. cf Gentile, *Genesi e struttura*, 'In fondo all'Io c'è un Noi' (At the base of the I, there is a We) (p.15) and 'Io è Noi' (I is We) (p.19).

73. G.W.F. Hegel, *Phänomenologie des Geistes*, hrsg. Johannes Hoffmeister, Bd. 5 of Hegel: *Sämtliche Werke* (Verlag von Felix Meiner, Hamburg, 1952) p.140.

74. The connection is made by Burgess, *1985*, ibid. pp.53, 70.

75. Yevgeny Zamyatin '*We*', trans. Bernard Guilbert Guerney (Penguin, Harmondsworth, 1977) pp.24, 138.

76. Nishida Kitarō, *Fundamentals of Philosophy*, trans. David Dilworth (Sophia University Press, Tokyo, 1970) p.87.

77. F. Nietzsche, *Also Sprach Zarathustra*, Erster Teil, Von Tausend und Einem Ziele.

78. J.-P. Revel, *The Totalitarian Temptation* (Penguin, Harmondsworth, 1978) p.281.

79. cf Nietzsche, *Also Sprach Zarathustra*, ibid. opening section of Von der Nächstenliebe analysing the 'bad self-love' hidden in love of one's neighbour.

INDEX

absolutism 51, 91, 159, 161
abstraction 51, 80, 121, 129, 166
academy in Japan 15-16
Adorno, Theodor 11n13, 76n56, 81
agriculturalism 42-3, 189
Aida, Yūji 21, 36n18, 43, 54n11, 180-1, 188-9, 191
aid agara 57, 154, 194-5, 217-18, 220
Ajättasattu complex 117-21, 155
akirame 57, 70-1
alienation 92, 110-12, 119, 121, 164, 211-12, 219
Alkmaion 38
amae 44, 57, 61-2, 121-77 *passim*
  and An'ya kōro 161-2
  and compulsion 131-2
  and dissatisfaction 131-2
  and Emperor system 135-6
  and freedom 61-2
  and heirarchy 137
  and iki 155-61
  and ki 130, 138
  and mono no aware 67
  and Morita therapy 168-9
  and paranoia 133-4
  and shyness 129-30
  and toraware 126
  and victimisation 132-4
  definition 122-3
  healthy vs. pathological 151-2
  historical roots 163-4
  see also Doi
Amaterasu Ōmikami 120, 143n22, 159
ambiguity 78, 88-9, 102, 108-9
Analects 97n33, 114, 180
Andreski, Stanislav 15, 34, 55n28, 99n60
animism 45, 51
anti-intellectualism 166-7, 201
Araki, Hiroyuki 58, 144n50
Arima, Tatsuo 66-7
artifice 51, 207
aru ga mama 166, 170, 207
Aruga, Kizaemon 54n14, 74n26, 226n54

Bairy, Maurice 148
Balint, Michael 123-5, 129

Barnlund, Dean 111, 157
Barthes, Roland 4, 14
Baudelaire, Charles 71-2, 161
beeinträchtigungswahn 133
Befu, Harumi 11n6, 59-60
Bellicosity 45
Benedict, Ruth 31, 115n31, 157
  Japanese discussion of 117-87
Bernstein, Basil 103-5, 112-14, 157
Bester, John 178
Böckh, August 208
bourgeoisie 45, 107-8, 112, 163-5, 201-3
Brown, Norman 53n5, 174n52
Brzezinski, Zbigniew 173n10
Burgess, Anthony 36n20, 227n74
bushidō 70-1, 205, 210

Carpenter, Charles R. 190, 192, 194
Carr-Greg, Charlotte 148
Chamberlain, Basil H. 210
cheng ming 97n33, n42, 216
chikō gōitsu 219
China 2, 13, 30, 35, 39, 47, 50, 55, 68, 86, 141, 155, 203
Chu Hsi 224n21
Clark, Gregory 26-7, 148
closed culture 51
coaxing *see under* amae
Coleridge, Samuel T. 170
concreteness 51
Conquest, Robert 52
continental culture 42-3, 91-3
continuity of Japanese culture 51, 193
contract 44, 92, 106, 112, 148
  see also kintract
corporations 19
  and paternalism 105-8
cultural Relativism 5-6, 28-34

dandy 70-2, 161
Dante, Alighieri 69
Darwin, Charles 35, 49, 193, 195
d'Aurevilly, Barbey 72
dependence *see* amae
desert culture 42, 54n9
de Vos, George 115n31
dochaku 35n1, 52

Index

Doi, Takeo 35, 61-2, 67, 99, 121-75 *passim*, 178-9, 186, 191, 213, 220
   foreign judgements on 147-8
   donative culture 51

Economic competition 21
egalitarianism 44, 87, 90, 178
Egami, Namio 28, 43, 54n10
ego 91, 93-4, 139-40, 152, 220, 222
Eliot, Thomas S. 69
emic 6, 9, 30, 59-60, 65, 226n51
empathy 91, 93-4, 99n60, 109-10
epistemology of the blood 25, 27, 36n2, 220
Erikson, Erik 21, 152, 186, 227n68
eurocentrism 3-7, 9, 12, 31, 33, 177, 179
Evans, Sir Arthur 27
evolution 35, 49, 84, 193, 195-6
exophoric speech 103

family, positional vs. personal 112-13
fascism
   and communal myths 106-7
   and emic theories 30, 154
   and language 81, 85, 87-8
   and nihonjinron 16-17, 193-4
father image 39-40, 45, 53, 87-8, 105-8, 111-12, 118, 135, 141, 154-5
Federn, Paul 117, 145n57
Fenellosa, Ernest 203
Ferrarotti, Franco 3-4
feudalism 33, 44-5, 63, 65, 70, 148, 160, 163-5, 202, 211
Fichte, Gottlieb 82-4, 86-7, 90, 96n19, 201
Fletcher, Sir Banister 34
foreign words *see* gairaigo
forest culture 42, 54n9
Frankl, Victor 168
freedom 61-2, 83
Freud, Anna 116
Freud, Sigmund 35, 49, 61, 117, 121-7, 139, 149, 158, 182, 193, 215, 217, 222
Fromm, Erich 7-8, 115n32
fūdo 41-2, 218
fuhen 34, 51
Fukuzawa, Yukichi 59

gairaigo 58, 77-8, 90, 104
   see also yamato kotoba
gekokujō logic 62, 142, 185
Gellner, Ernst 16

Genji Monogatari 67, 80
gemeinschaft 44, 136
genkō-itchi 100, 113, 219
Gentile, Giovanni 95n14, 227n62
Germany 53-4, 81-3, 106, 134, 201, 214-15
gesellschaft 44, 136
Gibney, Frank 147
gimu 106
giri 44, 105-6, 136, 139, 160, 178, 183
Goëthe, Johann, W. von 66, 97n33, 146n79, 176, 183
Goodall, Jane van Lawick 198
gōrishugi *see* rationality
group 22, 44, 49, 108, 134, 155, 195
   egotism of 140, 222
   narcissism of 211
guilt 44, 112
   and Ajattasattu complex 117-18
   and Naikan therapy 171
   and shame 177-87

Hagiwara, Sakutarō 87
haji *see* shame
Hamaguchi, Eshun 28-31, 44, 59, 109, 152-3, 213, 220-1
Hamann, Johann G. 96n19
Hamon, Hervé 20
haragei 79, 101-2, 108
harmony, of Japanese culture 51
Hasegawa, Nyozekan 214
Hearn, Lafcadio 75, 203-5, 212
Hegel, Friedrich 48, 221
Heidegger, Martin 68-73, 75-6, 81, 154, 215-18, 221
herodianism 47-8
heterogeneity 40, 51, 58, 195
hierarchy 44, 59-60, 135, 137
   see also verticality
higaisha-ishiki 132-4
Hirata, Atsutane 48
Hisamatsu, Sen'ichi 66, 85, 216
hitomishiri 129-30, 136
homogeneity 10, 51, 92
homosexuality 145n66, 158
Honda, Toshiaki 202
honne 105, 121, 144n41
hōon 136, 139
horizontality 44, 177
hsing ming 97n42
Hsu, Francis L.K. 44, 153, 221
humanitarianism 82-4
Huxley, Aldous 22

Identity
    concept of 21-2
    literature on 14-23
    of word and thing 85-6, 201
Ideology as means of social control
    6-7, 17-18, 20, 39-40, 65, 106-7,
    135, 206
ie 55n27, 57, 101
iki 57, 68-73, 155-61
Imanishi, Kinji 35, 191-7, 199n11,
    220
immaculateness 57-8
imperialism 2-3, 201-2
individualism 21-3, 44, 49, 106, 108,
    116, 172, 195, 209, 221-2
infantilisation 107, 139, 204, 219,
    222
Inoue, Takamaro 216
instinct 49, 116, 195
Ishida Eiichirō 199n11
ishin-denshin 79, 101, 103
island country 42-3, 91
Itoh, C. 19
ittaikan 103-4, 141
Iwakura, Tomohide 143n16
izon 123, 183
    see also amae

jama 134
Japan
    as Number One 105, 107-8, 222
    nihonjinron image of 42-6
Japanese language
    as a barrier 12, 18
    as material for nihonjinron 56-7
    as the Adamic vernacular 133-4
    see also language
jibun 79, 140
Jiménez, Juan R. 56
jinkaku 209, 221
jita-gōitsu 94, 99n70, 100, 104, 111,
    141, 220
jōmin 208
junnō 81, 139, 167

kagen-chinmoku 79, 101
    see also silence
Kamishima, Jirō 193, 221
kango 58, 80, 87-8, 90, 104, 133
    see also gairaigo
kanjinshugi 44, 221
Kant, Immanuel 85, 96n31, 184, 207
kantan-aiterasu 79, 101
Katō, Shūichi 51-2, 54n14

Kawai, Masao 192
Kawakami, Hajime 209-10, 221
Kawamura, Nozomu 11n8, 55n35
Kawashima, Takeyoshi 54n14,
    115n18, 173n11
Keene, Donald 52
keiyaku *see* contract
kenri 44, 106
ki 57, 130, 138
Kierkegaard, Søren 170
Kiernan, V.G. 18
Kindaichi, Haruhiko 54n7
Kimura, Bin 36n2, 152, 183, 220-1
Kimura, Shōsaburō 99n63, 109
kintract 44, 106
Kishimoto, Hideo 219
Kita, Ikki 205
Kitabatake, Chikafusa 47-8
kiyorakasa 57-8
kō *see under* public
kobun 107
kojinshugi *see* individualism
kokkaku 209, 221
kokuminsei 52, 79, 100
kokutai 45, 49-52, 73, 87-8, 92, 94,
    120, 136, 140, 203
kokutai no hongi 85, 88, 216
Kosawa, Heisaku 117-20, 136, 150-2,
    154-5, 215
Kōtoku Shūsui 205-6
Kuga, Katsunan 203
Kuki, Shūzō 68-73, 155-61, 211,
    215-16
Kumon, Shumpei 55n27, 221,
    227n71
Kure, Shūzō 170

Lacan, Jacques 147, 150
Laing, Ronald 100, 146n78
Language
    amuletic use of 105, 120, 177,
        184, 221
    formal vs. public 103-5, 112-13
    miscegenated vs. pure 100
    nihonjinron uses of 56-99 *passim*;
        and race 91; arguments from
        60; deficiency of 88-9; living
        vs. dead 81-4
Lannoy, Richard 155, 225n30
Lasch, Christopher 55n15, 116
Leach, Edmund 98n55
Lebra, Takie S. 33-4, 75n29, 103,
    127, 166
leucocytes and personality 200n36
Lévi-Strauss, Claude 14, 54n8

Index 231

Lewis, Oscar 29-30
Lifton, Robert 120, 147
logic 13, 32, 176
Löwith, Karl 217
loyalty, public vs. private 63-4

Maine, Henry 44
Mann, Thomas 97n33, 201, 206, 216
Maraini, Fosco 23n10
Marais, Eugene 192
Marcuse, Herbert 138
Marsh, Robert 148
marugakae 107, 112
Marui, Kiyoyasu 117
Maruyama, Masao 10, 75n39, 132-5, 163-4
Marx, Karl 61, 102, 107, 109, 114, 227n62
Marxism 2, 6, 33, 147, 210
masochism 98n52, 150-1
Masuda, Yoshio 54n9
maternal, image of 87, 112, 118-20
Matsumoto, Michirō 36n6, 102, 114n5
Mead, Margaret 182
meijitsu ittai 100, 113, 219
miai 112, 165
Michels, Roberto 106
middle-class 38-9
  see also bourgeiosie
Miller, Roy A. 23n8, 37n32, 55n29, 67, 73n1, 85-6, 91, 157
Mitamura, Engyō 209
Miyake, Setsurei 203
mizu-shōbai 160
Moloney, James M. 119, 121, 172
monkey 84, 192-3, 196-8
mono no aware 57, 65-8, 216
monotheism, of West 45
Moore, Charles 13, 26, 201
Mori, Arinori 20, 226n61
Mori, Jōji 115n25, 140
Mori, Mikisaburō 179-80
Mori, Ōgai 205
Morita, Shōma 165-6, 207, 215
Morita therapy 22-3, 165-71
Morris, Ivan 12
mother, image of 140-1
  in Japan 110-12
  in Shiga's An'ya kōro 161-3
  see also maternal
Motoori, Norinaga 48, 66-8, 86, 97n40, 208
Muraoka, Tsunetsugu 208

Naikan therapy 165, 170-2
Nagai, Kafū 205
Nakai, Kate W. 39
nakama 216-17
Nakane, Chie 31-3, 36n19, 44, 59, 137, 140, 177
Nakanishi, Susumu 10
narcissism
  and antagonism to father-image 39-40
  and desire for uniqueness 53n5
  and shame 185
  and socialisation 110, 136, 140-1
  beneath image of Japan 45
  Freud's view of 124
  iki as a disguise for 72
  in group 211, 222
  in preference for yamato kotoba 88
  transcendence of 150, 211-12, 220, 222-3
  vocabulary of 25, 174n52
nareai 126
national character 52, 88, 106-7
  see also kokuminsei
nationalism 2, 16, 38-9, 201-2
Natsume, Sōseki 205
Nature 42-3, 51, 163
Nauman, Nelly 57-8
neurosis and westernisation 119, 136, 225-6
Nichiren 47-8
Nietzsche, Friedrich 61, 214, 222
nihonjinron
  and national security 19
  and prehistory 120
  and science 188-200
  as alter ego of mandarins 40
  as anti-individualistic 21-2
  as revolt from reality 40
  as social force 15
  as totalitarian 52-3
  contrasted to seiyōron 30
  definition of 14
  difficulties in understanding 38, 153-4
  Doi's influence on 150
  psychological basis of 141, 155, 185
  quantity of 15
  related to prewar ideology 16-17, 218-19
  reworking samurai tradition 163
  theoretical weakness of 30-5
  writers of 15-16

nihonrashisa 21, 29
ningen 217, 220-1
ninjō 105-6, 136, 153, 156, 160
Ninomiya, Sontoku 106, 202
Nishida, Kitarō 35, 98n52, 191,
    194-5, 206-7, 215-16, 218, 220-2
Nitobe, Irazō 204-5, 212

Objectivity 46
Ogyū Sorai 59, 74
Okakura, Tenshin 160, 212
Okonogi, Keigo 74, 118, 120-1, 125,
    147, 150-2, 183
Olivetti, Angelo 106
omote 105, 114n13
Ōno, Setsuko 59-60
Ōno, Susumu 36n10, 113n2
Ōoka, Shōhei 11n12
Orient 1-4
    as utopian exemplar 2
Ortega y Gasset, José 11n8
Orwell, George 221
Osaragi, Jirō 156-7
oshaberi 46, 79, 86
Ōsugi, Sakae 100, 200, 205
oyabun 107

Pannunzio, Sergio 106
pastoralism of West 42-3
paternalism 105-6
patriarchy see under father
personality 28, 209-10
    linguistic theory of 93
phenomenalism 51, 166
physical contact of Japanese 111
Pike, Kenneth 29
polytheism in Japan 45
Price-Williams, Douglas 128
private 44, 63-5, 104-6, 108, 128,
    140, 164, 177, 185, 210, 217
psychoanalysis 116-76, *passim*
    early introduction in Japan 117
    expressing bourgeois individualism
        165
    see also amae, Doi
psychotherapy
    in Japan and USSR 22-3, 133
public 111, 119
    see also private

race, purity of 42, 91-2
rationality 38n18, 46, 68, 151
reality principle 138-40
rearing of child 110-11, 140
receptive culture 51

Redfield, Robert 5-6, 29-30
Reich, Wilhelm 142n1
relativism of Japanese culture 51
    of self-expression 91
Revel, J-P. 222
Reynolds, David 166-7
rinri 216-17
Rivarol, Antoine 89
Rousseau, J-J. 25, 176
rupture, as principle of West 51, 193

Sabata, Toyoyuki 30-1
Said, Edward 4
Sakagami Shōichi 188
Sakuta, Keiichi 177-8, 185
sankin-kōtai 164
Sartre, Jean-Paul 53n5, 61-2
Satō, Nobuhiro 202
Saul, Leon 158, 160
Saussure, Ferdinand 82, 96n26
seiyōron 30
selbstgleichschaltung 81, 85
selection of outside culture 49-52
shame 44, 167, 171, 176-87
Shaplen, Robert 147
shibumi 71, 155-6
Shiga Naoya 161, 174-5, 205
Shiga Shigetaka 41, 203
Shimazaki, Tōson 205
shinkeishitsu 165, 168-70, 207
shintō 48, 50, 206, 210
shiteki see private
Shiveley, Donald 223n7
shukaku-gōitsu 207, 220
silence, myth of 46, 79, 81, 85-6,
    101-4, 108, 113, 165
simple cognition 194, 220
situationalism 47, 79, 91
skinship 109, 111, 115n25
socialisation of child 110-11
    see also narcissism and
        socialisation
soto 105
species society 196
Sperba, Richard 117
Spitz, René 129-30, 150
subjectivity, of Japanese 46
subordination to group 22, 136, 140,
    211
Sugimoto, Yoshio 36n19, 74n12
Susanowo complex 145n57
Suzuki, Bunji 106
Suzuki, Daisetsu 8-9, 53n3, 209
Suzuki, Kantarō 101-2
Suzuki Takao, 36n2, 54n5, 88-94,

109, 113, 130, 133, 140, 167, 178, 213, 219-20
Swift, Jonathan 170

Tada, Michitarō 214
taijin-kyōfu 98n57, 129, 170
Tanabe, Hajime 194, 196
Tanizaki, Jun'ichirō 77-82, 85-6, 88-9, 95, 104, 113, 167, 205, 216
Tao Te Ching 114n4
tate *see* verticality, hierarchy
tatemae 105, 121, 144
Tayama, Katei 205
Thought policing 22, 86, 136-7, 224n15
Tokieda, Motoki 35
Tönnies, Ferdinand 44
Toqueville, Alexis de 44
toraware 126, 166, 168-9
Toynbee, Arnold 34, 46
transference 124-5
Trilling, Lionel 24n11
Tsuda, Sōkichi 185
tsūjin 71, 76, 174
tsumi *see* guilt
Tsunoda, Tadanobu 37n31, 189-91, 220
Tsurumi, Kazuko 11n8, 53n3, 158, 208
Turkle, Sherry 15

uchi 105
Ueyama, Shumpei 28, 36n9, 200n33
Ulpian 64
Umesao, Tadao 190-3, 199n11
unique
 definition of 34-5
 usage of word 25-6
uniqueness 25-35, 51, 203-5, 211
 as pathological 22
unity
 of child with mother 119, 161
 of logos and pathos 190-1
 of self and other 212, 218
 of subject and object 207, 219-20
 of thought and action 87
 see also chikō gōitsu, genkō-itchi, jita-gōitsu, meijitsu ittai, shukaku-gōitsu
universal validity 34, 51
ura 105
urbanity 71

van der Post, Laurens 58
vegetable culture 42
verticality 44, 57, 59, 177
 see also Nakane
Vogel, Ezra 120, 147

waga mama 61, 74n15, 140
Waley, Arthur 80
Wang Yang-Ming 87, 207, 219, 224n21
war
 and amae 148
 as racial conflict 45
watakushi *see* private
Watanabe, Shōichi 63-4, 77, 82-8, 113, 130, 133, 140, 178, 213, 219
Watsuji, Tetsurō 41, 66-8, 85, 152-4, 191, 194-5, 215-18, 220-1
Wen Shing Tseng 148
West, image of 30, 39-40, 42-3, 141-2, 156, 176, 212
Winnicott, David 126, 150
Wunderlich, Hans 27, 37n24

xenophobia 98n57

Yamada, Yoshio 218
Yamagato, Aritomo 206
yamato kotoba 64, 77-8, 80, 84-5, 88, 90, 123, 127-9, 133, 138, 165, 190, 219
 and infancy 111
 and public language 104
 definition of qualities 87, 100
 vs. gairaigo 58-60
Yanagita, Kunio 159, 208-9
yoko *see* horizontality
Yoshimoto, Inobu 171
Yūaikai 106

Zamyatin, Yevgeny 221
zealotism 46-7
Zen 3, 8-9